D1226744

Labor Shortages as America Approaches the Twenty-first Century

Labor Shortages as America Approaches the Twenty-first Century

Malcolm S. Cohen

Ann Arbor

THE UNIVERSITY OF MICHIGAN PRESS

Published in the United States of America by
The University of Michigan Press
Manufactured in the United States of America
♾ Printed on acid-free paper

1998 1997 1996 1995 4 3 2 1

A CIP catalogue record for this book is available from the British Library.

Library of Congress Cataloging-in-Publication Data

Cohen, Malcolm S.
Labor shortages as America approaches the twenty-first century / Malcolm S. Cohen.
p. cm.
Includes bibliographical references and index.
ISBN 0-472-10353-9 (alk. paper)
1. Labor market—United States. 2. Labor supply—United States. 3. Employment forecasting—United States. 4. Occupations—United States—Forecasting. I. Title.
HD5724.C64 1995
331.12′0973—dc20 94-36244
CIP

This book is dedicated to Robert M. Solow. I was fortunate enough to have him as a teacher and to learn from him as his research assistant and coauthor. His writings have continued to influence my understanding of economic phenomena.

Foreword

Robert M. Solow

There are two polar conceptions of what the discipline of economics is or ought to be. The first is Economics as Science. (The capital letters are essential.) In this view, the goal of economics is to derive a fairly complete theory of the economic world from a small number of axioms. This project has had quite a lot of success, in its own self-contained terms, leading up to the modern theory of general equilibrium.

The alternative conception can be summed up in Keynes's image of economics as dentistry. In this view, the goal of economics is to understand the working of hundreds of mechanisms that operate in economic life. These mechanisms—markets, decision procedures in firms and households, legal principles—are interrelated, but they can still be studied in a piecemeal way. To understand one of these mechanisms is to have an analytical picture of it, a theory, and some grasp of the relevant magnitudes, enough to account roughly for the range of observations. In the end, one goal of economics as dentistry is to know how to fix it if it hurts.

I am partial to this second conception of the nature of economics as a discipline. Malcolm Cohen's book is an excellent example of the economic dentist at work. It starts with a practical problem: the U.S. Immigration and Naturalization Service (INS) has to decide if there is a shortage of labor in certain specified occupations. Economics as Science will spend a lot of time exploring the possible meanings of "labor shortage" in a market economy, and could easily conclude that there is no such thing. In contrast, economics as dentistry will be more receptive to the idea that there may be peculiar mechanisms at work in some labor markets that could easily give rise to a state worth calling a shortage of certain skills. Even a partial understanding of those mechanisms may point the way to observable counterparts of those situations. Since every piece of the labor market may have its own idiosyncrasies, a collection of imperfect indicators is likely to be better than any single one. That is what this book offers.

Presumably a good dentist learns something new about oral life every time he or she is faced with a slightly nonroutine problem. Malcolm Cohen is a veteran specialist in the economics of labor markets; he will have accumulated much more experience than I have. I am an amateur in the economics of labor markets. I come to them primarily as a macroeconomist who is naturally curious about unemployment as an aggregative pathology of the economic system. (Characteristically, much of Economics as Science comes to the conclusion that there is no such thing.) What I need are some nearly universal mechanisms in the labor market that can be used in the diagnosis of macroeconomic problems. But I am willing to accept, if absolutely necessary, the conclusion that there are all sorts of labor markets and the details matter a lot.

The strong impression one gets from this book is that the details do matter a lot. There are hundreds of occupations to be dealt with. Each defines at least the possibility of a distinct labor market; no doubt some pairs of labor markets are more closely connected than others. At any given moment, some of those labor markets may be in one state and others in quite different states. They may evolve in the short run in quite diverse ways, depending on such factors as the geographical mobility of people and firms, interoccupational mobility, possibilities of substitution in technology and in consumption, the nature of the training process, and so on. One could imagine that this study, apart from performing its assigned task of helping the INS detect occupational shortages, might be the starting point of further studies of the dynamics of clusters of occupations and the people who fill them.

That would be entirely natural in the conception of economics as dentistry. Who among us has not had the experience of rising from the chair with a sense of relief as the dentist says, "Next!"? What I usually say at that point is, "Thank you, Dr. Cohen."

Preface

This book is the culmination of research initially started with Robert M. Solow in 1965 to estimate labor vacancies using help-wanted advertising. It continued with Arthur R. Schwartz in the 1970s and 1980s to estimate new hires using administrative records and later with Donald Grimes to estimate labor shortages. The U.S. Department of Labor awarded us grants in 1982, 1989, and 1992 to estimate labor shortages for administrative use in carrying out its mandate to identify occupations in which there are insufficient numbers of U.S. workers. Foreign workers in the identified shortage occupations may be certified for U.S. residency.

In the process of carrying out the research, I visited government officials in California, Texas, Illinois, Michigan, Massachusetts, Minnesota, Pennsylvania, and Washington, D.C., and talked by phone with officials in several other states. I participated in a conference sponsored by Senator Frank Lautenberg in New Jersey. I presented progress reports on the research at UCLA, the University of Michigan, the University of Maryland, and the American University as well as at a joint session of the Industrial Relations Research Association and the North American Economics and Finance Association. I spoke at a national meeting of state occupational information coordinators. I received valuable comments from participants at these gatherings.

It would be impossible to thank everyone who contributed in some way to the research, but I would like to mention particularly those who were most helpful. Alan Moss was the project monitor of the initial project in 1982 and continued to provide suggestions both for the research as it evolved and on the subsequent manuscripts. Tom Bruening, director of the Office of Foreign Labor Certification during the time of the second study, offered many helpful suggestions. Flora Richardson, current director of the Office of Foreign Labor Certification, provided much useful input, and her office was responsible for implementing the methodology. I would like to acknowledge the following members of her staff: Emily Biro, Michael Dougherty, Margaret Erickson, Dennis Gruskin, and Sarah Hoffman. Pat Stange, project monitor during the third study, also gave me many worthwhile comments.

Other Department of Labor employees who have been especially helpful are Bruce Alter, John Bregger, Sarah Carroll, John Castellani, Delores Dehaan, Alan Eck, Charlene Giles, Ruth Kapetan, Brian McDonald, Michael McElroy, Richard Mines, Paul Nelson, Janet Norwood, Richard Panati, Thomas Plewes, Walter Postle, Gary Reed, Neal Rosenthal, Robert Schaerfl, Shirley Smith, and Howard Wial. Other federal government employees providing input were Steve Baldwin, Aaron Bodin, Joe Gannon, Michael Harrigan, Richard Lee, Tom Scopp, and William Wascher.

Chris Arndt, Graham Burke, Robert Goddard, and Wendy Piper provided information about the Australian system.

University colleagues who offered comments at various stages of the research included Katharine Abraham, John Bound, Charlie Brown, James Duderstadt, George Fulton, William Kelly, Robert Lerman, William McKee, Daniel Mitchell, Greg Saltzman, Pat Scheetz, David Stevens, and Paul Weinstein. I also received useful input from members of the Young Scientists Network.

Richard Belous, Helen Kae Cleary, Angela Diaz, Abel Feinstein, Shirley Goetz, Mark Hughes, Mark Jordan, Eric Lyons, Joanne Palmieri, Steve Rosenow, Dale Shinn, Laura Steiner, Elliot Winer, and Katrina Wright provided other helpful comments or input.

I would like to thank several members of the Institute of Labor and Industrial Relations staff who were of great assistance. Jacqueline Murray provided many useful suggetions while editing the manuscript. I also received valuable research assistance from Donald Grimes, Peter Nicolas, Octavian Petrescu, and Susan Tuin.

Finally, I would like to thank the staff of the University of Michigan Press. Editor Colin Day gave me many useful suggestions. I also thank Laurie Ham for following through on the many details regarding publication.

Contents

CHAPTER 1

Introduction

Labor shortages in certain occupations have been recognized as a problem in times of economic expansion as well as contraction. For instance, there have been persistent shortages of nurses, physical therapists, and primary care physicians. The economic cycle does not have the same effect on all occupations. In fact, a deep economic recession could actually increase the demand for certain occupations, such as guards, mental health specialists, and unemployment claims processors. Other occupations tend to be relatively unaffected by changes in the business cycle.

Concern about labor shortages increases, however, when rapid economic growth has been sustained for a number of years. In the initial period of recovery following a downturn, labor demand can be met by slack labor. After the slack labor becomes employed, however, shortages can emerge as a problem.

Many variables determine whether shortages will actually occur. If labor supply grows fast enough to meet demand, shortages may never occur at all. Or shortages may occur in one part of the country but not in other parts. For example, major urban areas may have much less trouble recruiting primary care physicians than do rural areas. Likewise, shortages may occur in one submarket but not in other submarkets for the same occupation. For example, small biotechnology firms may have a difficult time attracting biologists, while research universities may have hundreds of biologist applicants for every tenure-track position.

This book explores the various aspects of labor shortages, from the theoretical considerations in chapter 2 to the empirical indicators constructed for all civilian occupational groups in chapter 5. The book can be useful to those interested in better understanding labor markets, to counselors advising people about prospects for different labor careers, to government and educational specialists planning training programs, and to job seekers and employers who simply want to know the results of the various occupational indicators.

Much of the research on labor indicators was sponsored by the U.S. Department of Labor for the purpose of identifying occupations having a shortage of U.S. workers. The methodology we developed could streamline the process by which certain categories of immigrants are admitted into the United States. Under current immigration law, aliens can be admitted to the United States according to different preference criteria, such as family reunification or labor market need. Generally, labor market need was determined on a case-by-case basis, with the requirement that employers prove there was a need for each immigrant they wanted to hire. The only exception to the case-by-case procedure was the Schedule A provision, which allowed for certification in occupations where there were insufficient numbers of U.S. workers to meet the need. (For a number of years, two occupations consistently on the Schedule A list were physical therapist and nurse, which have also ranked consistently at the top of the list according to our methodology.) There was no regular procedure, however, for reviewing the list to add or delete occupations. The Immigration Act of 1990 set up a pilot project to use labor market information to make a determination of labor shortages or surpluses "in up to 10 defined occupational classifications in the United States" (U.S. House 1992). The methodology described in this book was used by the Department of Labor to establish an initial list of shortage occupations. The definition of shortages is discussed in more detail in chapter 2.

It is not only to protect the U.S. labor force from loss of jobs to immigrant workers that the Department of Labor needs this kind of labor market information. The United States can enhance its competitive position in the global economy by judiciously choosing among the many applicants for immigration. Some of them are potential entrepreneurs or highly qualified professionals whose participation in the national economy would actually create jobs for unemployed domestic workers. For example, if there were a shortage of biotechnology specialists, an immigrant biotechnology specialist might invent new drugs, which would in turn create jobs in sales and marketing, as well as for support personnel.

Using labor market information to measure shortages is intended as a means of making the certification process faster, more efficient, and ultimately more equitable for all applicants, but it is not intended to replace the entire current procedure. We recognize that there are compelling reasons other than economic considerations for admitting some immigrants, such as family reunification or political sanctuary. The premise underlying the methodology described in this book is that, for those cases that are to be decided strictly for economic reasons, the procedure should be streamlined to admit those for whom the labor market has the greatest demand. Some job requirements, however, are too specialized to be measured by available labor market information. In those instances, a case-by-case analysis of an employer's job requirements may be the only way to determine whether a shortage exists.

The methodology described in this book provides a way to determine shortages at both national and state levels. When the methodology was applied for the period 1989–92, no occupational group was found to have a shortage in all states, and shortages could be identified for only parts of occupational groups in some states. Even at a time of relatively high unemployment, however, evidence of labor shortages was found in some occupational groups in some states. As the economy recovers, more states and more occupations will have shortages.

When making subgroup distinctions, it was often necessary to use criteria other than occupational codes as a method for classification. For example, for several science and engineering occupations, no shortages were identified at the bachelor's degree level, but there was evidence of potential shortages at more advanced degree levels and in certain specialty areas. As mentioned earlier, significant differences may exist between commercial and academic demand in a given occupation.

In the next chapter, our methodology is discussed and compared with other attempts to measure labor shortages, and various definitions of labor shortages are considered. Chapter 2 also presents a theoretical framework which, by considering the special factors that make labor markets different from other markets, counters the objection that labor shortages cannot exist since increased wages will bring supply and demand into equilibrium. Chapter 3 discusses indicators that can be used to measure labor shortages or surpluses at the occupational level. Chapter 4 presents detailed labor market indicators for 193 occupational groups, which measure surpluses or shortages for all major occupations in the United States. Chapter 5 analyzes the data from chapter 4, incorporating data from other studies, to predict future labor shortages or surpluses. Chapter 6 describes how labor market analysts can apply the analysis in this book to particular geographic areas or to finer delineations within occupational groups. Chapter 7 presents policy recommendations for achieving a better balance between supply and demand in U.S. labor markets and summarizes the results presented in the book. The indicators are general, however, and could be applied to other countries as well.

Our research on the measurement of shortages was originally undertaken in conjunction with the U.S. immigration program to improve the efficiency of making decisions on labor certifications. No single direct measure of labor shortages currently exists. Attempts to construct such measures are likely to be prohibitively expensive and inadequate. The closest thing to a direct measure of shortages would be job vacancies, but at present no such data are collected for the United States. Previous efforts to count job vacancies in the United States have been short-lived, very expensive, and not very promising.

Previous research has successfully used proxies for job vacancies. In this research, job vacancies were proxied by help-wanted advertising, which was explained by a model including the change in employment and unemployment rate. Although the model does not distinguish individual occupations, there is some evidence (discussed in the next chapter) that there are general relationships among all occupations, which would also be valid with respect to individual occupations.

Factors such as demographic changes, business growth or decline, the international economy, and diplomatic relationships among nations (discussed in chapter 5) can have a major impact on employment. Government policy also has a great deal of influence on the labor market. In the next few years we can expect major policy initiatives in areas such as government-sponsored research, medical care reform, defense cutbacks, new foreign trade treaties such as the North American Free Trade Agreement (NAFTA), and the transition from military to civilian use of resources. In chapter 5 we will examine some of the ways in which the unfolding of events in the coming years will have a bearing on labor shortages. We identify three possibilities:

1. Government policies could fail to address a mounting deficit and loss of U.S. competitiveness, which could lead to an economy generating far fewer jobs in the long run.
2. Government policies could address the deficit but ignore training needs, in which case we may not have the number of workers required to meet demand.
3. Government policies could successfully address the deficit, training needs, and U.S. competitiveness, in which case shortages could be averted and many jobs would be created.

To address training needs, it is useful to have a mechanism to measure and predict shortages and surpluses. Chapters 2 through 4 address this issue at the national level, and chapter 6 addresses it at the state level.

CHAPTER 2

Theory of Labor Shortages

This chapter deals with definitions of labor shortages, theories of labor shortages, and previous attempts to measure labor shortages; and it integrates theories of labor turnover and labor shortages. Empirical research conducted by the author on labor turnover is also presented. Theoretical explanations are offered as to why wages do not simply increase to eliminate labor shortages. Static and dynamic models are discussed.

Geographic distinctions are ignored in this chapter. Labor shortages can occur in some geographic areas even when there are no shortages in other areas. Shortages can also occur within subspecialties, or in one class of workers within an occupation. These issues are discussed in Chapter 6.

The Static Model of the Labor Market

The simplest economic model of supply and demand specifies that when a labor shortage first occurs, market forces will soon eliminate the shortage. This model, as illustrated by figures 2.1 and 2.2, does not allow for the possibility that a labor shortage could exist over the long run.

In figure 2.1, the wage level for a given occupation is set at W_0, and employer demand for workers is N_2 at that wage rate. Only N_1 workers are willing to supply labor for that wage. The difference between N_2 and N_1, then,

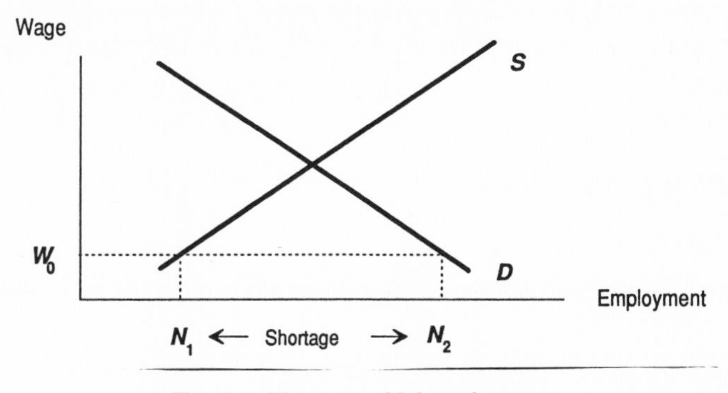

Fig. 2.1. Measure of labor shortage

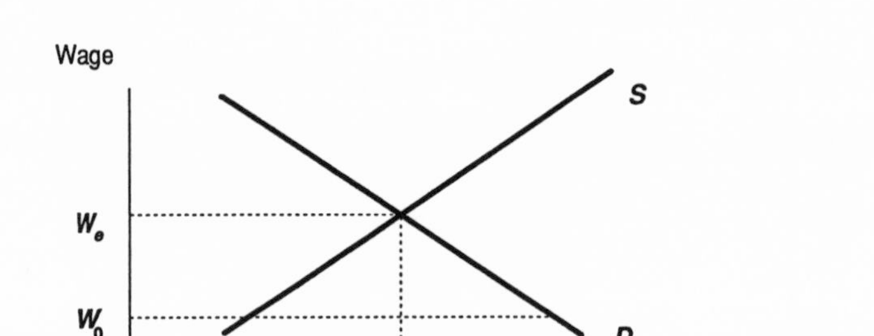

Fig. 2.2. Wage increase eliminates labor shortage

is a measure of the labor shortage; there are that many jobs being offered for which no workers are applying.

At this point, competitive market forces will drive up the wage rate, as illustrated in figure 2.2, to W_e, eliminating the shortage. This will result in more workers wishing to work at the higher wage and fewer workers demanded by employers.

A Dynamic Model of the Labor Market

The static view of labor markets illustrated in figures 2.1 and 2.2 does not take adequate account of the dynamics involved in labor market adjustment. Employers react to changing labor market conditions in a variety of ways, such as increasing wages or increasing search costs. Employers do not have perfect information about market conditions, and job seekers do not have perfect information about available jobs. There is a continuous process of adjustment to changing conditions, with many factors interacting at once. Labor market dynamics can explain labor shortages if adjustment speed is slow or if there are barriers to adjustment.

A dynamic view of labor market adjustment was suggested many years ago by Arrow and Capron (1959). According to their definition, "a steady upward shift in the demand curve will produce a shortage, that is, a situation in which there are unfilled vacancies in positions where salaries are the same as those currently being paid in others of the same type and quality." This concept is illustrated in figure 2.3.

Along the same lines as the Arrow-Capron definition, Blank and Stigler (1957) say that "a shortage exists when the number of workers available increases less rapidly than the number demanded at the salaries paid in the recent past."

A more recent approach to dynamic labor shortages was presented by Trutko et al. (1991). Their approach was to examine individual sources of

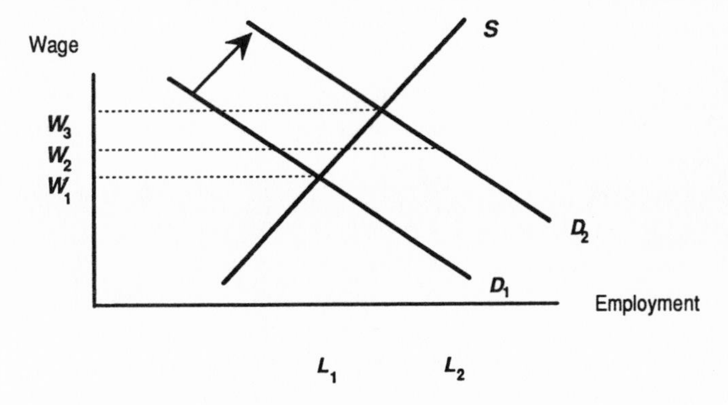

Fig. 2.3. Dynamic shortage

disequilibrium, such as increase in demand for labor, decrease in the supply of labor, or restrictions on prices, and suggest various approaches employers could take to alleviate shortages. Some of their suggestions were:

1. Increase recruiting effort.
2. Increase use of overtime.
3. Reduce minimum job qualifications.
4. Restructure work to use workers in other occupations.
5. Substitute machinery for labor.
6. Train workers.
7. Improve working conditions.
8. Offer bonuses to new employees.
9. Improve wages and fringe benefits.
10. Contract out work.
11. Turn down work.

Differences between Labor Markets and Product Markets

Labor markets simply do not behave in the same way as do product markets. When Willard Wirtz was secretary of labor in 1968, he even issued a directive to delete the use of the term *labor market* from Department of Labor publications because he didn't think labor should be viewed as a commodity being bought and sold in a market.

Robert Solow's Royer lectures at Berkeley (published as Solow 1990) go a long way toward discrediting the view that labor can be viewed as a commodity, such as fish, whose price fluctuates with supply and demand. Solow argued that traditional general equilibrium theory applied to labor markets has failed to explain the presence of unemployment. If labor markets cleared like fish markets, then when unemployment increased the price of labor would fall as unemployed workers bid down wages, and unemployment would disappear. The persistent unemployment of the past seems to contradict this theory of labor markets clearing.

Two explanations offered by Solow for the failure of labor markets to clear are the efficiency wage theory and the insider-outsider approach. A third notion alluded to by Solow, path dependence, is also discussed. This is not the place for an extensive essay on what has been so eloquently expressed by Professor Solow. Rather, we will briefly review these three concepts and discuss how they apply to a theory of labor shortages.

Efficiency Wage Theory

According to efficiency wage theories, a worker's productivity is a function of the variance of wages paid in the firm. Thus, if a worker feels unfairly compensated, that worker's productivity will decrease. If a labor shortage develops in one occupation in a firm, there may be a limit to which the firm can increase the relative wage of workers in that occupation before the productivity of workers in other nonshortage occupations is adversely affected. It may not be economical, however, to increase the wages of all workers in the firm.

According to a model developed by Akerlof and Yellen (1988), output is assumed to depend on the variance of wages in the firm. The smaller the wage differentials, the greater the labor efficiency. They assume

$$q = e(s^2\,[w])\,f(L_1, L_2)\ ;\ e < 0, f > 0 \qquad (1)$$

where q is output; L_1, L_2 is employment in occupations 1 and 2; e is a function of the variance in wages paid; w is wages; f is a function of labor inputs; and s^2 is the variance.

Here, as in typical models of production, increased labor input results in an increase in output ($f > 0$). In this model, however, there is an added element: the function $e(s^2\,[w])$, which shows that an increase in the wage gap across occupations would result in reduced output ($e < 0$). Thus, a selective increase in wages to attract workers to a specific occupation is inefficient for the firm because it may reduce productivity at the same time that it increases labor input.

Insider-Outsider Theory

The insider-outsider theory holds that insiders within the firm are stakeholders and to some degree are treated differently than are outsiders not yet in the firm

(Solow 1990). When applying this theory to explaining why, when unemployment exists, wages are not bid down, Solow offers several explanations. First, the insiders would resent a lowering of their wages, quite possibly resulting in a lowering of firm productivity. Second, a replacement of insiders with outsiders would deplete the firm of its specific talent. Third, a social norm may exist which prevents unemployed workers from offering their wages at less than the market price. The norm follows the consequences of the prisoners' dilemma.

According to the prisoners' dilemma, two prisoners are each offered a chance either to implicate the other prisoner in a crime or to deny that either prisoner committed the crime. If one prisoner implicates the other, that prisoner gets less jail time than would be received for denying that either prisoner committed the crime. If both prisoners implicate each other, however, they each get more jail time than they would if both prisoners deny the crime.

The argument applied to the social norm is that one job seeker asking a lower wage will be employed, but if all job seekers lower their wage offer, the result could be a lower wage for all workers in that job category. Because over the long run workers will be better off with some unemployment but a higher wage when they are employed, they may resist lowering their wage offer when they are unemployed.

Applying these theories to shortages yields a somewhat less compelling argument. Firms may not want to pay outsiders more than they pay insiders, to attract workers in short supply, unless they also increase the wages of insiders.

Firms that pay their chief executive officers one hundred times what they pay their highest-paid blue-collar workers may not be as concerned about efficiency wages. Insider-outsider theory may conflict in these cases with efficiency wage theory.

Industrial relations theories hold that worker involvement is a key to increased worker productivity. William Cooke found that productivity and quality performance increased in plants that established joint labor-management programs and that scheduled frequent meetings (Cooke 1990, Cooke and Meyer 1990). This conclusion was based on the perceptions of a sample of managers in 111 joint programs.

Path Dependence

In most dynamic models of the labor market, the history of the path to equilibrium does not play a significant role. When path dependence is a relevant factor, however, equilibrium may depend upon the starting point or the history of an event. For example, if employers find that there is a shortage initially, they may make organizational changes to deal with it. Suppose, for example, that hospitals need more nurses but are unable to hire enough to meet the need. The problem might be addressed by restructuring nursing occupations to assign some of the nurses' duties to less skilled medical personnel. Such action would lighten the nurses' load and thereby reduce the need for more nurses. Once this change has been made, equilibrium will shift to a different level, with demand being lowered from where it was before the initial shortage was perceived and action taken.

A Theory of Shortages

According to Abraham (1983), the vacancy rate in a steady state is computed according to the equation:

$$VR = NHR * d_v \quad (2)$$

where *NHR* is the new hire rate; d_v is the average length of time that a vacancy remains open; and *VR* is the vacancy rate.

The literature reviewed later in this chapter suggests that the rate of change of employment and the unemployment rate are good proxies for the new hire rate. Our interest in predicting labor market disequilibrium, however, requires estimation at the occupational level because new hire data are not available on an occupational level.

Blanchard and Diamond (1990) have utilized Current Population Survey data to estimate new hires. Their ingenious model requires the use of Current Population Survey gross flow data, which are inherently biased and would require a further correction, as suggested by Abowd and Zellner (1985). This approach would not work at the occupational level, however, since it is based on reinterview data available for less than 6 percent of the sample. Detailed occupational measures are barely significant, even using the entire sample.

It is reasonable to expect d_v to vary, as seasonal variation is extensive. Furthermore, the inclusion of both temporary and permanent new hires clouds the analysis. Most new hires are temporary—lasting less than nine months, according to our research (discussed at the end of this chapter).

Theories of the dual economy may well apply to temporary versus permanent new hires. Temporary new hires include contingent workers, who are less likely to receive extensive benefits and would not be regarded as insiders. Permanent new hires more generally include workers hired for the long term. These workers more often receive the full package of benefits and become regarded as insiders or stakeholders in the firm.

A firm is likely to fill a vacancy for a temporary worker in less time than is required to fill a vacancy for a permanent worker. Our research has shown that many new hires are temporary, and that the ratio of temporary to permanent new hires varies considerably by industry and, by inference, by occupation. Gross flow research by Blanchard and Diamond (1990) allows for two types of workers, primary and secondary. It is not at all clear whether we could refine the new hire estimates from the Current Population Survey to measure permanent versus temporary new hires, or whether this distinction would require establishment data.

If data were available, we could build a model to predict vacancies, then test the model's accuracy using actual data. With such a model, the following observations could be made:

1. An increase in vacancies in an occupation is an indication of a shift in demand. Unless that increase is accompanied by a subsequent shift in supply, it could signal a shortage. If it takes a long time for that shift in supply to occur, a temporary shortage could exist. If demand shifts again, faster than supply can catch up, the shortage could remain for a long time.
2. In a steady state, vacancies and new hires would be equal. If vacancies began to outpace new hires, a shortage would develop.
3. An increase in the length of time it takes to fill a vacancy could be evidence of a shortage.

Some occupations may be in a constant state of short supply. In these occupations, vacancies may already be high, the length of time to fill a vacancy may be long, and the number of new hires may be small compared to vacancies. We would want to measure vacancies, permanent and temporary new hires, and wages paid to new hires. Wages paid to new hires are important because increasing wages of new hires is one mechanism that can be used to attract new workers when shortages exist.

Another factor to be considered is replacement demand. In occupations with unusually high turnover, many vacancies can occur even when the total number of workers needed does not change. There would be a shortage in such occupations, however, if departing workers cannot be replaced as soon as desired.

Other Attempts to Measure Labor Shortages

In this section we review theoretical and empirical measures used in the past to describe labor shortages.

Unemployment Rate

It is generally agreed that when the unemployment rate is high, there is surplus labor. A low unemployment rate, however, does not necessarily mean a labor shortage. In the extreme case, if all workers who wanted jobs at a particular wage rate were able to find such jobs, and if employers could hire all the workers they wanted at that wage rate, supply and demand would be in equilibrium. The unemployment rate would be zero, yet there would be no labor shortage.

Similarly, if a great number of workers had to be located and interviewed before the right worker could be found for a particular job, and if employed workers could not easily search for this particular job, a labor shortage could exist even with a level of unemployment significantly above zero. Other problems with the unemployment rate as a sole indicator of shortages are discussed in Chapter 3.

Job Vacancy Surveys

It has been suggested that a job vacancy survey could definitively determine in which occupations shortages exist. The Bureau of Labor Statistics (BLS) used to collect such data but discontinued the practice in 1973. Since then BLS has carried out two pilot projects to determine the feasibility of collecting such data. The first pilot project study was published in 1981 and the second was published ten years later (U.S. Dept. of Labor 1981, 1991a).

Job vacancy data alone, however, would not be enough; they would need to be interpreted in conjunction with other labor market indicators. For example, if an occupation had a high job vacancy rate and a high unemployment rate, there may be imperfect information in the market that prevents workers and employers from being matched, or there may be rigidities in geographic mobility. A fuller analysis of labor market conditions would be required to understand the dynamics of the labor market for a particular occupation.

BLS developed two measures of labor vacancies in its 1991 survey: the vacancy fill rate and the duration of existing job openings. The vacancy fill rate is a measure of the new hires in a month divided by the number of jobs open at the end of that month. BLS defined a job as being open if "work would have started immediately or during the next pay period and if active recruiting of workers from outside the establishment took place." BLS further defined active recruiting to include "listings with private or public agencies, or school placement offices, help-wanted advertising, recruitment programs, or interview of applicants" (U.S. Dept. of Labor 1991a). The BLS definition excluded jobs to be filled by recalls, transfers, and promotions. The definition would also exclude jobs available only if the right candidate came along.

Unfortunately, the data collected in the BLS pilot were too limited to be used to determine whether any actual shortages existed in any occupations. It is interesting, however, to compare occupations identified by the BLS pilot as potentially having shortages to the shortage occupations identified using the measures developed for the project described in this book. BLS conducted such a test and found that several occupations were common to both lists. Further details of this comparison are presented in Chapter 5.

Occupational job vacancy data would be a useful addition to the information that could be relied upon in assessing shortages. The cost of a job vacancy survey, however, is likely to preclude its being initiated on a regular basis. The 1991 study indicated that it would cost $11–12 million to collect job opening data at the national level. Although the cost of collecting such data at the state and local level was not estimated in that study, the cost of a monthly survey was estimated by BLS in 1981 to be approximately $25–30 million per year ($44–53 million in 1991 dollars). At those prices, it is unlikely that any large-scale inquiry into job vacancies will be undertaken in the near future.

Even if money were no object and Congress were willing to spend $50 million a year to collect job vacancy data at a detailed occupational and geographic level, the data could still be misleading. For example, based on information I gathered in interviews at college job placement and labor certification offices, I learned that it may be necessary to subdivide occupational groups by educational attainment level to identify potential shortages. For example, there appeared to be a surplus of students with a B.A. in biology seeking work, while at the same time many employers had difficulty filling positions requiring a Ph.D. in biotech specialty fields. A job vacancy survey would not be of any help in providing statistically reliable information at this detailed a level.

Help-Wanted Advertising

In the absence of direct measures of job vacancies, indirect measures have been used. Robert Solow (1964) suggested, for example, using help-wanted advertising as a proxy for job vacancies to measure the Beveridge curve. (Lord Beveridge, a British politician and economist, suggested that a stable relation exists between job vacancies and unemployment. This relationship became known as the Beveridge curve.)

One measure of the availability of jobs is the help-wanted index developed by the National Industrial Conference Board. According to a recent study, while the unemployment rate declined from 7.5 percent in 1984 to 6.7 percent in 1991, help-wanted advertising, as measured by the index, declined from 130 in 1984 to 93 in 1991 (Medoff 1992). Our research, however, as reported in a later section, indicates that help-wanted advertising decreases as the economy moves further into a recession and steadily increases with the progress of a recovery. Our finding was that firms begin by using other informal methods and turn to help-wanted advertising later, presumably because their first efforts do not produce satisfactory results, or they use help-wanted advertising only to comply with job-posting requirements.

In 1967, Robert Solow and I used the National Industrial Conference Board's index of help-wanted advertising as a proxy for demand pressure in labor markets (Cohen and Solow 1967; see also Cohen and Solow 1970). We estimated a model to explain changes in help-wanted advertising as a function of changes in the unemployment rate, changes in the new hire rate, and a dummy variable equal to one in business cycle expansions and zero in contractions. In our model we normalized the help-wanted advertising index by adjusting it to reflect changes in the size of the civilian labor force.

The model did a credible job of explaining changes in help-wanted advertising. The signs on the coefficients were what would be expected with the change in normalized help-wanted advertising: Help-wanted advertising was inversely correlated with changes in new hires, and the dummy variable had a positive sign, suggesting that help-wanted advertising increases as the recovery progresses. The inference is that other recruitment methods, such as recalls and direct applications, are used first, and that help-wanted advertising is used more intensely as workers become harder to locate.

A misspecification in the Cohen-Solow study, mentioned by the authors (Cohen and Solow 1967) and also in a paper by Blanchard and Diamond on the Beveridge curve (1989), is that manufacturing new hires were used instead of total economywide new hires. Blanchard and Diamond constructed a measure of total new hires, using gross movements into and out of the labor force from the Current Population Survey. Their method makes use of a correction by Abowd and Zellner (1985) to account for biases in the gross flow computations. According to Blanchard and Diamond, a new hire is defined by counting workers who change from being unemployed or out of the labor force to being employed.

Specifying the equation to include total new hires instead of just manufacturing new hires reduces the importance of vacancies in explaining new hires relative to the unemployment rate. Blanchard and Diamond (1989) speculate that their result differs from the Cohen-Solow model because firms in manufacturing may have less trouble recruiting workers than firms in other industries. This view of the labor market would be consistent with efficiency wage theories, which were discussed in detail earlier in this chapter.

Katharine Abraham (1987) also used help-wanted advertising as a measure of job vacancies. In another study, however, she took an alternative approach to estimate vacancies, using data on job tenure from the Current Population Survey to calculate new hire rates (Abraham 1983). Data from various pilot surveys were used to compute the average time a job remains vacant. Abraham computed the vacancy rate using the steady state relation:

$$NHR\ d_v = VR, \tag{3}$$

where *NHR* is the new hire rate and d_v is the average length of time a job remains vacant.

In our comment on the Abraham article, we took issue with the steady state assumption as well as with the consistency of the vacancy-unemployment rate (Schwartz, Cohen, and Grimes 1986). We used administrative records from Social Security data and unemployment insurance wage records to measure new hires directly. Our conclusion was that there are far more new hires in the economy than are counted using methodologies such as Abraham's.

In our methodology, new hires were identified by checking a firm's employment record by employee identification number. If a worker did not appear in the firm's records in the previous four quarters, but did appear in the given quarter, the worker was considered a new hire. If a worker appeared in the previous quarter but not in the current quarter, the worker was considered a separation. The determination of a new hire was based on looking back four quarters. Lengthening the period resulted in a very small decrease in the new hire rate, but a large increase in the cost of making the computation. Furthermore, it may be of little relevance. It is likely that a worker who turns up again on a firm's records after more than four quarters is being hired anew rather than being recalled; hence, the new hire designation would be the most appropriate category for that worker. The number of such workers who are actually returning from an extended leave of absence would be too small to be significant and therefore would not justify the cost of culling them out of the new hire category.

Our survey of the literature indicates the absence of any generally available measure of labor shortage data. The use of wage records to generate new hire rates might be useful, except that no occupational data are available in wage records or Social Security records. The wage records could be used, however, to generate information on turnover by industry or geographic area.

New Hire Data Results

Our research on new hire behavior permits us to compute new hire rates for persons by industry, geographic area, income level, sex, race, and age, or for industries by industry and geographic area (Cohen 1985; Cohen and Schwartz 1979). Although our research is not directly applicable to measuring shortages in specific occupations, it does yield many insights into the functioning of labor markets relative to a theory of shortages.

First, we must define the term *new hires*. It can have several different connotations, depending on the context in which it is viewed. There are three cases relevant to this discussion, each of which involves a distinction between two measures of new hires: (1) number of hiring transactions versus number of individuals; (2) permanent new hires versus total new hires; and (3) job turnover versus occupational turnover. In each case, we seek to measure new hires in the way that gives the best insight into what is happening in the labor force.

When job changes are measured by counting hiring transactions, many people are counted more than once. In a study that I directed in 1975, it was estimated that the number of hiring transactions annually would be equivalent to 84 percent of total employment (Cohen and Schwartz 1980). That is, in a labor force of 100 million, 84 million hiring transactions would take place during the course of a year. When we attempted to measure job changes of individuals rather than transactions, using the same data, our finding was that 18 percent of workers in the labor force experienced a new hire transaction in 1975 in their primary job (Cohen 1985). The great discrepancy between the 84 percent and the 18 percent can be accounted for by two factors: (1) a small percentage of workers in the labor force hold many temporary jobs; and (2) multiple jobholders who change their secondary jobs are not included in the 18 percent.

Another way to refine new hire rates is to separate permanent new hires from the total. We defined a permanent new hire as a worker who remained with the company for at least two quarters beyond the quarter of hire. In 1975, only 35 percent of the new hires (equivalent to about 30 percent of total employment) were permanent by this definition. This ratio varies by industry, but the rate of permanent new hires tends to be more consistent than the total new hire rate across industries and would be more influenced by economic cycles.

Beginning in 1929 and continuing until 1981, BLS collected and published monthly data on labor turnover. The BLS turnover survey counted transactions rather than individuals, so its results should have been similar to our results.

During the period 1970 to 1979, BLS computed monthly labor turnover in manufacturing at 2.9 percent. If we extrapolate from this, we get an annual rate of about 35 percent. This can be compared to our measurement of hiring transactions, which was 84 percent. The BLS rate, however, was only for manufacturing and mainly for large, well-established firms. Our study, on the other hand, included nearly the entire private sector.

After the publication of our results in the *Monthly Labor Review* (Cohen and Schwartz 1980), BLS discontinued its survey and cited our research as one potential alternative source for labor turnover information. They concluded that “the new hire rates of the few small establishments of the BLS sample were two or three times higher than the corresponding rates of large establishments. In addition, many of the larger establishments in the sample were well established, and appeared to have less turnover than large establishments not in the sample" (Utter 1982).

Our research also indicates that turnover in service industries is higher than in manufacturing. For example, in the second quarter of 1974, the monthly rate was 9.2 percent in services and 5.4 percent in manufacturing.

All these comparisons give credence to our belief that our computations are reasonably accurate. Furthermore, our analysis is based on administrative records, which must be carefully monitored for accuracy since they are used to calculate workers' benefits.

The Social Security Administration discontinued collecting quarterly wage information. after 1976, but the employment services in all fifty states maintain wage records for the administration of their unemployment insurance programs. The information pertains to all workers covered by unemployment insurance, not just to unemployed workers. The coverage is quite extensive, including more than 98 percent of private wage and salary workers. Excluded are some railroad workers, federal employees, and certain workers in nonprofit institutions. Also excluded are workers earning virtually no wage and salary income, such as someone earning less than $50 in a calendar quarter from a single employer.

We compared new hire rates generated from Social Security records with wage records. We discovered some errors in the data because in many instances a state was tabulating the data for the first time in this format. These errors were later corrected. Overall, however, the results were generally comparable.

To update our new hire estimates from 1975 to the present, we developed a model based on the relationship between changes in employment and turnover measures. By definition, employment change can be decomposed into various flows:

$$\Delta E = NH + \text{recalls} - \text{quits} - \text{layoffs} - OS \tag{4}$$

where ΔE is change in employment; NH is new hires; and OS is other separations.

We can rewrite (4) as:

$$NH = \Delta E + Z \tag{5}$$

where Z = quits + OS + NL; and NL is net layoffs (layoffs − recalls).

To obtain rates, we divide both sides by E.

We do not have data on the individual components of Z, nor can we separate Z from NH. However, we can introduce a proxy for Z that has been an excellent explanatory variable for labor turnover.

According to Robert Hall (1972), "unemployment is one of the key variables in a theory of labor turnover because it serves as the main indicator of distress in labor markets." We can be more elaborate in our explanation of Z by paying more attention to the three components: quits, other separations, and net layoffs. Other separations are not readily explainable by any simple proxy, since other separations include diverse factors such as leave for military duty, retirement, death, and certain intercompany transfers. Net layoffs are likely to be positively correlated with the unemployment rate, since it is logical to expect more layoffs in an economic downturn than in a business recovery. Quits, on the other hand, are likely to be negatively correlated, since employees are reluctant to quit when unemployment is high.

Since our purpose is not to estimate the components of turnover, and since our sample does not distinguish among them, using the unemployment rate as a proxy for Z will probably suffice.

Rewriting (5), we get:

$$NHR = f(UR, \%E) \tag{6}$$

where NHR is the new hire rate; UR is the unemployment rate; and $\%E$ is percentage change in employment.

We had national quarterly data for NHR from 1972 to 1975, which enabled us to estimate a linear form of equation (6) for twelve quarters, ending in the second quarter of 1975. (For more details on the estimation, see Cohen and Schwartz 1983.) We then computed new hire rates for all fifty states for this period using the following equation:

$$\begin{aligned} NHR_t = a_1 &+ b_1\ \%\Delta E_t + b_2\ UR_{t-1} \\ &+ b_3\ S_1 + b_4\ S_2 \\ &+ b_5\ S_3 + b_6\ dummy + E_1 \end{aligned} \tag{7}$$

where $S_1 \ldots S_3$ are seasonal dummies; and *dummy* is a dummy variable for the first quarter of 1974, since serious data errors in the series were detected in this quarter.

To test the robustness of this model, we obtained new hire estimates from sixteen states. Spanning six years, these estimates included both business booms and recession years; they are compared to our new hire forecasts in table 2.1.

Considering that the state estimates are derived from an entirely different data source, a variance of 5 percent or less in two-thirds of the cases gives considerable confidence to our model. In Florida, the one case where our prediction was far too high, we discovered differences in the way the state computed the new hire rates. Upon further investigation, we even suspected that our forecast was more accurate than the actual estimate made by Florida.

Using the model, we estimated new hire rates and total new hires from 1981 to 1991 for each state. The new hire rates for each state are shown in table 2.2, and total new hires by state are shown in table 2.3. Figure 2.4 compares new hire rates state by state for 1989, the year before the start of the 1990–91 recession.

TABLE 2.1. Comparison of ILIR New Hire Forecasts with Actual Employment Service Potential New Hire Data

State	Period	Reported ESP New Hires	Predicted ILIR New Hires	% DIfference
Arkansas	Fiscal 1979	583,990	603,500	+3.34
California	Fiscal 1976	6,142,625	5,796,000	- 5.64
	Fiscal 1977	6,625,804	6,506,800	- 1.80
	Fiscal 1978	7,523,644	7,640,400	+ 1.55
	Fiscal 1979	8,366,534	8,226,400	- 1.67
Florida	Calendar 1980	2,673,019	3,790,500	+41.81
	Calendar 1981	2,918,487	3,729,700	+27.80
Idaho	Fiscal 1976	238,989	241,000	+ 0.84
Illinois	1979 3rd-4th Q	1,436,475	1,593,500	+10.93
Iowa	Fiscal 1981	587,016	582,500	- 0.77
Maine	Fiscal 1978	263,175	268,900	+2.17
Mississippi	1981 4th Q	101,921	107,400	+5.40
Missouri	1979 3rd-4th Q	718,946	670,400	- 6.75
	Calendar 1981	1,073,311	1,204,900	+12.26
Nevada	Fiscal 1976	309,100	298,300	- 3.48
	Fiscal 1979	452,679	476,800	+ 5.32
	Fiscal 1980	464,348	466,600	+ 0.48
	Fiscal 1981	438,880	477,600	+ 8.95
New Mexico	Fiscal 1979	410,927	412,000	+0.26
	Fiscal 1980	378,288	386,200	+2.10
North Carolina	1979 4th Q	392,663	370,300	- 5.71
North Dakota	Fiscal 1976	147,081	144,300	- 1.88
Pennsylvania	Fiscal 1976	2,051,553	2,147,100	+4.66
South Carolina	1979 1st-3rd Q	611,324	627,700	+ 2.68
	1981 2nd-4th Q	550,619	522,900	- 5.03
South Dakota	Fiscal 1979	177,433	155,800	-12.19
	Fiscal 1980	142,795	137,500	- 3.70
	Fiscal 1981	134,109	142,900	+ 6.57

Sources: Malcolm S. Cohen, "Deriving Labor Turnover Rates from Administrative Records," in *Record Linkage Techniques - 1985*, U.S. Department of the Treasury, Internal Revenue Service, Statistics of Income Division; and *A Summary of State ESP Data*, Institute of Labor and Industrial Relations, University of Michigan, November 1980.

TABLE 2.2. New Hire Rate in the Private Nonfarm Economy by State
(Quarterly rate per 100 employees)

State	1981	1982	1983	1984	1985	1986	1987	1988	1989	1990	1991
Alabama	18.3	15.2	14.7	18.8	19.1	19.3	20.5	21.4	22.0	21.7	19.6
Alaska	35.0	35.3	43.8	31.2	28.2	24.0	24.8	25.9	26.7	26.3	27.2
Arizona	26.7	22.3	24.5	29.4	28.8	28.0	28.9	29.1	30.0	29.4	27.1
Arkansas	21.2	17.2	15.9	21.3	21.7	22.3	23.9	25.3	26.2	25.8	23.1
California	23.3	20.6	21.0	24.5	24.1	24.1	25.2	26.1	26.3	25.4	23.3
Colorado	27.5	21.5	19.6	27.0	26.2	26.7	29.2	31.2	32.6	32.1	28.6
Connecticut	15.4	13.2	12.1	16.5	15.7	16.3	16.7	17.1	17.0	16.1	14.9
D.C.	21.3	19.2	18.3	22.7	22.6	23.0	24.3	24.9	25.0	24.1	22.3
Delaware	13.9	8.6	5.1	12.3	14.0	14.7	16.5	18.9	20.4	20.3	16.9
Florida	30.0	24.4	23.9	31.2	30.4	31.3	33.0	33.9	34.4	32.8	28.6
Georgia	21.3	17.2	16.4	22.9	22.6	22.9	24.4	25.2	26.0	25.2	22.0
Hawaii	18.9	17.1	18.1	19.7	20.7	20.7	21.7	21.8	23.1	21.9	19.9
Idaho	24.9	23.7	24.9	26.3	25.3	25.0	26.2	27.1	27.3	27.1	26.3
Illinois	16.9	13.9	14.8	18.4	17.4	18.1	19.3	20.1	20.1	19.8	17.6
Indiana	15.6	12.2	12.2	16.5	16.4	17.0	18.3	19.2	19.5	19.0	16.9
Iowa	16.7	13.9	12.7	16.8	17.0	17.5	18.8	19.9	20.3	20.1	18.1
Kansas	21.4	18.3	18.2	21.9	21.3	22.0	23.0	23.9	24.4	24.0	22.4
Kentucky	17.5	14.9	15.2	19.4	18.5	18.7	20.4	20.5	21.0	20.4	18.5
Louisiana	24.6	22.7	21.0	24.6	25.0	25.5	26.0	26.9	27.4	27.2	25.7
Maine	18.9	17.3	19.3	20.3	19.9	20.7	21.2	22.1	20.7	19.7	18.7
Maryland	19.4	17.6	20.3	21.6	20.9	21.3	21.7	21.8	21.3	20.2	18.1
Massachusetts	18.4	16.3	16.2	19.9	18.5	18.8	19.6	19.7	18.7	17.9	17.1
Michigan	14.5	11.5	12.1	15.9	16.3	16.0	16.9	18.1	18.6	17.8	15.9
Minnesota	16.3	13.6	13.7	17.3	16.7	17.2	18.4	19.1	19.4	19.2	17.4
Mississippi	19.9	16.6	17.4	20.6	20.7	20.4	22.2	22.9	23.2	22.9	21.0
Missouri	18.2	15.8	16.2	19.6	19.0	19.3	20.1	20.8	21.1	20.4	18.5
Montana	24.5	23.1	26.3	25.7	23.3	24.1	25.2	27.2	26.8	26.0	26.1
Nebraska	19.9	18.2	18.1	21.4	20.0	20.5	21.6	22.0	22.2	22.3	20.7
Nevada	32.2	27.1	29.9	34.0	33.7	34.6	36.2	37.4	37.8	36.4	33.1
New Hampshire	19.0	14.3	15.4	20.2	20.1	20.2	21.4	22.2	21.1	19.9	18.1
New Jersey	18.6	16.1	14.6	19.7	18.9	19.4	20.0	20.8	20.3	19.4	17.8
New Mexico	27.7	24.1	23.8	28.2	28.3	27.4	29.0	30.6	31.2	30.8	28.3
New York	17.0	14.3	13.7	17.5	17.2	17.5	18.3	18.8	18.8	18.3	16.2
North Carolina	17.9	13.7	13.6	18.9	19.0	19.5	21.0	22.2	22.5	21.5	19.0
North Dakota	22.5	19.8	23.9	20.2	19.4	18.9	20.7	19.8	19.6	20.7	20.5
Ohio	14.8	11.5	12.1	16.1	15.8	16.2	17.2	17.9	18.3	17.8	15.7
Oklahoma	26.1	20.5	20.3	24.2	22.8	22.4	25.1	26.4	26.8	26.8	24.5
Oregon	21.3	19.3	20.6	23.7	23.5	23.8	25.2	26.2	26.2	25.6	23.5
Pennsylvania	14.4	11.3	12.0	15.5	15.0	15.2	16.5	16.9	16.8	16.2	14.5
Rhode Island	18.1	14.3	13.8	19.0	18.9	19.2	20.2	21.5	21.6	20.9	18.4
South Carolina	18.0	14.4	14.2	18.6	18.6	19.2	20.5	21.5	22.0	21.7	18.9
South Dakota	19.5	18.1	20.7	21.7	19.5	20.7	21.5	21.8	22.3	22.3	21.2
Tennessee	18.9	15.6	15.9	19.8	19.6	20.0	21.2	21.8	22.1	21.3	19.7
Texas	26.3	22.9	21.6	26.1	26.0	26.0	27.4	28.6	29.2	29.1	27.0
Utah	23.4	20.3	20.2	24.4	23.6	23.4	24.4	26.0	26.7	26.4	24.3
Vermont	20.2	18.1	20.1	21.2	20.9	20.9	21.3	20.5	19.5	17.8	18.1
Virginia	17.6	14.8	14.7	19.5	19.4	19.6	20.5	21.4	21.7	20.7	18.3
Washington	21.2	20.4	22.5	23.2	22.7	22.9	23.7	23.5	23.8	22.7	21.7
West Virginia	15.7	11.8	14.3	16.5	16.0	15.4	16.4	16.5	16.9	16.7	15.6
Wisconsin	14.2	11.2	11.2	15.0	14.8	15.3	16.5	17.4	17.6	17.3	15.3
Wyoming	30.8	27.9	27.1	30.5	30.7	30.1	31.6	32.5	33.2	32.9	31.5
United States	19.9	16.8	16.9	20.9	20.5	20.8	21.9	22.7	23.0	22.4	20.3

Source: Estimated from regression models using unpublished employment data by industry and state from the U.S. Department of Labor, Bureau of Labor Statistics.

TABLE 2.3. Number of New Hires in the Private Nonfarm Economy by State (Annual total in thousands)

State	1981	1982	1983	1984	1985	1986	1987	1988	1989	1990	1991
Alabama	776	624	609	826	863	900	993	1,071	1,128	1,135	1,025
Alaska	180	200	265	198	183	146	143	152	168	174	186
Arizona	897	742	858	1,145	1,221	1,246	1,335	1,378	1,449	1,442	1,327
Arkansas	510	401	386	547	567	598	662	723	774	789	715
California	7,688	6,641	6,931	8,649	8,852	9,099	9,877	10,635	11,124	10,944	9,720
Colorado	1,158	926	851	1,254	1,227	1,233	1,347	1,463	1,581	1,597	1,442
Connecticut	776	660	614	881	864	919	966	1,007	994	918	801
D.C.	183	166	163	215	225	237	267	286	298	290	262
Delaware	188	117	69	174	204	220	255	301	329	331	268
Florida	3,742	3,050	3,116	4,440	4,544	4,871	5,437	5,815	6,127	5,960	5,050
Georgia	1,503	1,216	1,208	1,837	1,916	2,020	2,251	2,404	2,527	2,481	2,120
Hawaii	239	211	228	253	276	286	316	330	374	371	342
Idaho	258	232	250	276	270	258	273	296	315	330	330
Illinois	2,705	2,153	2,267	2,929	2,826	2,953	3,240	3,507	3,591	3,576	3,144
Indiana	1,107	833	836	1,189	1,208	1,278	1,439	1,571	1,648	1,631	1,440
Iowa	593	466	427	587	591	607	676	751	801	810	737
Kansas	653	540	540	680	666	696	741	795	834	840	786
Kentucky	681	562	569	771	755	776	889	931	988	985	894
Louisiana	1,306	1,179	1,050	1,262	1,268	1,223	1,217	1,291	1,340	1,376	1,320
Maine	256	233	267	295	298	325	352	387	371	347	314
Maryland	1,009	906	1,092	1,235	1,248	1,331	1,420	1,486	1,487	1,414	1,218
Massachusetts	1,679	1,479	1,503	1,976	1,884	1,955	2,094	2,148	2,025	1,850	1,663
Michigan	1,607	1,206	1,289	1,793	1,948	1,958	2,110	2,312	2,456	2,384	2,061
Minnesota	956	775	791	1,062	1,049	1,095	1,210	1,308	1,369	1,376	1,248
Mississippi	504	405	426	525	539	538	597	643	668	673	616
Missouri	1,190	1,006	1,046	1,347	1,338	1,392	1,495	1,591	1,651	1,615	1,429
Montana	209	191	220	219	196	198	207	231	237	235	242
Nebraska	393	350	349	433	415	426	460	485	506	525	489
Nevada	457	372	413	500	521	563	631	704	773	794	730
New Hampshire	258	193	219	312	326	347	383	408	386	347	296
New Jersey	1,909	1,654	1,539	2,213	2,185	2,294	2,430	2,593	2,549	2,389	2,090
New Mexico	387	335	335	422	439	428	455	497	520	531	489
New York	4,061	3,419	3,293	4,377	4,398	4,574	4,863	5,085	5,111	4,946	4,166
North Carolina	1,425	1,069	1,099	1,625	1,697	1,807	2,038	2,244	2,339	2,261	1,957
North Dakota	171	150	182	154	147	141	156	152	153	166	168
Ohio	2,160	1,601	1,671	2,326	2,347	2,452	2,677	2,876	3,009	2,967	2,565
Oklahoma	1,008	808	752	910	841	788	868	933	973	1,003	918
Oregon	698	593	639	774	782	820	903	991	1,045	1,053	966
Pennsylvania	2,328	1,760	1,858	2,477	2,426	2,505	2,786	2,932	2,989	2,892	2,540
Rhode Island	248	191	187	273	280	296	318	344	348	325	266
South Carolina	695	537	545	763	782	833	932	1,024	1,081	1,095	928
South Dakota	140	126	149	165	150	160	171	180	192	202	199
Tennessee	1,094	878	906	1,201	1,228	1,295	1,434	1,542	1,615	1,567	1,436
Texas	5,446	4,805	4,448	5,669	5,804	5,666	5,890	6,294	6,568	6,790	6,355
Utah	405	352	355	459	459	462	488	538	582	605	574
Vermont	136	121	137	152	156	164	177	176	172	152	148
Virginia	1,168	978	1,006	1,429	1,507	1,600	1,765	1,907	2,001	1,921	1,652
Washington	1,092	1,023	1,140	1,234	1,244	1,304	1,421	1,480	1,598	1,596	1,531
West Virginia	319	228	261	308	302	289	309	317	331	336	313
Wisconsin	915	699	703	987	984	1,044	1,164	1,282	1,344	1,354	1,193
Wyoming	222	192	167	188	191	173	169	177	185	190	186
United States	59,688	49,553	50,226	65,915	66,637	68,788	74,697	79,974	83,022	81,880	72,853

Source: Derived from data in table 2.2 and unpublished employment data by industry and state from the U.S. Department of Labor, Bureau of Labor Statistics.

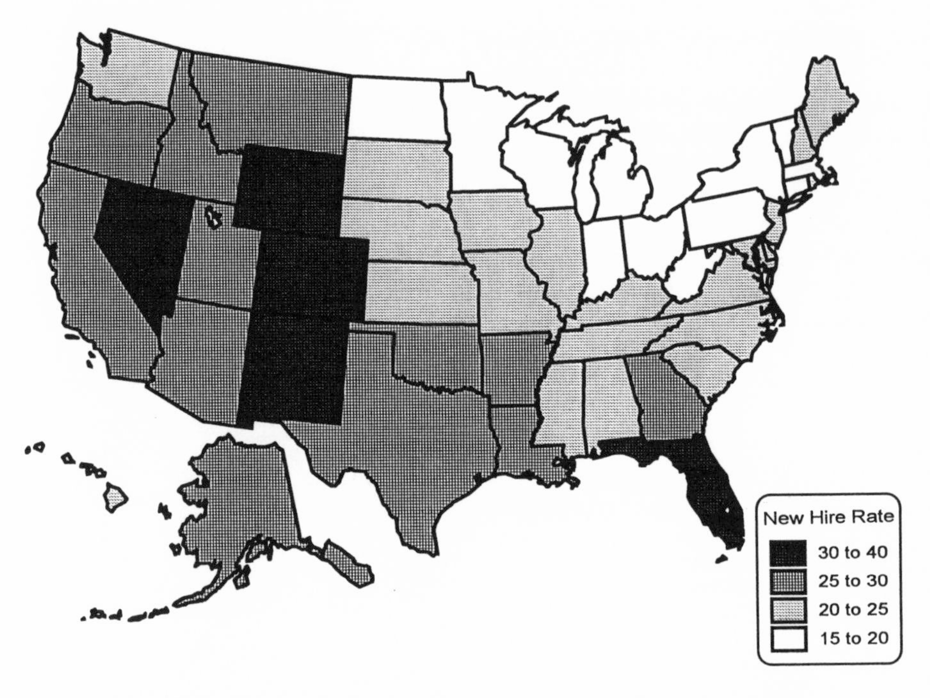

Fig. 2.4. New hire rate in the private nonfarm economy by state, quarterly rate per hundred employees, 1989

Table 2.2 and figure 2.4 illustrate the wide variability in hiring transactions across states. For example, in 1989, in Pennsylvania and West Virginia the quarterly new hire rates are below 17 percent, whereas in Nevada the rate exceeds 37 percent. Quarterly rates in excess of 25 percent mean that more hiring transactions take place in a state in a year than the total number of employed workers in the state. It would be incorrect to conclude that most people change jobs once each year. A more correct explanation would be that a large number of people work as contingent workers and move from job to job. This is consistent with the estimate I made for 1975, that only 18 percent of the work force changed principal jobs.

Table 2.3 shows the estimates of the total number of hiring transactions taking place in a year. For 1991, it had declined by nearly 7 million from its 1989 peak, but it still stood at nearly 73 million, which is surprisingly high for a recession year.

Summary

Various definitions of labor shortages were discussed in this chapter, and both static and dynamic models of labor shortages were presented. Several reasons why labor markets do not clear like product markets, such as efficiency wage theory, were offered to explain labor shortages. A model to explain job vacancies was introduced as a theoretical basis for measuring shortages. The model would use variables such as the unemployment rate and rate of change of employment. Changes in wages paid to new hires would be of importance in that they may be highly correlated with the change in the average wage, but unfortunately, such data are not readily available. Indirect measures of job vacancies, such as help-wanted advertising, were discussed, along with models used to explain variations in help-wanted advertising. Results of research on factors affecting new hires were presented. Distinctions were made between permanent and nonpermanent new hires.

Chapter 3 provides a detailed discussion of actual data available to measure shortages by occupation.

CHAPTER 3

Use of Labor Market Indicators to Measure Shortages

In theory, it should be easy to determine whether a labor shortage exists: Simply look at the demand and supply for labor in any occupation; if demand exceeds supply, then a shortage exists and policies could be implemented to reduce the shortage. Such policies might include increased compensation to workers entering the occupation, improved working conditions, increased worker training, or admission of more immigrants to work in the occupation.

In practice, there is a problem in measuring both supply and demand for labor. Demand is not directly observed. Employment would correspond to demand only if the labor market were in equilibrium; otherwise, demand could exceed or fall short of observed employment. We can derive demand by industry, assume occupational staffing patterns are fairly consistent, and get a measure of demand in which we have some confidence. Supply assumptions are more tenuous. For example, what is the supply of financial managers? A direct measure might be to take the sum of all MBAs with a degree in finance and all currently employed and unemployed financial managers; but should we also include people who are trained as financial managers but are working in other fields? What about students graduating with a degree in economics, who may or may not get jobs as financial managers? The case of financial managers is not unique; a direct measure of supply is simply not available for most occupations.

Since supply cannot be measured directly, the determination of labor market imbalances must rely upon *indicators*, or models using these indicators. The best-known example of such an indicator is the unemployment rate. A high unemployment rate in an occupation is an indicator that there are surplus workers in that occupation, and a low unemployment rate is an indicator of a labor shortage. Using only one indicator, however—even one as relevant as the unemployment rate—can still lead to an incorrect conclusion. A low unemployment rate could exist, for example, when supply and demand are in perfect balance.

We suggest, therefore, combining several labor market indicators to test for shortages. We have developed a number of indicators, which will be discussed later in this chapter. Ideally, these indicators could be combined in a model or models to measure excess demand. Some less formal attempts to combine the indicators are discussed in chapter 4.

We expect that for many occupations the indicators will point in one direction or another. If most or all of the indicators for an occupation are neutral or negative, then there is no labor shortage in that occupation. Conversely, if positive indicators dominate, the occupation is more likely to have a labor shortage. This would not necessarily indicate an across-the-board shortage, however. There could be shortages in an occupation in some parts of the country but not in others; or within an occupation, there might be a shortage at certain levels of education but not at others, or a shortage of workers with a particular skill. For example, there could be a shortage of computer programmers experienced in a particular computer language even when there is no overall shortage of programmers.

When the indicators are mixed, however, no conclusion is indicated. We suggest three steps that can be taken to further the analysis. First, an indicator can be deleted and the impact noted. Second, models can be built and refined to combine the indicators. Third, a detailed study of the occupation may help give a more thorough understanding of the factors at work. In all cases, the indicators should be viewed as the starting point for such analyses, not as the ultimate determining factor.

In this chapter we discuss some indicators and reliability measures that can be constructed from available data. In chapter 4 we present example results. Here we concentrate on national measurement; in chapter 6 we discuss measurement at the state level and construction of measures for more detailed occupations. In chapter 5 we discuss the probability of more prevalent shortages in the future, and the factors that could contribute to such shortages.

Available Data, Past and Present

It is useful to begin our discussion by first summarizing the data sources that could generate the indicators. Unfortunately, there has been a reduction in relevant labor market information collected since the early 1980s. Four major sources relevant to labor shortage determination have disappeared. These four sources are:

—a labor turnover survey which ascertained accessions, new hires, separations, and quits primarily for large firms in manufacturing;
—a job vacancy survey (a pilot for a new survey was completed in 1991);
—national job bank information collected from job banks throughout the

United States that reported jobs open for more than thirty days; and
—national supply data on vocational education completions.

Existing data that will be relied upon include:

1. Data on employment, unemployment, wages, and replacement demand from the Current Population Survey (CPS), a monthly survey of approximately 57,000 households conducted by the Census Bureau. Labor market indicators from the survey are published by the Bureau of Labor Statistics (see U.S. Dept. of Labor 1992f, 1994).
2. BLS employment forecast. Every two years, the Bureau of Labor Statistics publishes forecasts approximately 10 to 14 years into the future. The bureau uses an econometric model to forecast employment by industry, then uses current data from its Occupational Employment Statistics (OES) survey to obtain staffing patterns. These patterns are assumed to prevail in the future and are applied to predict future occupational employment in each industry. Employment is then summed up from each industry. In cases where technological or other changes are expected, the data from the OES staffing patterns matrix are adjusted to conform to new projections (see U.S. Dept. of Labor 1992c).
3. Labor certification data collected by the Employment and Training Administration of the U.S. Department of Labor.
4. Data collected by the Office of Education on graduations from a variety of programs, including community colleges, professional schools, and graduate programs. The biggest gap in the data is the lack of current information on vocational education and proprietary school graduates (see U.S. Dept. of Education 1988). These data are examined for a few occupations but not generally used.
5. Data on apprenticeship completers collected by the U.S. Department of Labor, Bureau of Apprenticeship and Training. These data are also examined for a few occupations but not generally used.

Due to lack of funds, many government agencies do not publish all the data they collect. They do, however, make the data available on request. Unpublished data of this nature were used in this study.

What Is an Occupation?

The *Dictionary of Occupational Titles* (*DOT*) (U.S. Dept. of Labor, Employment and Training Administration 1991) lists more than 20,000 occupational titles arranged into 12,741 different codes, and even at this level of detail, further distinctions can be made. For example, chefs can be classified by the country of the food they cook, such as Chinese, with further subcategories, such as Mandarin or Cantonese. Biologists with a bachelor's degree can be distinguished from biotech specialists with a Ph.D. Engineers have different subspecialties. Chapter 6 discusses analyzing occupations at levels of detail far greater than those dealt with in this chapter and the next.

Virtually every data source has a different way of classifying occupations. Some of the more comprehensive classification systems, along with the *DOT*, are the *Standard Occupational Classification* (*SOC*) system (U.S. Dept. of Commerce 1980); Census Bureau codes (which differ among years of collection—see U.S. Dept. of Commerce 1989), and Occupational Employment Statistics (OES) survey codes (U.S. Dept. of Labor 1992d). Some of the data on which we rely are from a forecast done by BLS called the BLS matrix, which combines OES codes. None of these systems corresponds exactly to any of the others. The closest match is between Census Bureau and *SOC* codes. Furthermore, the Office of Education has coding systems for graduates of training programs by course offering and field of study that do not correspond to any of the other classification systems (Malitz 1981).

The data currently available on educational graduates at the national level are inadequate for most occupations. A more detailed discussion of this topic can be found in Chapter 4.

To analyze data from the various occupational classification systems, agencies, and surveys, it is necessary to develop a crosswalk among these systems. Significant efforts in this regard have already been accomplished by the Bureau of Labor Statistics and the National Crosswalk Service Center of the Iowa State Occupational Information Coordinating Committee (SOICC) (1993). They in turn have drawn upon research by other state agencies and the U.S. Department of Labor.

Our study first examined the crosswalk from the Iowa Center and modified it for our purposes. The Iowa crosswalk is fairly useful between the *DOT* and the Census Bureau, but it is not very helpful when attempting to match census occupations into BLS occupational forecasting matrix occupations. BLS has developed a crosswalk between census occupations and OES coded occupations (U.S. Dept. of Labor 1991b). For certain occupations, however, such as engineering managers, the crosswalk may not be very helpful since the census and OES occupations do not mesh well.

To link census occupations with OES or BLS matrix occupations, we first grouped the 500 census occupations into 193 groups, and then assigned each of the 280 summary matrix codes to one of the 193 groups. The grouping was done using the crosswalks developed by BLS and the Iowa SOICC.

The groups were modified as data from the various systems were cross-checked with one another. Attempts were made to group together occupations with similar types of education and training requirements. For example, many unskilled occupations were grouped together, but different professional specialty occupations were grouped separately. It would have been ideal to separate occupations requiring different levels of education, but such labor market information was generally not available. A study we did to provide this information is discussed in Chapter 6.

Throughout the period of this research, many revisions were made to the various crosswalks used. It was not possible always to go back and reestimate all the indicators, but we did provide a summary of how all our occupational groups could be derived using the 1990 Census Bureau classification system shown in appendix A. Unfortunately, historical data cannot be constructed for all 1990 census categories. Data prior to 1992 rely on the 1980 census classification system.

Prerecession and Slow Economic Growth Indicators

During the first third of the decade of the 1990s, the economy was growing at too slow a pace to generate many shortages. During the period 1986–89, while the economy was growing faster, there was more potential for shortages to develop. Thus, we have divided the period for analysis into two subperiods, 1986–89 and 1990–93. We also show information for 1983–89.

We used the same categories consistently to construct our indicators. Thus, most occupations during 1990–93 would have lower scores, although the relative ranks could move up for some occupations.

Recommended Indicators

After carefully reviewing available labor market information in conjunction with the theoretical considerations discussed in Chapter 2, indicators were developed.

Every labor market statistic has some limitation. Our purpose is to permit a better understanding of how each indicator can be interpreted. When several indicators are combined with background information on the occupation and knowledge of workings of the labor market, useful distinctions can be drawn.

The recommended indicators for 1993 are as follows.

1. Occupational unemployment rate, 1992–93.
2. Change in occupational employment, 1989–92 and 1992–93 averaged.
3. Change in weekly wages of full-time workers by occupation, 1989–92 and 1992–93 averaged.
4. BLS predicted employment growth by occupation: long run, 1992–2005.

5. Replacement demand by occupation: net, 1990–2005; total, 1990–91.
6. Labor certifications by occupational group per 100,000 workers employed in that group, 1990–92.
7. Specific vocational preparation required for the same occupation.

The indicators could be updated annually except indicator 4, which currently is updated every two years, and indicator 5, which is updated every two to four years. Indicator 7 would be updated only if a new survey were completed of vocational preparation necessary for each occupation. Each indicator is discussed in more detail in the sections that follow.

In addition, we illustrate in table 4.15 another indicator, additions to labor supply by occupation compared to BLS projections. Our final decision was that this indicator was not sufficiently reliable for most occupations to warrant inclusion other than as an illustration for selected occupations.

Occupational Unemployment Rate

The most direct measure of labor shortages available is the occupational unemployment rate. These data are derived from the monthly Current Population Survey. The unemployment rate is low either when demand exceeds supply, or when supply and demand are in balance. In general, a low unemployment rate would suggest a labor shortage.

Our unemployment rate indicator is the average unemployment rate for the period 1992–93, based on the 1990 Census Bureau occupational classification system. We used this period because it is the only recent period for which consistent data are available. Data prior to 1992 are based on the 1980 Census Bureau occupational classification system, and after 1993, a new methodology was introduced to measure unemployment (U.S. Dept. of Labor 1994).

The major advantages to the measure are:

1. It is one of the principal explanatory variables suggested by the theoretical discussion in chapter 2.
2. It is the most direct measure currently available on occupational shortages.
3. It is collected monthly by a trained interviewer staff for more than 57,000 households throughout the United States.
4. Estimates are available within a month of the time data are collected.

Some of the major drawbacks to the measure are:

1. Surveyed subjects may provide incorrect information. The occupational classification is often made by a family member other than the

worker and can therefore be in error. Also, people tend to upgrade their occupational classification over their actual job title.

2. A person's occupation is defined by the most recent job rather than either the longest-duration job or the occupation for which that person is trained. For example, an unemployed auto worker who last worked one month as a sales clerk in retail trade would be classified as a sales worker rather than an auto worker.
3. The unemployment rate as officially measured by BLS does not correspond exactly to the theoretical measure of unemployment described here, namely, the excess of supply over demand at a given wage. Unemployment as officially measured by BLS distinguishes only whether respondents are looking for work, not at what wage they would look for work.
4. Unemployment may vary across occupations because of differences in search time unrelated to labor shortages. Unemployment may be caused by a lack of aggregate demand, or it may have structural or frictional causes. For our purposes, there is no need to distinguish between structural change and lack of aggregate demand because to the extent that either one causes unemployment in an occupation, a shortage in that occupation is unlikely. The problem arises with frictional unemployment. Frictional causes are related to the time workers spend looking for work between jobs and can vary by occupation. If low frictional unemployment in an occupation causes the occupation's overall unemployment rate to be low, then a low unemployment rate does not indicate a labor shortage in that occupation. Further research is needed to learn more about differences in frictional unemployment by occupation.
5. The count of unemployed persons does not include those who are working part time because they cannot find full-time work, or those who stop looking for work because they think work is not available.
6. Occupational classifications with respect to the unemployed apply only to persons who have worked two or more weeks full time in an occupation; they do not include recent entrants to that occupation who have never worked in the occupation. For example, a recent graduate of a dental school who has not yet worked as a dentist would not be counted as an unemployed dentist.
7. Unemployment rates do not measure underemployment. Highly educated workers may take jobs that do not fully use their training and that do not pay as well as other jobs for which they are qualified but which are unavailable.

The unemployment rate used in this study is computed from the Current Population Survey and is based on annual averages of twelve monthly surveys. The use of annual averages reduces the standard error of estimate by 50 percent over the standard error of estimate for single-month surveys. To further reduce the standard error of the unemployment rate, we calculated an average over two years. These standard errors are discussed in more detail in chapter 4.

Trend Change in Employment

The trend change in employment by occupation often reflects the trend in demand for workers in that occupation. An increase in employment suggests an increase in demand, whereas a decline in employment suggests a decline in demand. A labor shortage is more likely to occur if demand is increasing than if it remains constant or declines, because the supply of workers may not be sufficient to meet the growing demand.

Because the Current Population Survey's occupational definitions were changed in 1992 to reflect the 1990 Census Bureau classification system, we estimate the trend change in employment by averaging the change in employment equally from 1989–92 and 1992–93. This places a greater weight on the more current and more correctly classified data.

Our measure of employment by occupation is based on annual averages of twelve monthly surveys taken from the Current Population Survey. The advantages of this measure are:

1. It is one of the principal explanatory variables suggested by the theoretical discussion in chapter 2.
2. The data are collected monthly by a trained interviewer staff for more than 57,000 households throughout the United States.
3. Estimates are available within a month of the time the data are collected.

The disadvantages of the measure are:

1. Surveyed subjects may provide incorrect information. The occupational classification is often made by a family member other than the worker and can therefore be in error. Also, people tend to upgrade their occupational classification over their actual job title.
2. Employment changes do not always reflect changes in demand. For example, if labor supply were fixed, an increase in demand would not result in an increase in employment.

Trend Change in Wage Rates

According to traditional economic theory, if demand exceeds supply, wages will be bid up. Thus, rapidly rising wages are consistent with a labor shortage. If wages are bid up sufficiently, the labor shortage could be eliminated.

Economic theory suggests that the wages of newly hired workers could be higher as a result of bidding for scarce labor, but there are no data showing wages of newly hired workers apart from the total. If firms increase wages of newly hired workers, however, the average wage for all workers would go up unless the wages of existing workers declined or the mix of new and old workers changed enough to lower the average.

In most firms, when wages of entry-level workers increase, wages of other workers also increase to reestablish the wage differentials existing prior to the increase. Since we are dealing with economywide averages rather than firm averages, analysis of occupational wage changes is more complicated. For example, consider an economy with two sectors, large firms and small firms. Assume large firms pay more than small firms do, and that large firms are declining while small firms are growing. Even with declines in large firms, small firms may have difficulty finding workers and thus may bid up their wages. Average wages could still decline, however, if the increase in small-firm wages is not sufficient to make up for the sectoral shift. Average wages could be misleading in this instance; wages paid to newly hired workers would be more interesting.

From the Current Population Survey it is possible to obtain median wages for full-time workers. These data were historically computed only for occupations with 50,000 or more full-time workers employed; BLS computes but does not publish wages for occupations with fewer than 50,000 workers. Rather than rely on data for which the sample size was too small, we used a "hot deck" approach to estimate missing data using values from another cell that is expected to have similar characteristics. We used this hot deck approach to estimate the wages for missing cells, either by interpolating missing years or by using aggregate categories when subcategories were missing. For example, if the rate of change of wages was not available for the occupation "all other engineers," the rate of change of wages for "all engineers" was substituted. The extent to which these interpolations were made affected our confidence in the reliability of the measure and is discussed in the section of this chapter dealing with reliability of the data.

The advantages of this measure are:

1. Like the unemployment rate, this indicator reflects both demand and supply conditions, and the two indicators together yield more reliable information than either of them separately.

2. The data are collected monthly by a trained interviewer staff for approximately 14,000 households throughout the United States.
3. Estimates are available quarterly, within a month of the quarter in which the data are collected.

The disadvantages of this measure are:

1. Historical data are available only for occupations with 50,000 or more full-time workers.
2. Since data refer to usual weekly earnings, they may exclude data on commissions or other pay received irregularly.
3. Surveyed subjects may provide incorrect information.
4. Data reflect only changes in wages; they do not include changes in benefits or working conditions.
5. Wages may change for reasons other than fluctuations in supply and demand; for example, wages in unionized industries are determined by union contracts.
6. Data are for wage and salary workers only; they do not reflect changes in self-employed workers' wages.
7. Data are for average workers rather than newly hired workers.

BLS Predicted Employment Growth

The Bureau of Labor Statistics forecasts employment by occupation for the year 2005. An econometric model is utilized to project employment by industry to 2005, then a staffing patterns matrix from the bureau's OES survey is applied to 2005 industry estimates to get occupational employment estimates.

In some occupations where changes in staffing patterns are expected by 2005, or in other occupations where the staffing patterns are not ascertained by the Occupational Employment Survey, such as household domestic help, BLS makes adjustments to the matrix.

The Bureau publishes three estimates of employment growth from 1992 to 2005: low, moderate, and high. Because we judge the moderate estimate to be the most reasonable of the three, it is used as one of our indicators. The presumption is that the occupations with the highest projected occupational growth are the most likely to have a labor shortage.

The advantages of this measure are:

1. The projected change in employment provides a longer-term view of growth in demand for the occupation.
2. Projections used to determine future occupational employment are based on a comprehensive survey of current staffing patterns of U.S.

employers. Such an approach is less likely to have occupational classification errors than is a household survey.

A major disadvantage of this measure is that future projections are conditional and therefore always susceptible to error. A changing trend or government policy could radically change projections. For example, an expanded government medical care program could increase demand for medical practitioners, or medical cost containment might significantly reduce biotech research. Changes in political systems abroad could reduce demand for military goods and increase demand for domestic programs.

Replacement Demand

Differences in the rate at which workers leave an occupation could influence future shortages. The measure of this rate is called replacement demand.

BLS has developed two measures of replacement demand (U.S. Dept. of Labor 1992b). The first measure, based on total separations, includes all workers who leave an occupation. The second measure nets out the experienced workers entering an occupation from those leaving.

BLS estimates total separations by tracking workers surveyed in the Current Population Survey over a year, to determine how many have left their occupation. These data are then merged with a special CPS supplement that provides data on occupational transfers.

BLS represents net separations, in most cases, as the number of workers entering an occupation minus workers leaving over a five-year period, by five-year age group. For example, in 1985 there were 112,000 registered nurses in the 50–54 age group, and in 1990 there were 96,000, for a net separation of 15,000. BLS sums all age groups having negative employment change and treats the other age groups as having no change, to arrive at total net separations.

BLS measures net separations only over the long term; thus, this measure is more meaningful when looking at long-term shortages. To get at short-term shortages, the BLS measures total separations. Total separations can tell us something about short-term shortages. A large number of separations over the short term indicates high turnover, and most occupations with high turnover do not have an equally high rate of replacement; hence, high turnover suggests the possibility of a labor shortage.

Over the long term, net separations are most influenced by the aging of the work force. It is a given that older workers will retire, but whether there are trained workers available to replace them depends on the demand for labor some years earlier. For example, in a period when the construction industry is not doing well, young people will be discouraged from entering apprentice programs in that industry and will choose other careers. Eventually, however, even without a significant surge in the economy, the construction industry will lose workers through retirement and other inevitable factors, such as relocation or death. Over time, there will be a demand for new workers, but then there will be a shortage of journeymen because of all the potential apprentices who chose alternate careers.

For 1990–91, BLS matched workers in the CPS who were present in both years in the sample. Excluded from the match would be households that moved in 1991. Workers could be in the same occupation, enter a different occupation, become unemployed, or leave the labor force between 1990 and 1991. This sample was also merged with a January 1991 special supplement of occupational mobility. (Data derived from a special tabulation was provided to us by the BLS. The merge methodology that was applied to the 1990–91 data is described in U.S. Dept. of Labor, Bureau of Labor Statistics 1991b.)

To obtain a measure of total replacement demand, we counted all workers who left an occupation, then expressed the rate as a percentage of workers employed in the occupation in 1991.

The major advantage of this measure is that it takes account of occupational turnover, which is of far greater importance than growth in determining job openings for most occupations. For all U.S. occupations, 16.4 percent of all workers left their occupation from 1990 to 1991.

The disadvantages of the total measure are:

1. It omits workers who moved between 1990 and 1991.
2. It does not count workers who died between 1990 and 1991.
3. There are very large differences among occupations, some of which may be spurious.
4. The standard errors for these measures are larger than for the other measures, since the sample size is smaller.

Labor Certifications by Occupational Group

In compiling this indicator, we tabulated the number of aliens receiving permanent labor certifications by occupation, over a three-year period. The majority of certifications were for foreign-born, non-U.S. citizens working in the United States. Only a small number of certifications were for workers not yet in the United States. If the certification process has accurately reflected labor market conditions, an occupation with a large number of certifications, either in absolute terms or as a percentage of employment growth in that occupation, would be a positive indicator of shortages.

The major advantage of this indicator is that it summarizes independent determinations made on thousands of cases in which employers assert they cannot get U.S. workers.

The disadvantages of this indicator are:

1. Even if the current process of certification operates to identify local shortages, it may not properly identify national shortages. (State data are discussed in chapter 6.)
2. Current regulations used in labor certification may not always identify labor market shortages or surpluses. For example, certain occupations may have licensing requirements that require U.S. training. Foreign workers trained in the United States may qualify, but in some occupational areas, non-U.S. citizens typically may not receive such training.
3. If labor market information is used to determine shortages, there will be fewer certifications made on a case-by-case basis and the reliability of this indicator will be diminished over time.
4. Employers obtain labor certification through a legal process, which may generate different results than would an economic analysis.

Comparison of Labor Supply to BLS Projections and Replacement Demand

Although this indicator is one of those most commonly used, our analysis of it shows it to be one of the least reliable. Therefore, it is not included on our recommended list. This indicator is computed by comparing the ratio of annual additions to supply from training to projected openings. Openings are computed by adding replacement demand and projected employment growth.

The advantages of the indicator are:

1. When the data are available, the indicator provides a separate picture of both sides of the labor market—supply and demand.
2. When serious imbalances exist, the data are usually conclusive.
3. Several states have done extensive collection of these data.

The disadvantages are:

1. Additions to supply from training are not the only additions to supply. Workers may leave unemployment, change occupations, or reenter the labor force.
2. Data are not available on all sources of supply. For example, there are

virtually no data on graduates of proprietary schools. Vocational educational data have not been collected since 1982–83.

3. It is difficult to match data classification by course of study to data based on employment. For example, in what occupations do history majors work after they graduate? There are numerous choices.

Reliability Measures

To assess the reliability of the various indicators discussed in the previous section, three measures were constructed for each indicator where appropriate and possible. These measures are: (1) standard error, (2) coverage ratio, and (3) missing data match. These measures are discussed in turn.

Standard Error

Since many of the indicators are based on data from the Current Population Survey, which is a stratified random sample of the population, it is possible to compute the standard error of the estimate. For example, if the CPS-measured unemployment rate for an occupation is 6 percent with a standard error of 1 percent, then it can be shown statistically that 95 times out of 100, the unemployment rate measured from the population with no sampling error would be between 4 and 8 percent.

Coverage Ratio

The coverage ratio is a measure of how completely an indicator derived from administrative statistics covers the population. Unlike the other reliability measures, the coverage ratio is not estimated by occupational group. The problem is not sampling error but rather the failure of administrative records to account for the entire population. For example, the U.S. Employment Service (ES) places few if any lawyers, but it places many clerical workers. The coverage ratio for the Employment Service is approximately 5 percent of all new hires in the United States. This can be derived by dividing the total number of ES hiring transactions by the total number of new hires in the United States (see table 2.3).

Because the coverage ratio was low, we decided not to use as an indicator the data on unfilled openings sent to the interstate data clearance center in New York. New York receives data on hard-to-fill job openings from the other state employment services, but these services send only the data they choose to release. For example, only twelve job openings were reported to New York in 1988 by the Michigan Employment Security Commission.

Missing Data Match

For some of the occupations, data were incomplete, and we had to interpolate data or substitute data from more aggregate occupational categories. For the occupations where this adjustment was necessary, the reliability of the indicator is diminished.

More detail on these measures of reliability is provided in Chapter 4.

CHAPTER 4

The Indicator Results

In this chapter, estimates of the various indicators are presented. Not only do these results give us insights into which occupations represent potential shortages or surpluses, they also give us an opportunity to examine gaps in our knowledge of occupational information.

Results for each indicator are presented first, followed by a summary of the results for all of the combined indicators. The indicators are discussed in the same order as in chapter 3. For ease of reference, the indicators are:

—unemployment rates
—employment change
—change in wage rates
—BLS predicted employment growth
—replacement demand
—labor certifications
—annual flows of supply and demand

The last indicator, annual flows of supply and demand, is not used in the final index since it is incomplete for most occupations. An alternative indicator is used instead—skill level, measured by the amount of specific vocational training (SVP) required for an occupation.

Unemployment Rates

Table 4.1 summarizes occupational unemployment rates for 193 Census Bureau groupings of occupational classifications for various periods from 1983 to 1993. Table 4.2 provides a summary tabulation of the distribution of unemployment rates.

For both unemployment rates and employment growth rates, occupational groups were exact aggregations of detailed census occupations, and no matching error was committed by our process. Classification errors could have been committed by respondents, however, in identifying their own or their family members' occupation. (Minor changes were made in the 1990 census classifications compared with 1980, which could have caused some

TABLE 4.1. Average Annual Unemployment Rates and Labor Force, by Occupation

Occupation	Group Number	1983 - 89	1983 - 86	1987 - 89	1992 - 93	Labor Forc (thousands 1992
Executive, administrative, and managerial occupations						
Financial managers	007	2.4	2.1	2.8	3.3	532
Personnel and labor relations managers	008	3.1	3.7	2.3	5.2	110
Purchasing managers	009	1.9	2.2	1.6	3.5	118
Managers, marketing, advertising, and public relations	013	2.7	2.6	2.8	4.8	540
Administrators, education and related fields	014	1.4	1.6	1.1	1.8	618
Managers, properties and real estate	016	3.0	3.4	2.4	3.8	456
Other executive, administrative, and managerial	01A	2.7	3.0	2.3	3.5	8,857
Accountants and auditors	023	2.4	2.6	2.1	3.3	1,416
Management analysts	026	2.1	2.3	1.9	3.5	225
Personnel, training, and labor relations specialists	027	3.5	4.2	2.7	3.9	434
Buyers, wholesale and retail trade, except farm products	029	2.4	2.7	2.0	4.0	214
Purchasing agents and buyers, NEC	033	3.5	3.5	3.6	4.6	236
Construction inspectors	035	3.4	4.0	2.7	3.7	68
Other management-related occupations	03A	2.7	2.7	2.6	3.9	1,526
Professional specialty occupations						
Aerospace engineers	044	1.3	1.1	1.5	4.4	93
Chemical engineers	048	1.6	2.0	1.0	3.8	72
Architects, surveyors, and mapping scientists	04A	2.3	2.5	1.9	4.2	161
Civil engineers	053	2.6	3.0	2.1	3.3	224
Electrical and electronic engineers	055	1.5	1.6	1.5	3.7	546
Industrial engineers	056	2.5	2.9	1.8	4.7	214
Mechanical engineers	057	2.0	2.4	1.6	4.3	318
Other engineers	05A	3.0	3.6	2.2	3.8	353
Computer systems analysts and scientists	064	1.7	1.8	1.5	2.9	712
Operations and systems researchers and analysts	065	2.0	1.7	2.4	2.1	196
Statisticians, actuaries, and other mathematical scientists	06A	1.2	1.0	1.6	2.1	48
Chemists, except biochemists	073	2.1	2.7	1.3	1.6	122
Geologists and geodesists	075	3.8	4.2	3.3	4.5	55
Biological and life scientists	078	2.6	3.2	1.8	3.2	98
Other natural scientists	07A	1.1	1.2	0.8	1.4	194
Physicians	084	0.5	0.6	0.4	0.6	617
Dentists	085	0.4	0.2	0.6	0.3	163
Veterinarians	086	0.3	0.6	0.0	0.8	45
Optometrists	087	0.0	0.0	0.0	0.0	24
Registered nurses	095	1.5	1.7	1.1	1.2	1,825
Pharmacists	096	0.9	1.2	0.6	0.8	200
Dietitians	097	3.0	3.6	2.3	3.7	94
Inhalation therapists	098	2.7	3.2	2.1	1.1	77
Other therapists	09A	2.1	2.2	1.9	2.0	125
Physical therapists	103	1.4	1.2	1.6	2.2	106
Speech therapists	104	0.9	1.3	0.5	0.0	79
Physician's assistants	106	2.0	2.6	1.2	2.2	46
Teachers, secondary school	157	1.7	2.0	1.4	1.6	1,191
Teachers, special education	158	1.9	2.1	1.8	1.6	273
Teachers, NEC	15A	3.1	3.4	2.7	3.6	680
Teachers, prekindergarten, kindergarten, and elementary	15B	2.1	2.4	1.8	2.0	2,164
Teachers, college and university	15C	1.9	2.1	1.7	2.3	752
Counselors, educational and vocational	163	2.2	2.5	1.8	3.4	242
Economists	166	3.4	3.5	3.3	4.4	129
Psychologists	167	2.1	2.6	1.4	2.5	227

ᴀBLE 4.1 - *Continued*

cupation	Group Number	1983 - 89	1983 - 86	1987 - 89	1992 - 93	Labor Force (thousands) 1992
Other social scientists	16A	3.0	3.1	2.8	3.4	43
Librarians, archivists, and curators	16B	2.1	2.4	1.8	2.7	211
Social workers	174	3.4	4.1	2.5	3.4	612
Recreation workers	175	10.6	12.9	7.6	11.7	105
Clergy	176	0.6	0.7	0.5	0.6	318
Religious workers, NEC	177	2.3	2.8	1.7	1.4	70
Lawyers	178	0.9	1.0	0.9	1.2	762
Judges	179	0.0	0.0	0.0	0.0	35
Designers	185	3.6	4.3	2.7	4.4	570
Musicians and composers	186	5.5	6.8	3.7	4.0	197
Painters, sculptors, craft artists, and artist printmakers	188	2.8	3.2	2.2	4.3	232
Photographers	189	3.5	3.9	3.0	6.0	135
Other editors, reporters, authors, and technical writers	18A	2.9	3.5	2.1	3.3	459
Professional specialty occupations	18B	6.9	7.9	5.7	7.0	379
Public relations specialists	197	3.6	3.4	3.8	4.5	168
Announcers	198	5.8	6.2	5.2	9.2	58
chnicians and related support occupations						
Clinical laboratory technologists and technicians	203	2.3	2.3	2.3	3.0	311
Dental hygienists	204	0.8	0.8	0.8	0.6	74
Health record technologists and technicians	205	4.2	4.8	3.5	2.5	59
Radiological technicians	206	1.6	2.4	0.5	0.3	147
Licensed practical nurses	207	3.4	4.0	2.5	2.1	462
Health technologists and technicians, NEC	208	2.9	3.6	2.0	4.6	507
Electrical and electronic technicians	213	3.3	3.6	3.1	6.7	354
Other technicians and related support occupations	21A	3.7	4.1	3.1	4.1	274
Drafting occupations and surveying and mapping technicians	21B	4.4	5.3	3.3	6.8	352
Airplane pilots and navigators	226	2.8	3.3	2.3	2.5	100
Computer programmers	229	2.3	2.3	2.4	2.8	567
Other science technicians	22A	4.1	4.4	3.8	4.4	251
Legal assistants	234	3.6	3.9	3.2	5.0	252
Other technicians, except health engineering and science	23A	3.2	3.5	2.8	3.8	715
les occupations						
Insurance sales occupations	253	2.5	2.7	2.2	3.6	593
Real estate sales occupations	254	1.5	1.5	1.5	2.5	739
Securities and financial services sales occupations	255	1.9	1.6	2.3	3.6	334
Other sales occupations	25A	3.9	4.3	3.5	4.6	7,052
Sales workers, other commodities	274	6.4	7.1	5.3	7.3	1,497
Sales counter clerks	275	6.6	7.4	5.6	8.6	218
Cashiers	276	10.2	11.0	9.3	11.1	2,855
dministrative support occupations, including clerical						
Supervisors, administrative support	30A	2.2	2.2	2.2	3.3	787
Computer equipment operators	30B	3.8	4.1	3.3	5.3	702
Secretaries	313	4.0	4.6	3.3	5.1	3,908
Stenographers	314	1.7	2.1	1.3	0.5	72
Typists	315	6.7	7.7	5.2	7.5	591
Interviewers	316	6.4	6.7	5.9	8.3	165
Hotel clerks	317	8.7	9.7	7.3	8.3	116
Transportation ticket and reservation agents	318	3.1	3.0	3.2	4.0	262
Receptionists and information clerks, NEC	31A	6.8	7.7	5.6	7.8	1,252
Records processing occupations, except financial	32A	5.8	6.7	4.5	5.9	973
Financial records processing	33A	3.8	4.3	3.2	4.4	2,444

(*continued*)

TABLE 4.1 - *Continued*

Occupation	Group Number	1983 - 89	1983 - 86	1987 - 89	1992 - 93	Labor For (thousand 1992
Duplicating, mail, and other office machine operators	34A	7.8	8.2	7.3	6.2	77
Communication equipment operators	35A	5.9	6.1	5.5	6.1	241
Mail and message distributing operators	35C	4.5	4.7	4.2	5.0	954
Production coordinators	363	4.2	5.0	3.2	5.3	208
Material recording, scheduling, and distribution clerks	36A	6.4	7.1	5.6	7.6	1,796
General office clerks	379	5.7	6.3	4.9	6.6	772
Adjusters and investigators	37A	3.7	3.9	3.3	4.2	1,359
Bank tellers	383	3.6	3.9	3.3	3.6	485
Data-entry keyers	385	6.7	7.2	6.1	8.0	627
Statistical clerks	386	3.4	3.5	3.3	5.1	62
Teacher's aides	387	4.6	5.2	3.8	3.6	505
Miscellaneous administrative support	38A	3.9	4.4	3.3	4.2	1,406
Service occupations and farming						
Child care workers, private household	406	6.0	6.6	5.2	6.7	380
Private household cleaners and servants	407	6.4	6.9	5.7	6.6	518
Launderers, cooks, housekeepers, and butlers	40A	7.8	7.4	8.4	6.5	42
Police and detectives	41A	1.3	1.5	1.0	1.1	657
Firefighting and fire prevention occupations	41C	2.6	2.2	3.1	2.0	249
Correctional institution officers	424	2.0	2.3	1.6	1.5	300
Guards	42A	8.6	9.7	7.1	8.9	1,001
Supervisors, food preparation and service occupations	433	6.6	7.4	5.5	6.5	361
Bartenders	434	10.1	11.8	7.9	9.5	323
Waiters and waitresses	435	10.2	11.6	8.3	8.9	1,505
Food counter, fountain, and related occupations	438	11.8	12.5	10.9	11.4	357
Cooks, including short-order	43A	10.3	11.2	9.0	10.1	2,097
Food preparation and service occupations	43B	11.6	12.6	10.2	10.3	998
Waiter's/waitress's assistants	443	11.1	12.0	10.0	10.5	411
Dental assistants	445	4.4	4.5	4.3	4.1	174
Health aides, except nursing	446	5.1	5.9	4.1	5.2	385
Nursing aides, orderlies, and attendants	447	8.9	10.0	7.5	7.9	1,710
Cleaning and building service, except household	44A	10.2	11.5	8.5	10.0	3,141
Supervisors, cleaning and building service workers	44B	4.6	4.7	4.4	5.4	181
Barbers	457	1.5	1.8	1.1	1.7	87
Hairdressers and cosmetologists	458	3.3	3.6	2.9	3.1	786
Public transportation attendants	465	3.7	4.6	2.5	3.0	95
Welfare service aides	467	6.9	7.4	6.2	5.8	97
Child care workers, except private household	468	5.4	6.1	4.4	5.3	1,071
Personal service occupations, residual	46A	8.7	10.0	7.0	7.3	582
Farming, forestry, and fishing occupations	47A	7.8	8.6	6.8	8.1	3,762
Precision production, craft, and repair occupations						
Bus, truck, and stationary-engine mechanics	507	4.6	5.6	3.3	5.3	354
Small-engine repairers	509	6.2	7.1	5.1	4.0	58
Automobile mechanics, including apprentices	50A	5.8	6.7	4.5	6.7	962
Automobile body and related repairers	514	7.2	8.3	5.8	8.3	223
Heavy-equipment mechanics	516	7.1	9.0	4.6	8.3	171
Aircraft mechanics	51A	3.6	4.0	2.9	8.6	179
Electronic repairers, communications and industrial equipment	523	5.1	5.5	4.6	5.6	164
Data processing equipment repairers	525	2.8	2.7	3.0	4.8	153
Household appliance and power tool repairers	526	3.1	3.5	2.7	4.2	53
Telephone line installers and repairers	527	3.2	3.5	2.9	1.9	59
Telephone installers and repairers	529	1.9	2.1	1.6	2.4	176

BLE 4.1 - *Continued*

cupation	Group Number	1983 - 89	1983 - 86	1987 - 89	1992 - 93	Labor Force (thousands) 1992
Miscellaneous electrical and electronic equipment repairers	533	4.6	5.4	3.5	8.2	77
Heating, air conditioning, and refrigeration mechanics	534	4.0	4.3	3.5	5.3	256
Office machine repairers	538	2.8	2.3	3.5	3.3	61
Mechanics and repairers, except supervisors	53A	4.6	5.5	3.5	5.1	1,426
Millwrights	544	10.0	12.6	6.7	8.7	102
Supervisors, blue-collar	55A	3.4	3.9	2.8	4.7	2,429
Tile setters, hard and soft	565	10.3	11.4	8.9	13.5	68
Carpet installers	566	7.6	7.8	7.3	7.1	109
Brickmasons and stonemasons, including apprentices	56A	12.4	14.3	9.8	16.6	219
Carpenters and apprentices	56B	10.9	12.5	8.8	13.2	1,445
Drywall installers	573	12.6	14.4	10.1	19.6	147
Electrical power installers and repairers	577	3.5	4.0	2.7	3.6	108
Electricians and apprentices	57A	6.3	7.6	4.5	9.3	737
Painters, construction and maintenance, paperhangers, plasterers	57B	12.1	13.6	10.0	13.3	700
Concrete and terrazzo finishers	588	16.4	18.7	13.4	23.3	82
Glaziers	589	6.4	5.8	7.1	11.2	42
Plumbers, pipefitters, and steamfitters	58A	8.8	10.2	6.8	10.1	479
Insulation workers	593	14.5	16.7	11.5	21.7	71
Roofers	595	14.4	15.7	12.8	15.0	225
Other construction trades	59A	13.5	16.0	10.2	16.2	347
Extractive occupations	61A	17.8	20.5	14.3	15.1	125
Tool and die makers, including apprentices	63A	2.9	3.3	2.5	3.0	134
Machinists, including apprentices	63B	6.2	8.2	3.6	7.1	492
Other precision production occupations	65A	10.1	12.2	7.3	10.5	512
Precision woodworking occupations	65B	5.9	7.3	4.1	8.6	120
Sheet metal workers, including apprentices	65C	9.1	10.7	7.1	8.8	112
Upholsterers	668	5.2	6.0	4.2	5.7	74
Other precision textile, apparel, and furnishings machine workers	66A	6.1	7.4	4.3	6.8	188
Optical goods workers	677	3.7	3.9	3.4	5.4	67
Dental laboratory and medical appliance technicians	678	3.7	4.2	3.1	1.9	52
Butchers and meat cutters	686	8.6	9.1	8.1	7.7	310
Bakers	687	5.9	6.4	5.2	5.9	127
Precision workers, assorted materials	68A	7.1	8.1	5.7	8.5	151
Plant and system operators	69A	2.9	3.5	2.1	2.9	272
erators, fabricators, and laborers						
Metalworking and plasticworking machine operators	71A	10.2	12.4	7.2	9.0	462
Woodworking machine operators	72A	9.5	11.2	7.1	8.5	150
Metal and plastic processing machine operators	72B	11.2	13.6	8.1	11.2	174
Textile, apparel, and furnishings machine operators	73A	10.8	12.2	8.9	10.7	1,345
Printing machine operators	73B	4.5	4.6	4.3	6.5	472
Machine operators, assorted material	75A	9.8	11.5	7.6	9.4	2,775
Fabricators, assemblers, and handworking occupations	78A	12.0	14.0	9.3	11.9	2,179
Production inspectors, testers, samplers, and weighers	79A	9.1	10.4	7.3	10.0	995
Motor vehicle operators	80B	7.6	8.8	6.0	7.0	3,849
Rail transportation occupations	82A	6.0	7.6	3.8	4.1	73
Water transportation occupations	82B	12.5	14.7	9.6	12.6	61
Material moving equipment operators	85A	10.9	12.8	8.3	10.4	1,116
Handlers, equipment cleaners, helpers, laborers	86A	13.8	15.4	11.6	13.7	5,361

urce: Derived from unpublished data from the U.S. Department of Labor, Bureau of Labor Statistics.

matching errors in a few of our groups.) A further discussion of some of these problems follows at the end of this chapter.

The first column of table 4.1 identifies the occupations that can be analyzed using labor market information. The second column, Group Number, refers to the groupings developed for this study, which were derived from census codes. See appendix A for a description of these groups. In the next four columns, average annual unemployment rates are given for various subperiods between 1983 and 1993. For example, the average annual unemployment rate for financial managers was 2.4 percent between 1983 and 1989, 2.1 percent between 1983 and 1986, 2.8 percent between 1987 and 1989, and 3.3 percent between 1992 and 1993. The last column gives the total number of people in the labor force for each occupation listed.

As can be seen in table 4.1, there is a wide variation in unemployment rates by occupation. In general, managerial and professional occupations have lower unemployment rates, while construction trade occupations, machine operators, and laborers have higher unemployment rates. The occupations with the highest skill level generally have the lowest unemployment, which reflects the demand in our economy for highly educated workers. A low unemployment rate in an occupation is no guarantee, however, that workers trained in a given occupation will be able to find work in that occupation. Underemployment could result if workers cannot find work in their chosen occupation and must take jobs in other occupations for which they are overqualified.

The average unemployment rate declined between the 1983–86 period

TABLE 4.2. Distribution of Average Annual Occupational Unemployment Rates

Category	Percentage	1983 - 89	1983 - 86	1987 - 89	1992 - 93
7	Under 1.6	20	19	27	18
6	1.6 - 2.2	23	17	29	15
5	2.3 - 2.9	26	22	27	10
4	3.0 - 3.6	26	23	28	23
3	3.7 - 5.4	27	36	27	50
2	5.5 - 7.4	28	25	26	24
1	7.5 and Over	43	51	29	53
	Total	193	193	193	193
	U.S. Mean[a]	6.1%	6.9%	5.0%	6.4%

Source: Derived from data in table 4.1.
[a]Experienced unemployment rate

and the 1987–89 period, for most occupations. Among the exceptions were financial managers, operations and systems researchers, securities sales occupations, and office machine repairers.

From 1987–89 to 1992–93, the unemployment rate increased in nearly every occupation as the country faced slower economic growth. Unemployment decreased by more than 0.5 percent in a few occupations, such as inhalation therapists; health records technologists; stenographers; office machine operators; private household workers; launderers, cooks, housekeepers, and butlers; small-engine repairers; telephone line installers and repairers; dental lab technicians; firefighters; barbers; cleaning and building supervisors; and butchers. Some of these decreases could be due to sampling errors where the sample is small, as is the case for private household workers. Other decreases could be due to differences in occupational classification between the two periods.

The change in unemployment is not used as an indicator. Thus, even though the unemployment rate for launderers, cooks, housekeepers, and butlers declined by almost two percentage points from 1987–89 to 1992–93, it was still 6.5 percent during 1992–93 and would be in one of the groups with the highest unemployment rates.

The distribution of average unemployment rates is shown in table 4.2. Over the 1983–89 period, twenty occupations had an average unemployment rate of under 1.6 percent, and forty-three occupations had an average unemployment rate of 7.5 percent or greater. Between the 1987–89 and 1992–93 periods, the number of occupations in the low unemployment rate categories declined and the number of occupations in the higher categories increased. Thus, for example, in 1987–89, twenty-seven occupations had unemployment rates under 1.6 percent, and twenty-nine were 7.5 percent and over. By 1992–93, the number of occupations with unemployment at 1.6 percent or below had fallen to eighteen, and the number of occupations with unemployment at 7.5 percent or over had risen to fifty-three. Also included in table 4.2 is a category code or rank which will be used later in the chapter to summarize the various indicators. The indicator was constructed to divide all 193 occupations approximately evenly into seven groups, based on data for 1987–89, a period when the economy was relatively strong.

Unemployment rates were computed by aggregating total unemployment within a group and dividing by the total labor force of that group. These rates differ from rates computed by BLS because we only had data rounded to the nearest 1,000 workers. In most instances this makes little difference. For very small occupations, rates shown as 0 percent might be 1 percent if computed more accurately by BLS. The average of all occupational unemployment rates would be lower than the average U.S. unemployment rates because our data include only workers with an occupational attachment.

Although the Current Population Survey upon which the estimates are based has fluctuated from year to year in terms of the number of household interviews, the sample covered between 53,200 households and 57,800 households for the period in which our data were estimated. For the majority of the period, more than 57,000 households were interviewed. While the absolutely correct procedure would be to estimate separate standard errors each year, the potential bias in failing to do so is very small. Furthermore, standard errors are representative only, and do not pertain to the exact occupations estimated. Computation of exact standard errors would require a complex simulation process, which again would not yield significant differences from the approximations given here.

The standard errors for single-year estimates are shown in table 4.3. The base refers to the number of persons in the labor force in the given occupation. Standard errors for averages of multiyear periods would be lower than shown in table 4.3. Averaging the unemployment rate over two years reduces the standard error by 76 percent compared to the single-year values shown in table 4.3. An average over three years reduces the standard error by 63 percent; over four years, 55 percent. (These estimates were derived from unpublished Bureau of Census simulations provided by the Bureau of Labor

TABLE 4.3. Standard Errors for Unemployment Rates

Annual Base of Labor Force (in thousands)	Annual Unemployment Rate				
	1	2	5	10	15
25	1.61	2.26	3.52	4.85	5.74
50	1.14	1.60	2.49	3.43	4.06
100	0.80	1.13	1.76	2.42	2.87
500	0.36	0.50	0.79	1.08	1.28
1,000	0.25	0.36	0.55	0.76	0.91
2,000	0.18	0.25	0.35	0.54	0.65
4,000	0.13	0.18	0.28	0.39	0.42
6,000	0.10	0.15	0.22	0.31	0.37
10,000	0.08	0.12	0.17	0.24	0.29

Source: Derived from *Employment and Earnings,* U.S. Department of Labor, Bureau of Labor Statistics, December 1989, pp. 131 - 32. Base of 25,000 interpolated.

Statistics.) The 1990 census provides a sufficient sample size to permit calculation of unemployment rates for all groups with minimal statistical errors. In addition, unemployment rates will be available for approximately five hundred census occupations. Unfortunately, response errors to occupational classifications are much greater in the 1990 Census, as discussed in chapter 6.

Employment Change

Table 4.4 summarizes the change in employment by occupational group for the periods 1983–86, 1986–89, 1989–92, and 1992–93. The standard errors for the change in annual employment are very similar to the standard errors for unemployment rates shown in table 4.3, if growth rates are substituted for unemployment rates in table 4.3.

With the 1990 Census, it will be possible to compute employment changes for all 193 groups from 1980 to 1990, with minimal statistical errors. It will also be possible to compute employment changes for nearly five hundred detailed occupations, but classification response errors are likely to be more serious.

As mentioned earlier, underemployment could exist for some occupations with a low unemployment rate. Although we were unable to measure underemployment directly, we get a better picture of the supply and demand conditions for an occupation by considering other indicators, such as employment growth and wage change, than we would get from a single indicator.

The most rapidly growing occupations between 1986 and 1989 were computer systems analysts, physical and other therapists, physician's assistants, recreation workers, dental hygienists, health record technologists, airplane pilots, and optical goods workers, all with a compound average annual growth rate of more than 10 percent. The occupations with the largest declines in employment during this period include typists, duplicating machine operators, statistical clerks, telephone and telephone line installers and repairers, glaziers, extractive occupations, and rail and water transportation occupations, all declining by a compound annual rate of 5 percent or more from 1986 to 1989. We also computed the arithmetic average of the growth rates for 1989–92 and 1992–93. The occupations growing by an average of more than 10 percent were management analysts, biological and life scientists, other natural scientists, inhalation therapists, health technologists and technicians not elsewhere classified (NEC), stenographers, data-entry keyers, small-engine repairers, precision woodworking occupations, and water transportation occupations. During this same period, employment declined by 2 percent

TABLE 4.4. Average Annual Percentage Change in Employment, by Occupation

Occupation	Group Number	1983 - 86	1986 - 89	1989 - 92	1992 - 93	Avera 1989 -
Executive, administrative, and managerial occupations						
Financial managers	007	4.6	4.9	3.1	2.3	2.
Personnel and labor relations managers	008	2.5	3.9	-6.7	-7.7	-7.
Purchasing managers	009	6.8	3.2	0.9	-3.5	-1.
Managers, marketing, advertising, and public relations	013	3.6	5.3	0.1	-3.9	-1.
Administrators, education and related fields	014	6.4	5.4	1.1	5.0	3.
Managers, properties and real estate	016	5.9	7.6	-1.1	10.3	4.
Other executive, administrative, and managerial	01A	5.8	6.1	-0.6	4.1	1.
Accountants and auditors	023	4.4	4.1	-1.2	1.6	0.
Management analysts	026	12.3	-1.2	6.0	14.7	10.
Personnel, training, and labor relations specialists	027	2.3	7.0	-0.8	-3.6	-2.
Buyers, wholesale and retail trade, except farm products	029	5.5	-1.5	-1.4	10.2	4.
Purchasing agents and buyers, NEC	033	3.4	2.5	-3.5	16.1	6.
Construction inspectors	035	-1.3	6.1	2.7	-3.0	-0.
Other management-related occupations	03A	6.6	5.8	2.6	6.9	4.
Professional specialty occupations						
Aerospace engineers	044	5.1	6.4	-7.4	-6.7	-7.
Chemical engineers	048	-4.1	4.3	1.5	-17.1	-7.
Architects, surveyors, and mapping scientists	04A	4.4	4.9	-5.4	-7.2	-6.
Civil engineers	053	3.4	2.2	-4.5	1.8	-1.
Electrical and electronic engineers	055	6.9	1.3	-2.6	1.1	-0.
Industrial engineers	056	-1.1	-0.7	0.8	-1.5	-0.
Mechanical engineers	057	3.5	2.6	-0.8	-2.3	-1.
Other engineers	05A	3.0	-0.6	2.7	-5.0	-1.
Computer systems analysts and scientists	064	11.7	13.7	7.0	11.0	9.
Operations and systems researchers and analysts	065	11.2	7.0	-7.0	22.9	7.
Statisticians, actuaries, and other mathematical scientists	06A	4.3	-2.0	-0.7	-2.1	-1.
Chemists, except biochemists	073	7.9	-0.3	-0.5	10.8	5.
Geologists and geodesists	075	-9.0	2.0	0.0	3.8	1.
Biological and life scientists	078	5.7	5.8	7.3	20.0	13.
Other natural scientists	07A	1.7	3.7	5.6	19.3	12.
Physicians	084	-2.0	3.9	3.9	-1.5	1.
Dentists	085	1.6	8.8	-1.6	-6.2	-3.
Veterinarians	086	0.9	5.1	1.5	28.9	15.
Optometrists	087	12.6	-4.7	-2.6	8.3	2.
Registered nurses	095	2.7	2.4	4.1	3.0	3.
Pharmacists	096	0.8	2.4	4.4	-5.6	-0.
Dietitians	097	0.9	4.4	2.7	4.4	3.
Inhalation therapists	098	1.9	-4.8	6.9	19.5	13.
Other therapists	09A	-2.4	17.3	3.9	5.0	4.
Physical therapists	103	0.6	17.1	4.9	10.6	7.
Speech therapists	104	6.1	1.1	7.8	5.1	6.
Physician's assistants	106	-4.1	11.3	-10.1	0.0	-5.1
Teachers, secondary school	157	-0.4	0.7	-1.3	5.5	2.1
Teachers, special education	158	38.7	6.0	1.5	6.3	3.
Teachers, NEC	15A	1.8	6.4	6.7	7.6	7.
Teachers, prekindergarten, kindergarten, and elementary	15B	1.0	4.2	3.4	2.1	2.
Teachers, college and university	15C	1.8	3.5	1.3	4.9	3.1
Counselors, educational and vocational	163	-2.0	7.3	3.0	-4.3	-0.
Economists	166	4.2	3.2	0.0	-4.1	-2.0
Psychologists	167	6.9	8.4	2.0	8.1	5.0

ABLE 4.4 - *Continued*

ccupation	Group Number	1983 - 86	1986 - 89	1989 - 92	1992 - 93	Average 1989 - 93
Other social scientists	16A	7.5	5.3	0.0	0.0	0.0
Librarians, archivists, and curators	16B	-0.5	0.2	-0.8	7.7	3.5
Social workers	174	5.7	3.2	3.8	-0.7	1.6
Recreation workers	175	4.9	10.4	-2.7	-4.3	-3.5
Clergy	176	-0.9	5.6	-1.9	10.4	4.2
Religious workers, NEC	177	2.5	3.6	-4.4	4.3	0.0
Lawyers	178	0.3	6.2	0.5	3.2	1.9
Judges	179	-6.4	1.0	2.0	8.6	5.3
Designers	185	7.2	3.3	0.5	-0.2	0.2
Musicians and composers	186	1.9	1.2	3.4	-7.4	-2.0
Painters, sculptors, craft artists, and artist printmakers	188	0.5	6.6	-1.0	0.0	-0.5
Photographers	189	4.0	-4.1	4.8	4.7	4.7
Other editors, reporters, authors, and technical writers	18A	5.6	2.5	3.5	5.6	4.6
Professional specialty occupations	18B	7.1	6.6	2.2	0.0	1.1
Public relations specialists	197	0.0	0.4	0.4	-3.7	-1.7
Announcers	198	13.1	-2.5	1.3	-13.2	-6.0
chnicians and related support occupations						
Clinical laboratory technologists and technicians	203	3.8	2.6	-0.8	4.7	1.9
Dental hygier. .is	204	-3.7	10.7	-2.6	2.7	0.1
Health record technologists and technicians	205	1.4	14.5	-7.5	10.5	1.5
Radiological technicians	206	3.8	3.1	5.6	0.0	2.8
Licensed practical nurses	207	-2.0	-0.2	3.0	-6.2	-1.6
Health technologists and technicians, NEC	208	0.3	11.4	20.2	2.1	11.2
Electrical and electronic technicians	213	8.1	-0.2	0.4	-10.0	-4.8
Other technicians and related support occupations	21A	0.0	0.0	2.4	-2.7	-0.1
Drafting occupations and surveying and mapping technicians	21B	4.6	0.3	-3.7	-3.1	-3.4
Airplane pilots and navigators	226	4.6	11.3	-3.8	4.1	0.2
Computer programmers	229	7.4	0.7	-0.7	5.1	2.2
Other science technicians	22A	0.8	1.6	3.4	9.2	6.3
Legal assistants	234	11.2	6.1	4.7	5.4	5.0
Other technicians, except health engineering and science	23A	1.7	4.7	27.1	-37.9	-5.4
les occupations						
Insurance sales occupations	253	0.7	-1.6	2.3	1.7	2.0
Real estate sales occupations	254	8.9	1.6	-2.3	-1.3	-1.8
Securities and financial services sales occupations	255	10.1	2.2	2.2	10.2	6.2
Other sales occupations	25A	4.0	2.2	-6.9	2.3	-2.3
Sales workers, other commodities	274	-0.3	2.2	-3.0	2.7	-0.1
Sales counter clerks	275	6.3	4.2	1.2	-1.0	0.1
Cashiers	276	4.8	2.3	0.6	2.5	1.5
ministrative support occupations, including clerical						
Supervisors, administrative support	30A	2.5	0.4	1.0	2.5	1.8
Computer equipment operators	30B	12.3	0.7	-8.7	-9.5	-9.1
Secretaries	313	1.1	-0.1	-2.6	-3.1	-2.9
Stenographers	314	-10.2	-0.7	16.1	30.6	23.3
Typists	315	-1.3	-5.6	-9.2	-9.7	-9.5
Interviewers	316	-0.4	0.2	-6.4	-0.7	-3.5
Hotel clerks	317	6.4	4.9	6.3	-4.7	0.8
Transportation ticket and reservation agents	318	5.2	-0.6	30.7	0.8	15.7
Receptionists and information clerks, NEC	31A	4.8	3.8	2.4	2.6	2.5
Records processing occupations, except financial	32A	-0.8	0.2	2.5	-0.9	0.8
Financial records processing	33A	0.2	-1.1	-0.9	-2.6	-1.7

(continued)

TABLE 4.4 - *Continued*

Occupation	Group Number	1983 - 86	1986 - 89	1989 - 92	1992 - 93	Averag 1989 - 9
Duplicating, mail, and other office machine operators	34A	4.2	-5.5	3.5	-12.5	-4.5
Communication equipment operators	35A	-3.4	-3.0	2.5	-8.0	-2.7
Mail and message distributing operators	35C	4.2	1.8	-1.8	5.8	2.0
Production coordinators	363	-0.7	3.3	-0.3	1.0	0.3
Material recording, scheduling, and distribution clerks	36A	1.8	2.0	2.1	0.2	1.2
General office clerks	379	4.5	3.1	-4.0	2.0	-1.0
Adjusters and investigators	37A	6.9	9.4	6.4	5.5	6.0
Bank tellers	383	0.1	1.4	-2.4	-4.7	-3.5
Data-entry keyers	385	3.3	6.5	11.3	9.1	10.2
Statistical clerks	386	2.0	-5.5	-12.3	-13.8	-13.0
Teacher's aides	387	3.1	4.9	3.3	4.7	4.0
Miscellaneous administrative support	38A	18.5	6.0	9.8	-0.5	4.6
Service occupations and farming						
Child care workers, private household	406	-0.7	-3.6	-0.5	-2.3	-1.4
Private household cleaners and servants	407	1.0	-4.2	1.4	10.3	5.9
Launderers, cooks, housekeepers, and butlers	40A	-3.5	-1.9	-8.6	-17.9	-13.3
Police and detectives	41A	1.3	4.2	-0.4	11.7	5.7
Firefighting and fire prevention occupations	41C	4.9	-1.5	-0.3	0.4	0.1
Correctional institution officers	424	6.0	9.7	8.7	0.0	4.3
Guards	42A	1.4	2.2	3.3	-2.8	0.3
Supervisors, food preparation and service occupations	433	7.0	6.7	-1.7	-0.3	-1.0
Bartenders	434	-1.6	0.0	-3.3	10.3	3.5
Waiters and waitresses	435	1.1	-0.3	-0.5	3.3	1.4
Food counter, fountain, and related occupations	438	1.4	1.4	-3.7	16.1	6.2
Cooks, including short-order	43A	4.9	2.5	1.3	6.1	3.7
Food preparation and service occupations	43B	-0.9	0.5	4.8	0.0	2.4
Waiter's/waitress's assistants	443	-3.0	2.0	1.1	1.1	1.1
Dental assistants	445	2.7	3.8	-3.3	7.1	1.9
Health aides, except nursing	446	4.2	5.2	-4.4	-14.0	-9.2
Nursing aides, orderlies, and attendants	447	0.8	3.5	3.0	9.2	6.1
Cleaning and building service, except household	44A	1.3	1.5	-0.4	0.0	-0.2
Supervisors, cleaning and building service workers	44B	5.6	1.8	4.0	-13.9	-5.0
Barbers	457	0.0	-4.2	2.0	0.0	1.0
Hairdressers and cosmetologists	458	4.9	0.8	1.0	0.0	0.5
Public transportation attendants	465	4.1	6.6	1.9	14.3	8.1
Welfare service aides	467	4.2	3.0	-1.1	-20.7	-10.9
Child care workers, except private household	468	6.4	4.2	5.7	-1.4	2.1
Personal service occupations, residual	46A	-0.9	8.4	4.0	7.1	5.6
Farming, forestry, and fishing occupations	47A	-2.4	-0.2	0.3	-3.8	-1.7
Precision production, craft, and repair occupations						
Bus, truck, and stationary-engine mechanics	507	4.1	-1.7	1.3	3.3	2.3
Small-engine repairers	509	4.1	-2.9	-5.4	27.3	10.9
Automobile mechanics, including apprentices	50A	2.9	0.3	0.5	-4.5	-2.0
Automobile body and related repairers	514	-0.5	-0.9	1.9	-5.0	-1.5
Heavy-equipment mechanics	516	0.4	-0.8	-0.4	-3.2	-1.8
Aircraft mechanics	51A	0.9	6.3	6.2	-6.1	0.0
Electronic repairers, communications and industrial equipment	523	1.7	-0.2	-2.1	6.5	2.2
Data processing equipment repairers	525	10.7	4.6	-1.3	4.1	1.4
Household appliance and power tool repairers	526	-2.9	3.7	1.3	-19.6	-9.1
Telephone line installers and repairers	527	2.7	-5.5	2.4	-20.7	-9.1
Telephone installers and repairers	529	-2.6	-5.4	-3.8	9.3	2.8

BLE 4.4 - *Continued*

cupation	Group Number	1983 - 86	1986 - 89	1989 - 92	1992 - 93	Average 1989 - 93
Miscellaneous electrical and electronic equipment repairers	533	5.0	-3.3	2.0	-11.3	-4.7
Heating, air conditioning, and refrigeration mechanics	534	9.3	2.2	-4.8	8.7	2.0
Office machine repairers	538	-3.7	4.3	-4.1	0.0	-2.1
Mechanics and repairers, except supervisors	53A	0.4	3.4	-0.7	0.9	0.1
Millwrights	544	-0.7	3.2	-3.4	-5.5	-4.5
Supervisors, blue-collar	55A	3.8	1.8	-2.4	3.3	0.4
Tile setters, hard and soft	565	5.2	4.5	1.2	-5.1	-2.0
Carpet installers	566	5.7	1.6	-2.5	-6.9	-4.7
Brickmasons and stonemasons, including apprentices	56A	4.3	7.4	-6.3	3.3	-1.5
Carpenters and apprentices	56B	4.6	1.0	-3.3	3.2	-0.1
Drywall installers	573	18.5	-0.6	-9.2	16.4	3.6
Electrical power installers and repairers	577	0.6	-1.3	-0.3	6.8	3.2
Electricians and apprentices	57A	1.8	3.4	-1.9	0.5	-0.7
Painters, construction and maintenance, paperhangers, plasterers	57B	3.1	2.2	-1.0	1.2	0.1
Concrete and terrazzo finishers	588	10.8	-4.0	-8.5	27.1	9.3
Glaziers	589	7.2	-5.9	-2.6	-8.1	-5.3
Plumbers, pipefitters, and steamfitters	58A	2.2	-1.2	-2.2	2.1	-0.1
Insulation workers	593	2.3	2.2	-3.2	3.4	0.1
Roofers	595	12.0	-1.6	1.8	18.1	10.0
Other construction trades	59A	5.5	1.9	-3.0	0.0	-1.5
Extractive occupations	61A	-3.6	-6.7	-2.8	14.6	5.9
Tool and die makers, including apprentices	63A	1.3	-1.3	-4.2	2.3	-1.0
Machinists, including apprentices	63B	1.2	-0.6	-1.8	-2.9	-2.3
Other precision production occupations	65A	6.4	-0.9	-0.1	2.6	1.3
Precision woodworking occupations	65B	5.4	-2.3	4.7	16.5	10.6
Sheet metal workers, including apprentices	65C	2.6	1.0	-10.5	5.0	-2.8
Upholsterers	668	5.6	-3.5	-0.5	-10.0	-5.2
Other precision textile, apparel, and furnishings machine workers	66A	0.2	1.9	-5.1	-11.4	-8.3
Optical goods workers	677	1.2	11.3	-7.2	-6.3	-6.7
Dental laboratory and medical appliance technicians	678	3.2	-2.5	0.6	-1.9	-0.6
Butchers and meat cutters	686	1.1	-2.3	2.4	-5.9	-1.7
Bakers	687	1.6	0.9	2.0	-0.8	0.6
Precision workers, assorted materials	68A	2.4	3.7	-5.4	2.2	-1.6
Plant and system operators	69A	-1.5	1.8	1.8	1.5	1.7
rators, fabricators, and laborers						
Metalworking and plasticworking machine operators	71A	-1.0	-1.5	-5.4	-2.7	-4.0
Woodworking machine operators	72A	0.7	3.9	-6.7	0.7	-3.0
Metal and plastic processing machine operators	72B	-2.0	-0.4	-1.5	-2.6	-2.0
Textile, apparel, and furnishings machine operators	73A	-2.2	0.8	-4.0	-3.3	-3.7
Printing machine operators	73B	0.4	0.8	-2.2	-9.2	-5.7
Machine operators, assorted material	75A	1.6	1.2	-3.0	0.4	-1.3
Fabricators, assemblers, and handworking occupations	78A	2.5	2.9	-1.8	-1.2	-1.5
Production inspectors, testers, samplers, and weighers	79A	0.3	1.6	-2.6	0.8	-0.9
Motor vehicle operators	80B	4.0	2.0	1.0	3.5	2.2
Rail transportation occupations	82A	-4.8	-5.0	-8.8	1.4	-3.7
Water transportation occupations	82B	1.1	-7.8	4.7	16.7	10.7
Material moving equipment operators	85A	-1.1	4.3	-3.2	0.1	-1.5
Handlers, equipment cleaners, helpers, laborers	86A	4.1	1.4	-2.4	1.5	-0.5

rce: Derived from data provided by U.S. Department of Labor, Bureau of Labor Statistics.

or more a year in forty-seven occupations, compared to only twenty-five occupations in 1986–89.

The distribution of average annual employment change by occupation is shown in table 4.5. Over the entire 1986–89 period, annualized employment growth averaged 2.3 percent; twenty occupations grew by 7 percent or more. From 1989 to 1993, however, average annual employment growth was less than 1 percent. Again, a category code is introduced for use later in the chapter.

Changes in the 1990 census classification system mean that a few of the employment changes from 1989 to 1993 are simply statistical artifacts rather than true changes. Our use of groups rather than Census codes minimizes the effect of many of the changes. Two examples of cases where our indicator is unreliable are physician's assistants and transportation ticket and reservation agents. Ambulance drivers were included in the classification physician's assistants until 1992, when they were removed from that category. Auto club tour counselors were added under the classification transportation ticket and reservation agents in 1992. The problem is also minimized by averaging the 1989–92 and 1992–93 changes. Classification errors would be minimized if we used only the 1992–93 change, but then we would have the problem of increased sampling error. This problem is discussed in more detail later in this chapter.

TABLE 4.5. Distribution of Occupational Employment Changes

Category	Percentage	Average 1983 - 89	Average 1983 - 86	Average 1986 - 89	Average 1989 - 93
1	Declining by 2 or more	12	21	25	47
2	-0.1 to -1.9	24	19	28	39
3	0 to 1.9	46	49	39	37
4	2 to 3.4	39	21	32	19
5	3.5 to 4.9	31	32	28	17
6	5 to 6.9	26	27	21	15
7	7 or more	15	24	20	19
	Total	193	193	193	193
	U.S. Mean	2.6%	2.8%	2.3%	0.8%

Source: Derived from data in table 4.4.

Change in Wage Rates

The average annual percentage change in full-time median usual weekly earnings by occupation is shown in table 4.6 for the period 1983–89, for the subperiods 1983–86 and 1986–89, and for 1989–93. Also included in table 4.6 are the standard errors of the estimates for each occupation for the percentage change in wages between 1988 and 1989, and the missing data match value. The standard errors of the estimates are calculated using the standard error of a ratio formula (U.S. Dept. of Labor 1982). The standard errors are calculated using unpublished data provided to us by the Bureau of Labor Statistics. Standard errors for wage changes are higher than for employment estimates largely because earnings data are collected only from one-fourth of the sample in any given month. The missing data match value indicates how much data had to be interpolated. The higher the number, the more interpolation was necessary, and the less reliable is the indicator. A value of 1 means there were no missing data. A value of 2 means some middle-year data were missing. A value of 3 means an endpoint was missing. A value of 4 means another occupation was used to estimate but the match was considered close. A value of 5 means another occupation was used but the match was not as close as a 4; there was extensive estimation of the data.

According to table 4.7, the average annual change in full-time median weekly wages in the United States between 1983 and 1986 was 4.6 percent, compared to 3.8 percent from 1986 to 1993. In general, growth in median weekly wages was higher than average for managerial and professional occupations, and lower than average for trade and machine-working occupations. Occupations enjoying the highest wage growth from 1986 to 1989 were registered nurses, pharmacists, dietitians, therapists, physician's assistants, lawyers, judges, insurance salespeople, interviewers, private household workers, brickmasons, and dental lab technicians. Median weekly wages for carpet installers, photographers, and health record technologists probably declined over the period. For 1989–93, no medical occupations were in the top six occupations with annual wage growth exceeding 8 percent, yet many were still in the top wage category of growth greater than 6 percent. Of the twenty occupations counted in this top category, seven were medical related, two were other professionals, one was another technician classification, one was sales, two were administrative support, three were service, three were precision production, and one was a water transportation occupation.

The distribution of average annual growth in full-time median weekly wages is also shown in table 4.7. Over the 1983–93 period, the number of low-paying occupations increased every subperiod, from forty for categories 1 and 2 in 1983–86, to fifty-seven in 1986–89, to sixty-seven in 1989–93.

TABLE 4.6. Average Annual Percentage Change in Median Full-time Weekly Wages, by Occupation

Occupation	Group Number	1983 - 89	1986 - 89	1989 - 93	Standard Error[a]	Match[b]
Executive, administrative, and managerial occupations						
Financial managers	007	5.2	4.5	3.9%	4.9	1
Personnel and labor relations managers	008	5.3	2.5	2.0%	9.8	1
Purchasing managers	009	2.3	0.9	4.4%	11.0	1
Managers, marketing, advertising, and public relations	013	4.7	3.5	3.1%	3.7	1
Administrators, education and related fields	014	5.9	5.3	2.2%	2.8	1
Managers, properties and real estate	016	4.0	4.2	4.8%	4.7	1
Other executive, administrative, and managerial	01A	3.9	4.3	3.5%	0.6	5
Accountants and auditors	023	4.0	3.0	4.1%	1.8	1
Management analysts	026	3.5	6.9	2.8%	7.1	1
Personnel, training, and labor relations specialists	027	4.9	4.5	2.0%	4.9	1
Buyers, wholesale and retail trade, except farm products	029	6.4	6.2	1.0%	5.8	1
Purchasing agents and buyers, NEC	033	4.6	4.6	2.8%	3.4	1
Construction inspectors	035	5.2	5.6	2.3%	0.9	3
Other management-related occupations	03A	3.9	2.9	3.9%	0.8	1
Professional specialty occupations						
Aerospace engineers	044	4.0	4.2	5.9%	3.5	1
Chemical engineers	048	4.2	3.8	5.4%	3.9	1
Architects, surveyors, and mapping scientists	04A	5.0	5.0	0.1%	9.2	4
Civil engineers	053	4.2	5.9	4.2%	3.0	1
Electrical and electronic engineers	055	4.6	4.5	4.0%	1.8	1
Industrial engineers	056	5.0	4.2	4.9%	3.3	1
Mechanical engineers	057	4.3	3.7	4.0%	2.9	1
Other engineers	05A	4.4	4.4	4.1%	1.1	5
Computer systems analysts and scientists	064	5.2	4.1	3.7%	2.3	1
Operations and systems researchers and analysts	065	2.0	2.4	4.6%	3.8	1
Statisticians, actuaries, and other mathematical scientists	06A	4.2	3.4	4.1%	1.9	5
Chemists, except biochemists	073	3.7	1.7	4.2%	5.9	1
Geologists and geodesists	075	3.8	4.0	11.0%	3.3	5
Biological and life scientists	078	5.7	4.4	2.3%	9.7	1
Other natural scientists	07A	3.8	4.0	3.0%	3.3	5
Physicians	084	7.9	6.6	6.5%	8.6	1
Dentists	085	7.6	6.4	6.0%	6.8	5
Veterinarians	086	7.6	6.4	6.0%	6.8	5
Optometrists	087	7.6	6.4	6.0%	6.8	5
Registered nurses	095	6.2	7.3	4.8%	1.5	1
Pharmacists	096	6.5	7.2	5.1%	2.9	1
Dietitians	097	6.9	8.4	3.7%	1.8	3
Inhalation therapists	098	7.5	8.1	4.1%	3.7	1
Other therapists	09A	6.5	8.1	4.6%	3.0	5
Physical therapists	103	7.3	9.7	7.6%	3.1	3
Speech therapists	104	7.4	9.9	7.5%	3.1	4
Physician's assistants	106	6.6	8.3	4.6%	1.4	3
Teachers, secondary school	157	5.8	4.3	3.5%	2.1	1
Teachers, special education	158	6.9	5.6	4.5%	2.5	1
Teachers, NEC	15A	3.6	2.8	2.6%	5.5	5
Teachers, prekindergarten, kindergarten, and elementary	15B	5.5	5.7	2.5%	1.1	4
Teachers, college and university	15C	6.4	5.8	2.8%	3.6	1
Counselors, educational and vocational	163	6.4	6.6	0.9%	2.8	1
Economists	166	2.6	0.0	3.0%	4.6	1
Psychologists	167	4.9	2.1	2.8%	9.1	1
Other social scientists	16A	4.7	2.3	2.4%	3.1	5
Librarians, archivists, and curators	16B	4.4	4.4	4.5%	4.3	1

TABLE 4.6 - *Continued*

Occupation	Group Number	1983 - 89	1986 - 89	1989 - 93	Standard Error[a]	Match[b]
Social workers	174	4.7	3.2	3.9%	3.5	1
Recreation workers	175	3.7	4.0	-0.2%	4.3	3
Clergy	176	4.4	1.2	5.0%	3.9	1
Religious workers, NEC	177	3.2	1.7	0.2%	1.9	5
Lawyers	178	8.0	8.9	4.1%	1.3	1
Judges	179	7.7	9.0	4.2%	1.3	5
Designers	185	3.8	-0.1	3.9%	2.5	1
Musicians and composers	186	3.7	2.4	4.1%	1.5	5
Painters, sculptors, craft artists, and artist printmakers	188	2.1	3.5	3.9%	9.2	1
Photographers	189	0.1	-3.8	6.6%	7.2	1
Other editors, reporters, authors, and technical writers	18A	4.3	5.1	5.8%	3.5	5
Professional specialty occupations	18B	5.6	5.4	3.9%	0.5	5
Public relations specialists	197	4.4	3.6	1.6%	7.7	1
Announcers	198	3.7	2.4	4.1%	1.5	5
Technicians and related support occupations						
Clinical laboratory technologists and technicians	203	4.6	2.9	5.9%	3.5	1
Dental hygienists	204	4.4	5.0	4.8%	1.7	5
Health record technologists and technicians	205	0.7	-2.2	2.3%	1.7	4
Radiological technicians	206	4.3	4.3	7.7%	4.1	1
Licensed practical nurses	207	4.1	5.7	5.3%	2.3	1
Health technologists and technicians, NEC	208	3.5	2.4	3.8%	4.1	1
Electrical and electronic technicians	213	3.8	2.4	3.7%	2.5	1
Other technicians and related support occupations	21A	4.9	4.5	3.7%	0.4	5
Drafting occupations and surveying and mapping technicians	21B	4.6	5.7	1.5%	3.3	5
Airplane pilots and navigators	226	5.2	2.3	7.7%	10.7	3
Computer programmers	229	4.2	5.3	5.4%	1.7	1
Other science technicians	22A	4.3	4.0	1.3%	6.0	5
Legal assistants	234	6.8	8.0	3.4%	4.5	1
Other technicians, except health engineering and science	23A	4.7	5.0	-1.6%	2.2	5
Sales occupations						
Insurance sales occupations	253	5.1	7.1	2.4%	3.7	1
Real estate sales occupations	254	4.7	3.4	4.8%	2.0	1
Securities and financial services sales occupations	255	3.8	2.3	4.7%	9.2	1
Other sales occupations	25A	3.9	3.0	4.4%	0.9	5
Sales workers, other commodities	274	4.0	4.8	4.0%	3.1	1
Sales counter clerks	275	2.7	4.0	7.7%	5.0	1
Cashiers	276	3.0	3.7	2.8%	1.6	1
Administrative support occupations, including clerical						
Supervisors, administrative support	30A	4.7	4.9	4.5%	2.1	5
Computer equipment operators	30B	3.8	3.8	5.1%	2.2	5
Secretaries	313	4.5	4.4	4.2%	1.1	1
Stenographers	314	4.5	4.2	8.4%	0.9	4
Typists	315	4.5	4.1	4.2%	1.8	1
Interviewers	316	6.1	7.0	1.7%	4.3	1
Hotel clerks	317	3.8	2.6	3.3%	2.4	3
Transportation ticket and reservation agents	318	0.4	-2.3	1.6%	5.6	1
Receptionists and information clerks, NEC	31A	3.6	2.6	5.1%	1.9	5
Records processing occupations, except financial	32A	3.1	2.7	4.8%	1.9	1
Financial records processing	33A	3.7	3.0	4.6%	1.0	1
Duplicating, mail, and other office machine operators	34A	4.3	4.0	2.0%	8.4	5
Communication equipment operators	35A	1.7	0.2	5.7%	3.5	1
Mail and message distributing operators	35C	3.6	3.5	4.4%	1.2	1
Production coordinators	363	3.0	-1.4	4.0%	4.9	1

(*continued*)

TABLE 4.6 - *Continued*

Occupation	Group Number	1983 - 89	1986 - 89	1989 - 93	Standard Error[a]	Match[b]
Material recording, scheduling, and distribution clerks	36A	2.7	2.1	3.4%	1.9	1
General office clerks	379	4.2	3.2	3.0%	2.1	1
Adjusters and investigators	37A	3.5	3.6	3.6%	1.8	1
Bank tellers	383	4.4	4.6	2.6%	2.2	1
Data-entry keyers	385	3.7	3.0	3.2%	2.0	1
Statistical clerks	386	4.9	4.7	4.1%	4.4	1
Teacher's aides	387	5.1	5.7	3.6%	4.2	1
Miscellaneous administrative support	38A	4.3	3.7	9.2%	1.0	5
Service occupations and farming						
Child care workers, private household	406	9.9	11.8	4.6%	9.5	1
Private household cleaners and servants	407	4.5	8.0	2.6%	4.9	1
Launderers, cooks, housekeepers, and butlers	40A	5.1	9.3	4.3%	5.5	5
Police and detectives	41A	4.6	4.9	6.1%	1.9	1
Firefighting and fire prevention occupations	41C	5.1	5.6	4.3%	3.8	1
Correctional institution officers	424	5.5	6.0	3.7%	3.3	1
Guards	42A	3.6	1.7	4.8%	3.1	1
Supervisors, food preparation and service occupations	433	1.6	4.0	4.0%	4.2	1
Bartenders	434	3.3	3.8	4.9%	4.8	1
Waiters and waitresses	435	3.8	5.7	3.2%	2.9	1
Food counter, fountain, and related occupations	438	2.1	3.2	4.5%	4.1	1
Cooks, including short-order	43A	3.9	3.3	3.8%	1.6	5
Food preparation and service occupations	43B	3.7	4.3	1.4%	1.1	1
Waiter's/waitress's assistants	443	3.2	6.7	1.7%	4.9	1
Dental assistants	445	5.2	4.8	3.8%	3.9	1
Health aides, except nursing	446	4.6	4.6	2.5%	3.3	1
Nursing aides, orderlies, and attendants	447	4.2	5.8	3.6%	2.3	1
Cleaning and building service, except household	44A	3.4	3.1	2.8%	1.5	1
Supervisors, cleaning and building service workers	44B	4.0	3.4	2.0%	5.5	1
Barbers	457	2.8	2.2	5.4%	2.3	5
Hairdressers and cosmetologists	458	3.1	3.4	4.4%	3.2	1
Public transportation attendants	465	2.8	2.2	34.2%	2.3	5
Welfare service aides	467	4.4	4.9	5.5%	2.6	3
Child care workers, except private household	468	2.5	0.2	7.5%	4.0	1
Personal service occupations, residual	46A	2.3	0.6	4.6%	7.7	5
Farming, forestry, and fishing occupations	47A	3.9	4.3	2.3%	2.0	1
Precision production, craft, and repair occupations						
Bus, truck, and stationary-engine mechanics	507	2.4	2.3	2.7%	3.5	1
Small-engine repairers	509	4.1	3.4	4.0%	2.0	5
Automobile mechanics, including apprentices	50A	4.4	5.4	2.7%	2.9	1
Automobile body and related repairers	514	4.8	3.4	1.0%	4.8	1
Heavy-equipment mechanics	516	3.6	4.8	1.7%	3.3	1
Aircraft mechanics	51A	3.8	3.4	11.0%	1.7	3
Electronic repairers, communications and industrial equipment	523	8.2	6.1	2.4%	6.9	1
Data processing equipment repairers	525	4.2	3.2	1.0%	4.7	1
Household appliance and power tool repairers	526	3.4	1.7	0.8%	1.4	5
Telephone line installers and repairers	527	3.9	3.1	3.3%	4.1	1
Telephone installers and repairers	529	3.2	0.9	3.3%	2.4	1
Miscellaneous electrical and electronic equipment repairers	533	2.3	2.4	5.4%	3.5	1
Heating, air conditioning, and refrigeration mechanics	534	4.1	3.3	3.5%	4.4	1
Office machine repairers	538	2.9	3.4	3.1%	9.3	1
Mechanics and repairers, except supervisors	53A	3.4	3.2	3.3%	1.3	5
Millwrights	544	4.4	2.4	3.9%	7.0	1
Supervisors, blue-collar	55A	3.2	5.0	1.1%	3.0	5

TABLE 4.6 - *Continued*

Occupation	Group Number	1983 - 89	1986 - 89	1989 - 93	Standard Error[a]	Match[b]
Tile setters, hard and soft	565	2.9	2.9	-0.1%	1.7	5
Carpet installers	566	0.9	-1.8	8.9%	1.9	3
Brickmasons and stonemasons, including apprentices	56A	4.5	7.3	-1.5%	3.7	1
Carpenters and apprentices	56B	3.9	4.4	2.6%	1.5	1
Drywall installers	573	0.9	2.5	-0.2%	6.3	1
Electrical power installers and repairers	577	4.2	2.7	5.8%	4.7	1
Electricians and apprentices	57A	2.6	1.4	2.7%	2.1	1
Painters, construction and maintenance, paperhangers, plasterers	57B	3.9	5.7	3.4%	2.2	5
Concrete and terrazzo finishers	588	2.1	5.2	1.2%	1.8	3
Glaziers	589	2.9	2.9	3.0%	1.7	5
Plumbers, pipefitters, and steamfitters	58A	3.7	1.7	1.2%	2.9	1
Insulation workers	593	1.9	3.1	4.2%	4.1	3
Roofers	595	3.9	5.2	-1.1%	11.6	1
Other construction trades	59A	4.1	5.6	3.2%	2.0	1
Extractive occupations	61A	2.3	2.2	2.2%	6.0	3
Tool and die makers, including apprentices	63A	5.3	5.4	1.6%	3.8	1
Machinists, including apprentices	63B	3.3	3.5	2.4%	3.0	1
Other precision production occupations	65A	2.9	3.7	1.1%	1.4	5
Precision woodworking occupations	65B	1.3	5.1	0.7%	11.0	3
Sheet metal workers, including apprentices	65C	2.8	4.4	2.8%	5.6	1
Upholsterers	668	2.7	4.2	2.1%	6.1	5
Other precision textile, apparel, and furnishings machine workers	66A	2.7	4.2	2.1%	6.1	5
Optical goods workers	677	3.8	2.7	4.1%	3.3	5
Dental laboratory and medical appliance technicians	678	6.2	7.4	6.4%	3.6	5
Butchers and meat cutters	686	-1.0	0.4	4.0%	3.9	1
Bakers	687	1.4	-1.9	5.7%	8.7	1
Precision workers, assorted materials	68A	4.8	4.6	1.7%	3.4	5
Plant and system operators	69A	3.4	2.0	3.5%	3.3	1
Operators, fabricators, and laborers						
Metalworking and plasticworking machine operators	71A	3.0	1.0	2.3%	2.8	5
Woodworking machine operators	72A	4.6	3.5	3.9%	4.2	1
Metal and plastic processing machine operators	72B	2.0	0.0	3.3%	5.7	1
Textile, apparel, and furnishings machine operators	73A	3.3	3.8	3.2%	1.5	1
Printing machine operators	73B	3.6	3.4	1.6%	3.4	1
Machine operators, assorted material	75A	2.1	1.8	3.3%	1.1	1
Fabricators, assemblers, and handworking occupations	78A	3.1	2.4	2.3%	2.1	1
Production inspectors, testers, samplers, and weighers	79A	2.9	1.9	3.2%	2.9	1
Motor vehicle operators	80B	3.8	4.3	2.7%	1.3	5
Rail transportation occupations	82A	4.6	3.8	2.3%	6.1	5
Water transportation occupations	82B	3.5	-1.9	6.9%	10.4	4
Material moving equipment operators	85A	3.1	2.4	2.2%	1.7	1
Handlers, equipment cleaners, helpers, laborers	86A	2.9	3.1	2.0%	1.2	5

Source: Derived from data provided by U.S. Department of Labor, Bureau of Labor Statistics.

[a]Standard error is for a one-year change based on 1988 - 89 data. Standard errors of a change over several years are about half of the standard error shown in the table.

[b]The match is a measure of how accurately the wage estimate reflects the data used for the group: 1 = no data missing, 2 = some middle-year data missing, 3 = endpoint missing, 4 = close match using another occupation for estimate, 5 = extensive estimation of data.

TABLE 4.7. Distribution of Average Annual Growth in Median Full-time Weekly Wages, by Occupational Group

Category	Percentage	1983 - 89	1983 - 86	1986 - 89	1989 - 93
1	Under 2.0	11	19	26	29
2	2.0 - 2.9	26	21	31	38
3	3.0 - 3.6	29	24	31	27
4	3.7 - 4.3	51	20	30	40
5	4.4 - 4.9	34	41	21	23
6	5.0 - 5.9	19	37	26	16
7	6.0 and over	23	31	28	20
	Total	193	193	193	193
	U. S. Median	4.1%	4.6%	3.7%	3.8%

Source: Derived from data in table 4.6.

Unlike the employment change, average median wage increases were about the same for 1986–89 and 1989–93: 3.7 to 3.8 percent.

BLS Predicted Employment Growth and Replacement Demand

The average annual predicted growth in employment and net replacement demand from 1990 to 2005 are shown in table 4.8, along with total replacement estimated for 1990 to 1991. Replacement demand measures job openings required to replace workers changing occupations or leaving the labor force.

The predicted growth is based on the Bureau of Labor Statistics forecast. The bureau makes a low, moderate, and high forecast; however, only the moderate forecast is used here. The method used to predict growth and replacement is described in *Occupation Projections and Training Data* (U.S. Dept. of Labor 1992b). The method used to compute replacement is further described in *Total and Net Occupational Separations: A Report on Recent Research* (U.S. Dept. of Labor 1991b). Net replacement demand is used as the primary indicator, but an alternative computation is made using total replacement demand. Total replacement demand can be computed only in years when a special CPS supplement was conducted on job mobility. The latest such supplement was January 1991.

The two indicators are useful measures of predicted demand due to job growth, and demand due to the need to replace persons leaving an occupation. It should be noted that replacement demand is generally larger than job growth.

Match indicators were constructed for replacement demand. The missing data match value indicates how much data had to be interpolated. The higher the number, the more interpolation was necessary, and the less reliable is the indicator. A 1 indicates an exact match, a 4 means an exact match to BLS but BLS used a proxy, and a 5 means an estimate without an exact match even to a BLS proxy. Since the replacement demand indicator is based on a smaller sample than the other measures, and is only for time periods four years apart, more aggregate measures were used to represent smaller occupations. Hence, the match indicator is especially important when interpreting these estimates.

For BLS predicted employment, a crosswalk between Census Bureau and BLS matrix classification systems was used. The crosswalk is based on one developed by BLS. Detailed predictions of employment change from 1992 to 2005 are computed for approximately five hundred occupations.

Table 4.8 summarizes the two measures of demand by occupation. The occupations that are expected to have the most rapid job growth between 1990 and 2005 are computer systems analysts and scientists, operations and systems researchers, physical therapists, radiological technicians, and welfare service aides. Occupations in which employment is expected to decline by an average of more than 1 percent include communication equipment operators; statistical clerks; private household child care workers; private household cleaners and servants; telephone and telephone line installers and repairers; other precision production occupations; textile, apparel, and furnishings machine operators; and fabricators, assemblers, and handworking occupations.

Replacement demand values tend to be very low in professional occupations, where workers have a high degree of training specific to the occupation and therefore do not change occupations frequently. The total replacement demand value is much higher in low-training occupations such as child care workers in private households (52.3 percent) and food counter workers (44.0 percent), where many young people have their first jobs and turnover is very high.

There is little evidence to suggest that total replacement demand changes rapidly over time. Therefore, it is possible that labor markets will adjust to the occupational replacement demand ratios in different occupations. In this case, replacement demand might not be useful as a shortage indicator. To the extent that replacement demand is negatively correlated with skill levels, it may even be a contrary indicator.

The other measure of replacement demand is net replacement. This is lower than gross replacement because it is reduced by the number of people

TABLE 4.8. Annual Average Measures of Demand, by Percentage

Occupation	Group Number	Moderate Job Growth Annual 1992 - 2005	Annual Replacement Demand Value Total 1990 - 91	Annual Replacement Demand Value Net 1990 - 2005	Match Indicator, Replacement Demand[a]
Executive, administrative, and managerial occupations					
Financial managers	007	1.7	6.7	1.6	1
Personnel and labor relations managers	008	1.7	7.4	2.4	1
Purchasing managers	009	1.0	4.3	2.1	1
Managers, marketing, advertising, and public relations	013	2.4	8.5	2.1	1
Administrators, education and related fields	014	1.6	7.8	2.3	1
Managers, properties and real estate	016	2.3	9.4	1.4	1
Other executive, administrative, and managerial	01A	1.6	7.4	1.6	5
Accountants and auditors	023	2.2	10.5	1.5	1
Management analysts	026	2.8	14.2	1.1	1
Personnel, training, and labor relations specialists	027	2.2	8.8	1.9	1
Buyers, wholesale and retail trade, except farm products	029	1.0	12.5	2.0	1
Purchasing agents and buyers, NEC	033	-0.2	9.1	1.7	1
Construction inspectors	035	2.1	5.2	2.5	1
Other management-related occupations	03A	2.3	9.7	1.5	5
Professional specialty occupations					
Aerospace engineers	044	1.0	3.4	2.3	4
Chemical engineers	048	1.4	4.0	2.3	4
Architects, surveyors, and mapping scientists	04A	1.4	9.9	1.5	4
Civil engineers	053	1.6	6.4	2.2	1
Electrical and electronic engineers	055	1.7	3.4	2.1	1
Industrial engineers	056	1.2	1.8	2.3	1
Mechanical engineers	057	1.4	4.0	2.5	1
Other engineers	05A	1.8	5.3	2.3	5
Computer systems analysts and scientists	064	5.9	6.6	0.9	1
Operations and systems researchers and analysts	065	3.7	5.9	1.3	1
Statisticians, actuaries, and other mathematical scientists	06A	1.1	6.2	1.4	4
Chemists, except biochemists	073	1.5	5.6	3.1	4
Geologists and geodesists	075	1.6	5.6	3.1	4
Biological and life scientists	078	1.7	5.6	3.1	4
Other natural scientists	07A	1.5	5.6	3.1	4
Physicians	084	2.3	3.1	2.4	1
Dentists	085	0.4	3.1	2.4	4
Veterinarians	086	2.1	3.1	2.4	4
Optometrists	087	1.2	3.1	2.4	4
Registered nurses	095	2.7	5.7	1.6	1
Pharmacists	096	2.0	1.7	2.2	1
Dietitians	097	1.8	5.5	2.0	1
Inhalation therapists	098	3.1	8.2	2.2	4
Other therapists	09A	3.3	8.2	2.2	4
Physical therapists	103	5.0	8.2	2.2	4
Speech therapists	104	3.2	8.2	2.2	4
Physician's assistants	106	2.3	8.2	1.7	4
Teachers, secondary school	157	2.4	8.7	2.3	4
Teachers, special education	158	4.4	6.2	0.8	1
Teachers, NEC	15A	2.2	11.1	0.9	5
Teachers, prekindergarten, kindergarten, and elementary	15B	2.0	10.0	1.8	5
Teachers, college and university	15C	1.8	12.6	3.2	1
Counselors, educational and vocational	163	2.2	11.9	1.9	1
Economists	166	1.8	19.2	2.8	1
Psychologists	167	3.1	4.9	0.8	1
Other social scientists	16A	1.5	10.2	2.1	4
Librarians, archivists, and curators	16B	0.9	10.3	2.1	4

TABLE 4.8 - *Continued*

Occupation	Group Number	Moderate Job Growth Annual 1992 - 2005	Annual Replacement Demand Value Total 1990 - 91	Annual Replacement Demand Value Net 1990 - 2005	Match Indicator, Replacement Demand[a]
Social workers	174	4.0	9.0	1.0	1
Recreation workers	175	2.5	17.7	1.3	4
Clergy	176	2.0	5.2	1.6	1
Religious workers, NEC	177	2.0	13.9	1.3	4
Lawyers	178	2.1	3.9	2.0	1
Judges	179	0.2	4.5	2.1	4
Designers	185	1.3	12.9	1.4	1
Musicians and composers	186	1.7	15.3	2.0	1
Painters, sculptors, craft artists, and artist printmakers	188	1.6	13.6	2.1	1
Photographers	189	1.7	12.6	2.3	1
Other editors, reporters, authors, and technical writers	18A	1.7	12.0	1.7	5
Professional specialty occupations	18B	2.7	13.7	2.0	4
Public relations specialists	197	1.8	16.4	3.1	1
Announcers	198	1.7	13.7	2.0	4
Technicians and related support occupations					
Clinical laboratory technologists and technicians	203	1.8	7.2	2.0	1
Dental hygienists	204	2.8	8.8	1.7	4
Health record technologists and technicians	205	3.8	8.8	1.7	4
Radiological technicians	206	3.8	8.8	1.7	4
Licensed practical nurses	207	2.6	8.0	1.7	1
Health technologists and technicians, NEC	208	3.0	12.1	0.9	1
Electrical and electronic technicians	213	1.6	8.4	1.3	1
Other technicians and related support occupations	21A	1.1	11.1	2.4	4
Drafting occupations and surveying and mapping technicians	21B	0.8	14.9	3.3	1
Airplane pilots and navigators	226	2.4	4.0	2.8	4
Computer programmers	229	2.1	9.3	2.2	1
Other science technicians	22A	1.7	8.3	2.6	4
Legal assistants	234	3.5	11.1	0.7	1
Other technicians, except health engineering and science	23A	2.6	11.4	1.7	5
Sales occupations					
Insurance sales occupations	253	1.1	7.8	2.6	1
Real estate sales occupations	254	1.1	14.8	1.5	1
Securities and financial services sales occupations	255	2.2	11.2	1.2	1
Other sales occupations	25A	1.4	18.2	2.4	5
Sales workers, other commodities	274	1.3	32.5	2.7	1
Sales counter clerks	275	2.4	30.3	1.4	1
Cashiers	276	1.7	32.2	3.2	1
Administrative support occupations, including clerical					
Supervisors, administrative support	30A	1.7	8.2	2.4	4
Computer equipment operators	30B	-4.0	15.6	0.9	4
Secretaries	313	0.8	13.8	2.2	1
Stenographers	314	-0.1	19.2	2.2	4
Typists	315	-1.3	22.3	1.9	1
Interviewers	316	1.6	23.8	2.5	1
Hotel clerks	317	2.7	26.3	1.7	4
Transportation ticket and reservation agents	318	3.0	10.2	1.8	1
Receptionists and information clerks, NEC	31A	2.3	26.1	1.4	1
Records processing occupations, except financial	32A	1.1	23.3	2.8	4
Financial records processing	33A	0.2	16.4	2.3	4
Duplicating, mail, and other office machine operators	34A	0.9	15.6	3.2	4
Communication equipment operators	35A	-2.5	13.9	2.6	4
Mail and message distributing operators	35C	0.3	10.7	2.2	5
Production coordinators	363	1.0	15.7	2.5	1

(*continued*)

TABLE 4.8 - *Continued*

Occupation	Group Number	Moderate Job Growth Annual 1992 - 2005	Annual Replacement Demand Value Total 1990 - 91	Net 1990 - 2005	Match Indicator, Replacement Demand[a]
Material recording, scheduling, and distribution clerks	36A	0.9	18.4	1.9	5
General office clerks	379	1.7	21.6	1.5	1
Adjusters and investigators	37A	2.2	14.8	1.2	5
Bank tellers	383	-0.4	22.6	3.7	1
Data-entry keyers	385	1.3	25.3	1.6	1
Statistical clerks	386	-0.4	7.2	2.3	1
Teacher's aides	387	2.8	18.0	1.7	1
Miscellaneous administrative support	38A	0.4	14.9	0.6	1
Service occupations and farming					
Child care workers, private household	406	-3.3	52.3	3.5	1
Private household cleaners and servants	407	-3.0	20.2	1.2	1
Launderers, cooks, housekeepers, and butlers	40A	-1.6	20.2	1.2	4
Police and detectives	41A	1.0	2.9	3.3	4
Firefighting and fire prevention occupations	41C	1.2	3.2	3.5	4
Correctional institution officers	424	4.2	8.7	1.3	1
Guards	42A	3.1	25.0	2.5	4
Supervisors, food preparation and service occupations	433	2.4	19.2	1.3	1
Bartenders	434	-0.7	28.7	3.2	1
Waiters and waitresses	435	2.4	32.2	3.9	1
Food counter, fountain, and related occupations	438	1.4	44.0	4.2	1
Cooks, including short-order	43A	2.4	36.2	3.6	4
Food preparation and service occupations	43B	2.7	32.4	3.0	4
Waiter's/waitress's assistants	443	2.0	31.9	4.2	1
Dental assistants	445	2.6	16.7	2.2	1
Health aides, except nursing	446	4.8	18.8	0.9	1
Nursing aides, orderlies, and attendants	447	3.8	18.5	1.4	1
Cleaning and building service, except household	44A	1.3	22.5	1.9	4
Supervisors, cleaning and building service workers	44B	2.2	9.5	2.4	1
Barbers	457	-0.1	6.0	1.5	4
Hairdressers and cosmetologists	458	2.4	13.1	1.1	1
Public transportation attendants	465	3.2	19.1	1.6	1
Welfare service aides	467	6.6	13.7	1.7	1
Child care workers, except private household	468	4.0	34.7	1.0	1
Personal service occupations, residual	46A	2.7	22.2	1.4	4
Farming, forestry, and fishing occupations	47A	0.3	19.7	1.6	4
Precision production, craft, and repair occupations					
Bus, truck, and stationary-engine mechanics	507	1.7	2.8	2.8	1
Small-engine repairers	509	1.1	11.6	3.0	4
Automobile mechanics, including apprentices	50A	1.6	13.4	2.9	1
Automobile body and related repairers	514	2.1	11.3	2.6	1
Heavy-equipment mechanics	516	0.3	12.8	2.8	1
Aircraft mechanics	51A	0.9	4.6	2.4	4
Electronic repairers, communications and industrial equipment	523	0.1	13.5	1.7	1
Data processing equipment repairers	525	2.9	7.0	1.0	1
Household appliance and power tool repairers	526	0.0	7.3	3.1	4
Telephone line installers and repairers	527	-2.1	0.2	2.2	4
Telephone installers and repairers	529	-4.1	0.2	2.2	1
Miscellaneous electrical and electronic equipment repairers	533	0.2	8.5	2.2	1
Heating, air conditioning, and refrigeration mechanics	534	2.0	6.2	1.1	1
Office machine repairers	538	0.6	1.5	2.2	4
Mechanics and repairers, except supervisors	53A	1.3	8.1	2.1	5
Millwrights	544	0.6	12.8	3.0	1
Supervisors, blue-collar	55A	0.9	7.4	2.6	4

TABLE 4.8 - *Continued*

Occupation	Group Number	Moderate Job Growth Annual 1992 - 2005	Annual Replacement Demand Value Total 1990 - 91	Annual Replacement Demand Value Net 1990 - 2005	Match Indicator, Replacement Demand[a]
Tile setters, hard and soft	565	1.6	1.9	2.1	4
Carpet installers	566	1.5	8.5	2.3	1
Brickmasons and stonemasons, including apprentices	56A	1.8	16.6	1.9	1
Carpenters and apprentices	56B	1.4	15.5	1.8	1
Drywall installers	573	2.4	20.7	1.7	1
Electrical power installers and repairers	577	0.5	5.6	3.0	1
Electricians and apprentices	57A	1.4	6.0	2.2	1
Painters, construction and maintenance, paperhangers, plasterers	57B	1.9	13.8	2.0	4
Concrete and terrazzo finishers	588	0.9	1.8	3.2	1
Glaziers	589	2.1	13.5	2.1	4
Plumbers, pipefitters, and steamfitters	58A	0.6	12.0	2.2	1
Insulation workers	593	2.5	30.1	4.2	1
Roofers	595	1.5	27.7	1.3	1
Other construction trades	59A	2.0	12.3	2.0	5
Extractive occupations	61A	-0.2	18.2	1.8	4
Tool and die makers, including apprentices	63A	-0.5	3.4	2.6	1
Machinists, including apprentices	63B	-0.1	7.4	2.4	1
Other precision production occupations	65A	-0.2	11.3	2.6	5
Precision woodworking occupations	65B	1.6	18.6	3.5	4
Sheet metal workers, including apprentices	65C	1.2	16.7	2.9	1
Upholsterers	668	0.9	8.3	2.6	1
Other precision textile, apparel and furnishings machine workers	66A	-0.5	10.4	2.6	4
Optical goods workers	677	2.1	14.8	2.7	4
Dental laboratory and medical appliance technicians	678	0.3	14.8	2.7	4
Butchers and meat cutters	686	-1.2	15.8	2.7	1
Bakers	687	0.4	17.8	1.6	1
Precision workers, assorted materials	68A	0.7	15.0	2.7	4
Plant and system operators	69A	0.8	4.6	2.8	4
Operators, fabricators, and laborers					
Metalworking and plasticworking machine operators	71A	-0.5	11.4	2.2	5
Woodworking machine operators	72A	-1.7	18.0	2.9	4
Metal and plastic processing machine operators	72B	0.1	11.2	3.3	4
Textile, apparel, and furnishings machine operators	73A	-1.7	18.8	2.2	5
Printing machine operators	73B	1.5	10.2	2.2	4
Machine operators, assorted material	75A	-0.5	17.0	2.1	4
Fabricators, assemblers, and handworking occupations	78A	0.3	15.8	1.8	4
Production inspectors, testers, samplers, and weighers	79A	-0.8	11.7	2.4	4
Motor vehicle operators	80B	1.7	16.6	1.7	4
Rail transportation occupations	82A	1.5	3.4	3.1	4
Water transportation occupations	82B	0.6	12.8	2.3	4
Material moving equipment operators	85A	1.0	10.8	1.9	4
Handlers, equipment cleaners, helpers, laborers	86A	1.2	27.3	2.1	5

Source: Derived from *Occupational Projections and Training Data*, Bulletin 2401, U.S. Department of Labor, Bureau of Labor Statistics; from *Total and Net Occupational Separations*, U.S. Department of Labor, Bureau of Labor Statistics; and from unpublished data.

[a]The match indicator is a measure of how accurately the replacement demand estimate reflects the data used for the group: 1 = an exact match, 4 = close match using another occupaton (proxy) for estimate, 5 = estimate without exact match even to proxy.

who enter an occupation. Net replacement demand for legal assistants, computer scientists, special education teachers, psychologists, and computer operators is less than 1 percent per year. Net replacement demand is more than 4 percent per year for waiters and waitresses and assistants, food and fountain counter workers, and insulation workers.

Additional research on occupational mobility could have a high payoff in terms of understanding labor supply and demand issues.

Tables 4.9 and 4.10 show distributions of BLS annual projected growth and annual replacement demand. Again, category ranks are provided for later use.

TABLE 4.9. Distribution of Annual Projected BLS Growth Employment, by Occupational Group

Category	Percentage	1992 - 2005
1	0 or less	26
2	0.1 - 0.9	29
3	1.0 - 1.2	17
4	1.3 - 1.4	12
5	1.5 - 1.9	39
6	2.0 - 2.3	26
7	2.4 and higher	44
	Total	193
	U.S. Growth	1.54%

Source: Derived from data in table 4.8.

TABLE 4.10. Distribution of Annual Replacement Demand, by Occupational Group

Category	Percentage 1990 - 91	Total 1990 - 91	Percentage 1992 - 2005	Net 1992 - 2005
1	Under 5	27	Under 1.4	35
2	5.0 - 7.9	29	1.4 - 1.5	27
3	8.0 - 9.9	27	1.6 - 1.9	31
4	10.0 - 12.9	32	2.0 - 2.1	25
5	13.0 - 15.9	27	2.2 - 2.4	23
6	16.0 - 21.9	27	2.5 - 2.7	30
7	22 and over	24	2.8 and over	22
	U.S. Mean	16.6%		2.0%

Source: Derived from data in table 4.8.

Labor Certifications

Labor certifications by occupational group are shown for 1988 and 1990–92 in table 4.11. The table also shows the average number of permanent certifications per 100,000 workers in the labor force for 1990–92. For example, from 1990 to 1992, there were 423 permanent certifications for workers in the financial manager occupation, an average of 28 certifications each year.

From 1990 to 1992, there were 1,375 certifications per 100,000 workers in the labor force for computer systems analysts and scientists, more than for any other occupation. Private household workers came in a close second, with 1,201 certifications. Biological and life scientists came in third at 888, more than twice as many as the next closest occupation. The number of certifications as a percentage of total employment is used as an indicator of labor shortage under the assumption that immigrants are being certified because employers are unable to find U.S. workers in those occupations where large numbers of certifications are being made.

One difficulty with certifications as an indicator of shortages is that certain occupations that require licensing or particular knowledge of U.S. laws and regulations receive few, if any, certifications. For example, no judges were certified in 1990–92, but only because an alien would be so unlikely to meet the requirements for becoming a U.S. judge. Therefore, the number of certifications would be irrelevant as a measure of shortage for judges.

Table 4.12 (see p. 72) presents the distribution of certifications per 100,000 workers in the labor force for 1990–92. Only thirty-two occupations had more than 50 certifications per 100,000 workers in the labor force. For all occupations, the mean was 29 per 100,000 workers in the labor force.

Annual Flows of Supply and Demand

We attempted to match annual flows of labor supply to annualized long-term demand for employment in certain selected occupational groups to illustrate the construction of this indicator. For some occupations, such as dental hygienists, this process is fairly straightforward. Training data are readily available. A comparison of annualized dental hygienist demand to graduates of dental hygienist programs is easy to make. It is also useful, however, to look at replacement demand for the occupation as well when undertaking the analysis. For other occupations, such as marketing, advertising, and public relations managers, there are many sources of supply. We do not know how many graduates from each source of supply end up in the occupation. For some courses of study, such as liberal arts graduates, the matching is nearly impossible.

TABLE 4.11. Permanent Labor Certifications 1988 and Fiscal Years 1990 - 92 and Annual Average per Labor Force 1990

Occupation	Group Number	Permanent Certifications 1988	Labor Force 1990 (in thousands)	Total Permanent Certifications 1990 - 92	Average Annu Certification per 100,00 Workers in Labor Forc 1990 - 92
Unknown or not matched		125			
Executive, administrative, and managerial occupations					
Financial managers	007	117	506	423	28
Personnel and labor relations managers	008	12	125	49	13
Purchasing managers	009	8	112	33	10
Managers, marketing, advertising, and public relations	013	332	533	912	57
Administrators, education and related fields	014	54	562	177	10
Managers, properties and real estate	016	25	447	70	5
Other executive, administrative, and managerial	01A	1,129	8,909	2,736	10
Accountants and auditors	023	491	1,476	1,856	42
Management analysts	026	38	203	223	37
Personnel, training, and labor relations specialists	027	14	412	29	2
Buyers, wholesale and retail trade, except farm products	029	108	226	164	24
Purchasing agents and buyers, NEC	033	71	267	249	31
Construction inspectors	035	3	71	9	4
Other management-related occupations	03A	156	1,338	776	19
Professional specialty occupations					
Aerospace engineers	044	89	111	187	56
Chemical engineers	048	141	72	790	366
Architects, surveyors, and mapping scientists	04A	253	177	623	117
Civil engineers	053	426	238	1,456	204
Electrical and electronic engineers	055	2,008	591	4,287	242
Industrial engineers	056	205	212	788	124
Mechanical engineers	057	400	322	1,826	189
Other engineers	05A	317	354	1,702	160
Computer systems analysts and scientists	064	1,117	615	8,866	1,375
Operations and systems researchers and analysts	065	21	215	141	22
Statisticians, actuaries, and other mathematical scientists	06A	136	49	416	283
Chemists, except biochemists	073	166	127	1,123	295
Geologists and geodesists	075	61	54	245	151
Biological and life scientists	078	207	76	2,024	888
Other natural scientists	07A	234	150	1,111	247
Physicians	084	178	578	951	55
Dentists	085	45	163	165	34
Veterinarians	086	15	58	40	23
Optometrists	087	3	23	9	13
Registered nurses	095	2,599	1,692	a	a
Pharmacists	096	102	171	352	69
Dietitians	097	15	84	56	22
Inhalation therapists	098	5	63	16	8
Other therapists	09A	24	111	130	39
Physical therapists	103	157	92	a	a
Speech therapists	104	11	65	46	24
Physician's assistants	106	2	68	25	12
Teachers, secondary school	157	128	1,228	400	11
Teachers, special education	158	37	275	197	24
Teachers, NEC	15A	337	568	1,226	72
Teachers, prekindergarten, kindergarten, and elementary	15B	213	1,999	788	13
Teachers, college and university	15C	1,650	781	6,839	292
Counselors, educational and vocational	163	13	219	117	18
Economists	166	182	118	914	258
Psychologists	167	42	214	134	21

TABLE 4.11 - *Continued*

Occupation	Group Number	Permanent Certifications 1988	Labor Force 1990 (in thousands)	Total Permanent Certifications 1990 - 92	Average Annual Certifications per 100,000 Workers in Labor Force 1990 - 92
Other social scientists	16A	22	38	129	113
Librarians, archivists, and curators	16B	46	213	177	28
Social workers	174	45	578	219	13
Recreation workers	175	2	108	16	5
Clergy	176	74	327	137	14
Religious workers, NEC	177	25	98	63	21
Lawyers	178	60	737	290	13
Judges	179	1	27	0	0
Designers	185	220	549	435	26
Musicians and composers	186	83	167	154	31
Painters, sculptors, craft artists, and artist printmakers	188	40	224	278	41
Photographers	189	7	127	30	8
Other editors, reporters, authors, and technical writers	18A	130	443	398	30
Professional specialty occupations	18B	229	338	696	69
Public relations specialists	197	26	167	89	18
Announcers	198	16	55	27	16
Technicians and related support occupations					
Clinical laboratory technologists and technicians	203	54	304	377	41
Dental hygienists	204	0	88	24	9
Health record technologists and technicians	205	5	71	1	0
Radiological technicians	206	22	123	66	18
Licensed practical nurses	207	102	451	46	3
Health technologists and technicians, NEC	208	29	290	170	20
Electrical and electronic technicians	213	42	362	113	10
Other technicians and related support occupations	21A	35	284	93	11
Drafting occupations and surveying and mapping technicians	21B	105	376	152	13
Airplane pilots and navigators	226	15	117	25	7
Computer programmers	229	296	612	1,476	80
Other science technicians	22A	48	251	157	21
Legal assistants	234	23	236	80	11
Other technicians, except health engineering and science	23A	65	390	16	1
Sales occupations					
Insurance sales occupations	253	11	613	18	1
Real estate sales occupations	254	3	769	0	0
Securities and financial services sales occupations	255	23	308	79	9
Other sales occupations	25A	541	8,653	1,558	6
Sales workers, other commodities	274	112	1,588	201	4
Sales counter clerks	275	4	209	14	2
Cashiers	276	6	2,753	37	0
Administrative support occupations, including clerical					
Supervisors, administrative support	30A	57	787	88	4
Computer equipment operators	30B	8	848	17	1
Secretaries	313	384	4,099	667	5
Stenographers	314	4	59	5	3
Typists	315	21	675	39	2
Interviewers	316	5	227	2	0
Hotel clerks	317	2	99	23	8
Transportation ticket and reservation agents	318	6	124	6	2
Receptionists and information clerks, NEC	31A	22	1,177	50	1
Records processing occupations, except financial	32A	33	959	50	2
Financial records processing	33A	120	2,503	274	4
Duplicating, mail, and other office machine operators	34A	16	77	14	6

(*continued*)

TABLE 4.11 - *Continued*

Occupation	Group Number	Permanent Certifications 1988	Labor Force 1990 (in thousands)	Total Permanent Certifications 1990 - 92	Average Annual Certifications per 100,000 Workers in Labor Force 1990 - 92
Communication equipment operators	35A	0	234	6	1
Mail and message distributing operators	35C	3	1,013	7	0
Production coordinators	363	13	205	56	9
Material recording, scheduling, and distribution clerks	36A	25	1,733	131	3
General office clerks	379	25	813	73	3
Adjusters and investigators	37A	4	1,168	12	0
Bank tellers	383	0	484	3	0
Data-entry keyers	385	5	517	6	0
Statistical clerks	386	0	90	2	1
Teacher's aides	387	5	508	23	2
Miscellaneous administrative support	38A	10	1,032	12	0
Service occupations and farming					
Child care workers, private household	406	1,388	334	2,983	298
Private household cleaners and servants	407	4,008	428	15,423	1,201
Launderers, cooks, housekeepers, and butlers	40A	2,808	63	168	89
Police and detectives	41A	0	677	0	0
Firefighting and fire prevention occupations	41C	0	268	0	0
Correctional institution officers	424	0	245	0	0
Guards	42A	4	871	17	1
Supervisors, food preparation and service occupations	433	369	363	96	9
Bartenders	434	2	336	6	1
Waiters and waitresses	435	65	1,508	163	4
Food counter, fountain, and related occupations	438	25	359	444	41
Cooks, including short-order	43A	2,911	1,981	4,784	80
Food preparation and service occupations	43B	505	904	1,679	62
Waiter's/waitress's assistants	443	80	398	150	13
Dental assistants	445	35	192	108	19
Health aides, except nursing	446	73	469	134	10
Nursing aides, orderlies, and attendants	447	590	1,558	1,959	42
Cleaning and building service, except household	44A	333	3,231	1,654	17
Supervisors, cleaning and building service workers	44B	44	155	5	1
Barbers	457	14	93	31	11
Hairdressers and cosmetologists	458	104	753	300	13
Public transportation attendants	465	0	103	0	0
Welfare service aides	467	0	100	1	0
Child care workers, except private household	468	21	936	57	2
Personal service occupations, residual	46A	66	543	769	47
Farming, forestry, and fishing occupations	47A	385	3,634	1,318	12
Precision production, craft, and repair occupations					
Bus, truck, and stationary-engine mechanics	507	105	326	94	10
Small-engine repairers	509	11	71	25	12
Automobile mechanics, including apprentices	50A	590	911	835	31
Automobile body and related repairers	514	218	215	300	47
Heavy-equipment mechanics	516	29	160	40	8
Aircraft mechanics	51A	22	131	18	5
Electronic repairers, communications and industrial equipment	523	95	189	152	27
Data processing equipment repairers	525	1	161	0	0
Household appliance and power tool repairers	526	22	52	32	21
Telephone line installers and repairers	527	1	63	3	2
Telephone installers and repairers	529	0	196	3	1
Miscellaneous electrical and electronic equipment repairers	533	52	68	93	46
Heating, air conditioning, and refrigeration mechanics	534	41	277	49	6

ABLE 4.11 - *Continued*

ccupation	Group Number	Permanent Certifications 1988	Labor Force 1990 (in thousands)	Total Permanent Certifications 1990 - 92	Average Annual Certifications per 100,000 Workers in Labor Force 1990 - 92
Office machine repairers	538	11	77	16	7
Mechanics and repairers, except supervisors	53A	226	1,368	600	15
Millwrights	544	129	101	67	22
Supervisors, blue-collar	55A	703	2,470	1,058	14
Tile setters, hard and soft	565	30	72	55	25
Carpet installers	566	14	116	18	5
Brickmasons and stonemasons, including apprentices	56A	10[illegible]	221	272	41
Carpenters and apprentices	56B	152	1,510	229	5
Drywall installers	573	56	171	23	4
Electrical power installers and repairers	577	2	124	4	1
Electricians and apprentices	57A	31	743	80	4
Painters, construction and maintenance, paperhangers, plasterers	57B	64	678	127	6
Concrete and terrazzo finishers	588	87	81	0	0
Glaziers	589	9	47	7	5
Plumbers, pipefitters, and steamfitters	58A	28	492	63	4
Insulation workers	593	11	59	4	2
Roofers	595	22	245	33	4
Other construction trades	59A	123	359	206	19
Extractive occupations	61A	11	138	1	0
Tool and die makers, including apprentices	63A	74	156	108	23
Machinists, including apprentices	63B	81	514	208	13
Other precision production occupations	65A	346	482	694	48
Precision woodworking occupations	65B	233	105	429	136
Sheet metal workers, including apprentices	65C	10	133	24	6
Upholsterers	668	68	70	87	41
Other precision textile, apparel, and furnishings machine workers	66A	815	193	882	152
Optical goods workers	677	14	64	17	9
Dental laboratory and medical appliance technicians	678	45	63	110	58
Butchers and meat cutters	686	15	277	101	12
Bakers	687	148	122	300	82
Precision workers, assorted materials	68A	99	167	169	34
Plant and system operators	69A	7	273	8	1
erators, fabricators, and laborers					
Metalworking and plasticworking machine operators	71A	231	503	212	14
Woodworking machine operators	72A	27	183	34	6
Metal and plastic processing machine operators	72B	68	182	160	29
Textile, apparel, and furnishings machine operators	73A	686	1,406	1,830	43
Printing machine operators	73B	133	477	177	12
Machine operators, assorted material	75A	228	2,978	425	5
Fabricators, assemblers, and hand working occupations	78A	478	2,165	1,757	27
Production inspectors, testers, samplers, and weighers	79A	162	1,007	177	6
Motor vehicle operators	80B	12	3,683	45	0
Rail transportation occupations	82A	1	85	0	0
Water transportation occupations	82B	7	56	46	27
Material moving equipment operators	85A	12	1,160	61	2
Handlers, equipment cleaners, helpers, laborers	86A	588	5,543	1,041	6
tal certified with occupational designations			124,067	100,971	29

urce: Derived from data provided by the U.S. Department of Labor, Employment and Training Administration.

hese occupations are not certified by DOL because they are presumed to be shortage occupations. They were signed a rank of 7 due to the large number of qualifying aliens admitted by the Immigration and Naturalization Service.

TABLE 4.12. Distribution of Certifications per 100,000 Workers in Labor Force, by Occupation

Rank	Certifications per 100,000 Workers in Labor Force	1990 - 92 Average per 1990 Labor Force
1	Fewer than 5	57
2	5 - 9	27
3	10 - 19	36
4	20 - 29	21
5	30 - 49	20
6	50 - 99	12
7	100 and over	20
	Total	193
	Mean	29

Source: Derived from data in table 4.11.

Table 4.14 illustrates the match between labor supply from education and training programs and selected occupational groups. To obtain sensible results, we further grouped some of our 193 occupations into even smaller clusters, then matched these clusters to Office of Education program codes (CIP codes). We picked a few dozen occupations to illustrate this process. Table 4.13 illustrates the crossover between our clusters, the occupational groups in our clusters, and the Office of Education fields of study we used to compute training supply.

Table 4.14 provides supply data for the various clusters identified in table 4.13. Sources of supply identified in table 4.14 include apprenticeship, vocational education graduates, and postsecondary programs by length of program and level of degree. The categories included are less than 1 year, 1 to 4 years, associate degree, B.A., M.A., and doctor's degrees. The data for vocational education awards in table 4.14 are for a much earlier time period than are the data used for demand.

Some obvious sources of data are missing from table 4.14. These include graduates of proprietary schools, Job Training and Partnership Act programs not separately reported, military training, and immigrants (legal or illegal). Also missing from table 4.14 are reentrants to the labor force and employed workers who transfer into an occupation from some other occupation. As indicated by the high replacement demand for some occupations shown in

TABLE 4.13. Occupational Clusters Used in Supply and Demand Analysis

Cluster Name	Cluster Number	Occupations in Cluster	Occupational Group Code	CIPCODE	Title
Correctional institution officers	424	Corrections	424	43.0101	Correctional administration
				43.0102	Corrections
Office machine repairers	538	Office machine repair	538	47.0102	Business machine repairers
Personnel	C01	Personnel and labor relations managers	008	07.0500	Personnel and training programs
		Personnel and labor relations specialists	027	06.0600	Human resource development
				06.1100	Labor and industrial relations
				06.1600	Personnel management
Carpentry	C03	Carpenters including apprentices	56B	46.0200	Carpentry
		Drywall installers	573		
Police and detectives	41A	Police and detectives	41A	43.0107	Law enforcement
				43.0108	Law enforcement and security services/admin.
Plumbers, pipefitters, and steamfitters	58A	Plumbers, pipefitters, and steamfitters	58A	46.0500	Plumbing, pipefitting, and steamfitting
Bus, truck, and stationary-engine mechanics	507	Bus and truck, diesel engine mechanics	507	47.0605	Diesel engine mechanics
Brickmasons and stonemasons	56A	Masonry including apprentices	56A	46.0101	Brickmasonry, stonemasonry, and tile setting, general
Sheet metal workers	65C	Sheet metal workers including apprentices	65C	48.0506	Sheet metal
Electricians	C04	Electricians including apprentices	57A	46.0300	Electrical and power transmission installers
		Electrical powerline installers and repairers	577		
Social workers	174	Social workers	174	44.0700	Social work
Accountants and auditors	023	Accountants and auditors	023	06.0200	Accounting
Secretarial and clerical	C02	Secretaries	313	07.0100	Accounting, bookkeeping, and related programs
		Stenographers	314	07.0300	Business data processors and equipment operators
		Typists	315	07.0600	Secretarial and related programs
		Receptionists	31A	07.0700	Typing, general office, and related programs
		Records processors, excluding financial	32A	07.9900	Business and office, other
		Financial records processors	33A		
		General office clerks	379		
Hairdressers and cosmetologists	458	Beauticians	458	12.0403	Cosmetology
Physical therapists	103	Physical therapists	103	17.0813	Physical therapy
Heating, air conditioning, and refrigeration mechanics	534	Heating, air conditioning, and refrigeration mechanics	534	47.0200	Heating, air conditioning, and refrigeration mechanics
Small-engine repairers	509	Motorcycle, boat, small-engine repairers	509	47.0606	Small engine repair
Dental assistants	445	Dental assistants	445	17.0101	Dental assisting
Electronic repairers, communications and industrial equipment	523	Electronic repairers, communications and industrial equipment	523	47.0103	Communications electronics
				47.0105	Industrial electronics
Machinists	C05	Tool and die makers including apprentices	63A	48.0507	Tool and die making

(continued)

TABLE 4.13 - *Continued*

Cluster Name	Cluster Number	Occupations in Cluster	Occupational Group Code	CIPCODE	Title
		Machinists including apprentices	63B	48.0503	Machine tool operators / machine shop
Aerospace engineers	044	Aerospace engineers	044	14.0200	Aerospace, aeronautical and astronautical engineering
Automobile mechanics	50A	Auto mechanics including apprentices	50A	47.0604	Automobile mechanics
Precision woodworking	65B	Woodworking	65B	48.0700	Woodworking
Automobile body and related repairers	514	Auto body repairers	514	47.0603	Auto body repair
Chemical engineers	048	Chemical engineers	048	14.0700	Chemical engineering
Household appliance and power tool repairers	526	Household appliance and power tool repairers	526	47.0106	Major appliance repair
				47.0108	Small appliance repair
Firefighting and fire prevention	41C	Firefighters	41C	43.0200	Fire protection
				43.0201	Fire control and safety
Architects	04A	Architects	04A	04.0000	Architecture and environmental design
Biological and life scientists	078	Biological and life sciences	078	26.0000	Life sciences

Source: Derived from data provided by the National Crosswalk Service Center of the Iowa State Occupational Information Coordinating Committee and the U.S. Department of Labor, Bureau of Labor Statistics.

TABLE 4.14. Sources of Supply - Education and Training Completions

Cluster Name	Cluster Number	Apprentice Programs 1988	Voc. Ed. Awards 1982 - 83	Postsecondary Education, Academic Year 1989 - 90						TOTAL
				Awards		Assoc.	B.A./B.S.	M.A./M.S.	Doc.	
				< 1 yr.	1 - 4 yrs.	Degree	Degree	Degree	Degree	
Correctional institution officers	424	301	0	1,930	0	480	609	146	0	3,466
Office machine repairers	538	0	477	54	202	24	0	0	0	757
Personnel	C01	0	925	209	0	288	4,901	1,990	37	8,350
Carpentry	C03	2,802	27,377	801	1,695	352	0	0	0	33,027
Police and detectives	41A	286	0	2,495	3,486	4,556	1,543	64	0	12,430
Plumbers, pipefitters, and steamfitters	58A	3,179	6,236	4,048	733	76	0	0	0	14,272
Bus, truck, and stationary-engine mechanics	507	132	7,556	3,109	3,113	654	0	0	0	14,564
Brickmasons and stonemasons	56A	317	8,183	43	78	18	0	0	0	8,639
Sheet metal	65C	1,400	2,443	59	320	7	0	0	0	4,229
Electricians	C04	6,290	20,097	4,155	5,112	562	2	0	0	36,218
Social workers	174	0	0	71	86	1,066	9,892	10,649	277	22,041
Accountants and auditors	023	0	0	1,452	1,978	5,828	45,038	3,290	60	57,646
Secretarial and clerical	C02	0	549,827	50,691	48,317	40,485	2,246	27	0	691,593
Hairdressers and cosmetologists	458	160	35,662	37,101	44,587	202	0	0	0	117,712
Physical therapists	103	0	0	0	110	269	3,532	919	2	4,832
Heating, air conditioning, and refrigeration mechanics	534	193	15,235	5,684	5,077	904	1	0	0	27,094
Small engine repairers	509	0	8,175	3,769	588	14	0	0	0	12,546
Dental assistants	445	0	8,073	2,656	3,745	359	0	0	0	14,833
Electronic repairers, communications & industrial equip.	523	332	9,958	620	856	750	4	0	0	12,520
Machinists	C05	2,823	28,347	1,484	3,383	945	1	0	0	36,983
Aerospace engineers	044	0	0	1	0	12	3,051	1,029	178	4,271
Automobile mechanics	50A	140	74,538	8,723	8,140	2,355	0	0	0	93,896
Precision woodworking	65B	92	7,970	112	319	44	0	3	0	8,540
Automobile body and related repairers	514	32	22,324	1,256	2,308	242	0	0	0	26,162
Chemical engineers	048	0	0	0	0	35	3,527	1,040	564	5,166
Household appliance and power tool repairers	526	0	2,928	241	315	16	0	0	0	3,500
Firefighting and fire prevention	41C	1,321	16,637	3,001	777	1,616	156	6	0	23,514
Architects	04A	10	0	258	2,492	2,067	9,348	3,505	97	17,777
Biological and life scientists	078	0	0	103	60	1,055	38,040	4,893	3,853	48,004

Source: Unpublished data from the U.S. Department of Labor, Bureau of Apprenticeship and Training, and *Occupational Projections and Training Data*, Bulletin 2251 (April 1986) and Bulletin 2401 (May 1992), U.S. Department of Labor, Bureau of Labor Statistics.

table 4.8, occupational shift is an important source of supply as well as demand.

Table 4.15 illustrates the match between supply from training institutions and demand. Employment growth, column (1), is computed by multiplying 1990 employment times the 1990–2005 annual growth rate from table 4.8. Replacements, column (2), are computed by multiplying net annual replacement demand from 1990 to 2005 as a percentage of employment times 1990 employment. Openings, column (3), are the sum of employment growth and replacements. The annual supply, column (4), is the sum of graduates from all training institutions.

The measures are computed as:

—the ratio of supply to total openings;
—the ratio of supply to openings from growth.

The occupations appear in table 4.15 in the order of the ratio of supply to total openings, column (5). A small ratio indicates low supply relative to openings. A large ratio indicates a large supply relative to openings.

Occupations appearing to be in relatively short supply based on table 4.15 are correctional officers, office machine repairers, police and detectives, and personnel. Occupations appearing to be in relative oversupply include small-engine repairers, hairdressers and cosmetologists, electronic repairers, and biological and life scientists.

It must be emphasized that for the data to be utilized in a serious manner, a careful analysis would be required of each occupation to determine if the missing sources of supply account for the excess demand, if changes have occurred to numbers graduating from the various educational programs shown in table 4.14, and if the replacement demand estimates are accurate. For example, the initial analysis shows a relative oversupply of biologists. If large numbers of graduates holding a bachelor's degree in biology go on to medical school, then this supply measure overestimates the number of graduates available to work as biologists.

Because data on replacement are probably less reliable than data on growth of employment, ratios were also computed comparing supply to openings due to growth, column (6). According to this measure, correctional institution officers and personnel are in very short supply, with annual supply falling short of the openings that result from employment growth in that occupation.

Within a given cluster, there should be no double-counting of students. However, some training programs may be counted in more than one cluster. Wherever possible, we attempted to delete duplicates by counting only major clusters, but this was not always possible. Another source of double-counting

TABLE 4.15. Comparison of Annual Supply and Demand, by Occupational Cluster

Cluster Name	Cluster Number	(1) Growth of Employment	(2) Replacements	(3) Openings (1)+(2)	(4) Annual Supply	(5) Ratio (4):(1)	(6) Ratio (4):(3)
Correctional institution officers	424	7,744	3,146	10,890	3,466	0.45	0.32
Office machine repairers	538	608	1,672	2,280	757	1.25	0.33
Police and detectives	41A	10,095	22,209	32,304	12,430	1.23	0.38
Personnel	C01	9,135	10,547	19,682	8,350	0.91	0.42
Carpentry	C03	14,382	27,081	41,463	33,027	2.30	0.80
Physical therapists	103	3,458	2,002	5,460	4,832	1.40	0.88
Plumbers, pipefitters, and steamfitters	58A	5,915	10,010	15,925	14,272	2.41	0.90
Sheet metal workers	65C	976	3,538	4,514	4,229	4.33	0.94
Aerospace engineers	044	1,308	2,507	3,815	4,271	3.27	1.12
Bus, truck, and stationary-engine mechanics	507	4,095	8,820	12,915	14,564	3.56	1.13
Accountants and auditors	023	28,760	21,570	50,330	57,646	2.00	1.15
Electricians	C04	12,592	18,986	31,578	36,218	2.88	1.15
Social workers	174	13,536	5,640	19,176	22,041	1.63	1.15
Brickmasons and stonemasons	56A	2,316	3,667	5,983	8,639	3.73	1.44
Firefighting and fire prevention	41C	3,945	9,205	13,150	23,514	5.96	1.79
Dental assistants	445	3,740	4,114	7,854	14,833	3.97	1.89
Machinists	C05	3,720	15,664	19,384	36,983	9.94	1.91
Precision woodworking	65B	776	3,395	4,171	8,540	11.01	2.05
Household appliance and power tool repairers	526	-50	1,550	1,500	3,500	-70.00	2.33
Chemical engineers	048	497	1,633	2,130	5,166	10.39	2.43
Secretarial and clerical	C02	69,502	208,836	278,338	691,593	9.95	2.48
Automobile mechanics	50A	11,206	24,998	36,204	93,896	8.38	2.59
Automobile body and related repairers	514	2,613	5,226	7,839	26,162	10.01	3.34
Architects	04A	2,040	2,550	4,590	17,777	8.71	3.87
Heating, air conditioning, and refrigeration mechanics	534	3,471	2,937	6,408	27,094	7.81	4.23
Small-engine repairers	509	402	2,010	2,412	12,546	31.21	5.20
Hairdressers and cosmetologists	458	11,010	8,074	19,084	117,712	10.69	6.17
Electronic repairers, communications and industrial equip.	523	-1,638	3,094	1,456	12,520	-7.64	8.60
Biological and life scientists	078	1,480	2,294	3,774	48,004	32.44	12.72

Source: Derived from data in table 4.14.

is that graduates at one level do not always enter the job market, but instead enter more advanced training. In addition, it should be noted that some graduates may already be employed in the occupation. When this approach is used in a mechanical manner, without careful analysis and supplementation of data, I have no confidence in the results.

Skill Level of the Job

Although not a shortage indicator per se, the level of skill required by the job is a policy variable relevant to the admission of immigrants as well as to the funding of education and training programs. To the extent that it takes longer to train workers, it may be more difficult to find U.S. workers to fill a shortage if one occurs in such an occupation. In fact, the *Economic Report of the President* states: "Immigrants with more education or training will likely make the greatest contributions to the U.S. economy, suggesting that basic skill levels could be one guide to admitting new immigrants under a skill-based criteria" (President 1990).

When combining the various indicators, we have added as an index the training time required for the specific occupational group. The training time was based on the specific vocational preparation (U.S. Dept. of Labor, Employment and Training Administration 1991). This preparation includes vocational education, apprentice training, in-plant training, on-the-job training, and experience in other jobs. Each of the 12,741 detailed occupations was assigned a code from 1 to 9, based on the amount of training time required. For example, occupations requiring 3 to 6 months were coded 4. The midpoint of the range was then assigned to each of the 12,741 occupations. Thus, a code 4 would receive a 4.5. The 12,741 occupations were then averaged over the 193 occupational groups. Since we had no information on employment for each of the 12,741 occupations, the computed average was unweighted.

Table 4.16 summarizes the distribution of occupations by month of training. A new seven-point ranking was assigned to each occupational group.

Summary of Indicators

A summary ranking of the indicators used in this study is shown in table 4.17. In the table, the various rankings used in tables 4.2, 4.5, 4.7, 4.9, 4.10, 4.12, and 4.16 are added up. The distributions selected in the various tables were based on several criteria: approximate equality of the distributions, use of natural groups—such as distinguishing between positive and negative employment growth or breaks on whole numbers, such as employment growth from 0 to 2 percent. A rank of 7 designates the indicator we thought most consistent with a labor shortage. A rank of 1 is designated as the most consistent with a labor surplus. The ranges were established in 1990, based on economic conditions during 1986–89, when labor shortages were more prevalent. Thus, it could happen that no occupation receives a 7 for a particular indicator for 1989–92.

The top three occupations are other natural scientists, veterinarians, and physical therapists. The next eleven occupations are physicians, registered nurses, speech therapists, chemists, biological and life scientists, computer programmers, computer systems analysts and scientists, operations researchers, geologists, radiological technicians, and airplane pilots and navigators. All the occupations except physical therapists require an average of at least three years of college. In fact, all the top twenty-seven occupations require some college. This may seem tautological, since skill level was one of the indicators. If we delete skill, however, and look at the top twenty-six ranked occupations, ignoring skill as an indicator, all but one of the occupations requires some college. All the twenty-seven top occupations on the original list are related to medicine, science, or computers.

The only top occupation not requiring college is public transportation attendants, but that may be only because of a statistical anomaly. The criterion used by the Bureau of Labor Statistics for including an occupation in its annual average estimates for weekly full-time wages is that there must be at least 50,000 people represented by the sample. In 1992 there were 49,000

TABLE 4.16. Distribution of Specific Vocational Preparation across Occupations

Rank	Specific Vocational Preparation	Count
1	Less than 6 months	27
2	6 - 13.9 months	29
3	14 - 23.9 months	24
4	24 - 32.9 months	28
5	33 - 39.9 months	27
6	40 - 59.9 months	28
7	60 months or more	30
	Total	193

Source: Derived from the *Dictionary of Occupational Titles*, 4th ed., 1991, U.S. Department of Labor, Employment and Training Administration.

TABLE 4.17. Ranks Used in Computing Labor Market Indicators, Sorted in Rank Order

Group Number	Occupation	Net Replacement Demand 1990 - 2005	Spec. Voc. Prep. (Months)	Average Certifications per 100,000 Workers in Labor Force 1990 - 92	Average Annual Employment Change 1989 - 93	Average Annual Unemployment Rates 1992 - 93	Projected Job Growth 1992 - 2005	Average Annual Wage Change 1989 - 93	Sum of Indicators
07A	Other natural scientists	6	7	7	7	7	5	3	42
086	Veterinarians	3	7	4	7	7	6	7	41
103	Physical therapists	2	4	7	7	6	7	7	40
084	Physicians	3	7	6	3	7	6	7	39
095	Registered nurses	2	6	7	5	7	7	5	39
104	Speech therapists	2	6	4	6	7	7	7	39
073	Chemists, except biochemists	4	6	7	6	6	5	4	38
078	Biological and life scientists	6	7	7	7	4	5	2	38
229	Computer programmers	5	6	6	4	5	6	6	38
064	Computer systems analysts and scientists	1	6	7	7	5	7	4	37
065	Operations and systems researchers and analysts	3	5	4	7	6	7	5	37
075	Geologists and geodesists	5	7	7	3	3	5	7	37
206	Radiological technicians	3	6	3	4	7	7	7	37
226	Airplane pilots and navigators	6	7	2	3	5	7	7	37
09A	Other therapists	2	6	5	5	6	7	5	36
15C	Teachers, college and university	6	7	7	4	5	5	2	36
176	Clergy	2	7	3	5	7	6	6	36
41A	Police and detectives	7	5	1	6	7	3	7	36
096	Pharmacists	2	6	6	2	7	6	6	35
053	Civil engineers	5	7	7	2	4	5	4	34
085	Dentists	5	7	5	1	7	2	7	34
678	Dental laboratory and medical appliance technicians	7	4	6	2	6	2	7	34
056	Industrial engineers	6	7	7	2	3	3	5	33
097	Dietitians	5	7	4	5	3	5	4	33
157	Teachers, secondary school	5	5	3	4	6	7	3	33
158	Teachers, special education	1	5	4	5	6	7	5	33
18A	Other editors, reporters, authors, and technical writers	1	7	5	5	4	5	6	33
014	Administrators, education and related fields	5	7	3	4	6	5	2	32
026	Management analysts	1	6	5	7	4	7	2	32
048	Chemical engineers	4	7	7	1	3	4	6	32
055	Electrical and electronic engineers	4	7	7	2	3	5	4	32
087	Optometrists	3	5	3	4	7	3	7	32
098	Inhalation therapists	2	3	2	7	7	7	4	32
15A	Teachers, NEC	1	6	6	7	4	6	2	32
166	Economists	6	7	7	1	3	5	3	32
167	Psychologists	1	7	4	6	5	7	2	32

Group Number	Occupation	Net Replacement Demand 1990 - 2005	Spec. Voc. Prep. (Months)	Average Certifications per 100,000 Workers in Labor Force 1990 - 92	Average Annual Employment Change 1989 - 93	Average Annual Unemployment Rates 1992 - 93	Projected Job Growth 1992 - 2005	Average Annual Wage Change 1989 - 93	Sum of Indicators
178	Lawyers	2	7	3	3	7	6	4	32
65B	Precision woodworking occupations	6	5	7	7	1	5	1	32
013	Managers, marketing, advertising, and public relations	3	7	6	2	3	7	3	31
023	Accountants and auditors	2	7	5	3	4	6	4	31
044	Aerospace engineers	5	7	6	1	3	3	6	31
057	Mechanical engineers	4	7	7	2	3	4	4	31
16B	Librarians, archivists, and curators	4	6	4	5	5	2	5	31
43A	Cooks, including short-order	5	3	6	5	1	7	4	31
465	Public transportation attendants	4	1	1	7	4	7	7	31
007	Financial managers	2	7	4	4	4	5	4	30
05A	Other engineers	2	7	7	2	3	5	4	30
06A	Statisticians, actuaries, and other mathematical scientists	1	7	7	2	6	3	4	30
16A	Other social scientists	3	6	7	3	4	5	2	30
189	Photographers	5	4	2	5	2	5	7	30
18B	Professional specialty occupations	3	5	6	3	2	7	4	30
208	Health technologists and technicians, NEC	1	4	4	7	3	7	4	30
314	Stenographers	4	3	1	7	7	1	7	30
509	Small-engine repairers	7	3	3	7	3	3	4	30
179	Judges	2	7	1	6	7	2	4	29
203	Clinical laboratory technologists and technicians	2	4	5	3	4	5	6	29
255	Securities and financial services sales occupations	1	5	2	6	4	6	5	29
438	Food counter, fountain, and related occupations	7	1	5	6	1	4	5	29
457	Barbers	7	3	3	3	6	1	6	29
577	Electrical power installers and repairers	6	6	1	4	4	2	6	29
016	Managers, properties and real estate	1	6	2	5	3	6	5	28
01A	Other executive, administrative, and managerial	3	7	3	3	4	5	3	28
03A	Other management-related occupations	1	6	3	5	3	6	4	28
106	Physician's assistants	2	5	3	1	6	6	5	28
15B	Teachers, prekindergarten, kindergarten, and elementary	2	5	3	4	6	6	2	28
174	Social workers	1	6	3	3	4	7	4	28
177	Religious workers, NEC	1	6	4	3	7	6	1	28
188	Painters, sculptors, craft-artists, and artist printmakers	3	6	5	2	3	5	4	28
204	Dental hygienists	1	3	2	3	7	7	5	28
234	Legal assistants	1	5	3	6	3	7	3	28
41C	Firefighting and fire prevention occupations	7	4	1	3	6	3	4	28
445	Dental assistants	5	3	3	3	3	7	4	28

TABLE 4.17 - *Continued*

Group Number	Occupation	Net Replacement Demand 1990 - 2005	Spec. Voc. Prep. (Months)	Average Certifications per 100,000 Workers in Labor Force 1990 - 92	Average Annual Employment Change 1989 - 93	Average Annual Unemployment Rates 1992 - 93	Projected Job Growth 1992 - 2005	Average Annual Wage Change 1989 - 93	Sum of Indicators
46A	Personal service occupations, residual	1	2	5	6	2	7	5	28
507	Bus, truck, and stationary-engine mechanics	6	5	3	4	3	5	2	28
566	Carpet installers	6	5	2	1	2	5	7	28
033	Purchasing agents and buyers, NEC	4	6	5	6	3	1	2	27
186	Musicians and composers	2	7	5	1	3	5	4	27
22A	Other science technicians	4	4	4	6	3	5	1	27
30A	Supervisors, administrative support	5	4	1	3	4	5	5	27
424	Correctional institution officers	1	2	1	5	7	7	4	27
593	Insulation workers	7	4	1	3	1	7	4	27
008	Personnel and labor relations managers	6	6	3	1	3	5	2	26
009	Purchasing managers	3	6	3	2	4	3	5	26
163	Counselors, educational and vocational	3	7	3	2	4	6	1	26
185	Designers	2	6	4	3	3	4	4	26
207	Licensed practical nurses	2	2	1	2	6	7	6	26
43B	Food preparation and service occupations	6	1	6	4	1	7	1	26
458	Hairdressers and cosmetologists	2	2	3	3	4	7	5	26
534	Heating, air conditioning, and refrigeration mechanics	3	5	2	4	3	6	3	26
687	Bakers	3	4	6	3	2	2	6	26
82B	Water transportation occupations	1	4	4	7	1	2	7	26
029	Buyers, wholesale and retail trade, except farm products	6	3	4	5	3	3	1	25
04A	Architects, surveyors, and mapping scientists	3	6	7	1	3	4	1	25
406	Child care workers, private household	7	1	7	2	2	1	5	25
50A	Automobile mechanics, including apprentices	7	3	5	1	2	5	2	25
544	Millwrights	7	6	4	1	1	2	4	25
573	Drywall installers	7	3	1	5	1	7	1	25
198	Announcers	7	3	3	1	1	5	4	24
21A	Other technicians and related support occupations	4	5	3	2	3	3	4	24
317	Hotel clerks	7	1	2	3	1	7	3	24
318	Transportation ticket and reservation agents	3	2	1	7	3	7	1	24
433	Supervisors, food preparation and service occupations	2	5	2	2	2	7	4	24
447	Nursing aides, orderlies, and attendants	1	1	5	6	1	7	3	24
468	Child care workers, except private household	1	1	1	4	3	7	7	24
533	Miscellaneous electrical and electronic equipment repairers	5	4	5	1	1	2	6	24
55A	Supervisors, blue-collar	6	6	3	3	3	2	1	24
56A	Brickmasons and stonemasons, including apprentices	5	5	5	2	1	5	1	24
63A	Tool and die makers, including apprentices	6	6	4	2	4	1	1	24

Group Number	Occupation	Net Replacement Demand 1990 - 2005	Spec. Voc. Prep. (Months)	Average Certifications per 100,000 Workers in Labor Force 1990 - 92	Average Annual Employment Change 1989 - 93	Average Annual Unemployment Rates 1992 - 93	Projected Job Growth 1992 - 2005	Average Annual Wage Change 1989 - 93	Sum of Indicators
205	Health record technologists and technicians	1	4	1	3	5	7	2	23
275	Sales counter clerks	3	1	1	3	1	7	7	23
42A	Guards	4	2	1	3	1	7	5	23
435	Waiters and waitresses	7	1	1	3	1	7	3	23
514	Automobile body and related repairers	5	3	5	2	1	6	1	23
51A	Aircraft mechanics	4	4	2	3	1	2	7	23
523	Electronic repairers, communications and industrial equipment	4	5	4	4	2	2	2	23
527	Telephone line installers and repairers	6	5	1	1	6	1	3	23
538	Office machine repairers	7	4	2	1	4	2	3	23
53A	Mechanics and repairers, except supervisors	4	3	3	3	3	4	3	23
57B	Painters, construction and maintenance, paperhangers, plasterers	5	4	2	3	1	5	3	23
69A	Plant and system operators	6	3	1	3	5	2	3	23
035	Construction inspectors	3	5	1	2	3	6	2	22
254	Real estate sales occupations	3	3	1	2	5	3	5	22
274	Sales workers, other commodities	7	2	1	2	2	4	4	22
31A	Receptionists and information clerks, NEC	2	2	1	4	1	6	6	22
37A	Adjusters and investigators	1	2	1	6	3	6	3	22
387	Teacher's aides	1	1	1	5	4	7	3	22
443	Waiter's/waitress's assistants	7	1	3	3	1	6	1	22
529	Telephone installers and repairers	3	5	1	4	5	1	3	22
588	Concrete and terrazzo finishers	6	4	1	7	1	2	1	22
589	Glaziers	5	4	2	1	1	6	3	22
677	Optical goods workers	2	4	2	1	3	6	4	22
73B	Printing machine operators	6	4	3	1	2	5	1	22
027	Personnel, training, and labor relations specialists	2	6	1	1	3	6	2	21
197	Public relations specialists	3	4	3	2	3	5	1	21
213	Electrical and electronic technicians	1	5	3	1	2	5	4	21
23A	Other technicians, except health engineering and science	3	5	1	1	3	7	1	21
25A	Other sales occupations	3	3	2	1	3	4	5	21
32A	Records processing occupations, except financial	5	2	1	3	2	3	5	21
35C	Mail and message distributing operators	5	1	1	4	3	2	5	21
363	Production coordinators	4	2	2	3	3	3	4	21
38A	Miscellaneous administrative support	1	2	1	5	3	2	7	21
434	Bartenders	7	1	1	5	1	1	5	21
44B	Supervisors, cleaning and building service workers	5	3	1	1	3	6	2	21
565	Tile setters, hard and soft	5	4	4	1	1	5	1	21

(continued)

TABLE 4.17 - *Continued*

Group Number	Occupation	Net Replacement Demand 1990 - 2005	Spec. Voc. Prep. (Months)	Average Certifications per 100,000 Workers in Labor Force 1990 - 92	Average Annual Employment Change 1989 - 93	Average Annual Unemployment Rates 1992 - 93	Projected Job Growth 1992 - 2005	Average Annual Wage Change 1989 - 93	Sum of Indicators
595	Roofers	2	4	1	7	1	5	1	21
68A	Precision workers, assorted materials	6	4	5	2	1	2	1	21
21B	Drafting occupations and surveying and mapping technicians	6	5	3	1	2	2	1	20
253	Insurance sales occupations	4	2	1	4	4	3	2	20
276	Cashiers	7	1	1	3	1	5	2	20
407	Private household cleaners and servants	1	1	7	6	2	1	2	20
446	Health aides, except nursing	2	2	3	1	3	7	2	20
526	Household appliance and power tool repairers	6	4	4	1	3	1	1	20
65C	Sheet metal workers, including apprentices	6	5	2	1	1	3	2	20
686	Butchers and meat cutters	6	3	3	2	1	1	4	20
30B	Computer equipment operators	5	2	1	1	3	1	6	19
313	Secretaries	4	3	2	1	3	2	4	19
33A	Financial records processing	4	2	1	2	3	2	5	19
385	Data-entry keyers	1	2	1	7	1	4	3	19
467	Welfare service aides	1	1	1	1	2	7	6	19
47A	Farming, forestry, and fishing occupations	6	3	3	2	1	2	2	19
516	Heavy equipment mechanics	7	4	2	2	1	2	1	19
525	Data processing equipment repairers	1	3	1	3	3	7	1	19
56B	Carpenters and apprentices	4	4	2	2	1	4	2	19
59A	Other construction trades	2	2	3	2	1	6	3	19
63B	Machinists, including apprentices	4	6	3	1	2	1	2	19
65A	Other precision production occupations	4	4	5	3	1	1	1	19
66A	Other precision textile, apparel, and furnishings machine workers	3	3	7	1	2	1	2	19
72B	Metal and plastic processing machine operators	6	2	4	1	1	2	3	19
35A	Communication equipment operators	6	1	1	1	2	1	6	18
379	General office clerks	3	2	1	2	2	5	3	18
383	Bank tellers	7	2	1	1	4	1	2	18
57A	Electricians and apprentices	3	5	1	2	1	4	2	18
668	Upholsterers	3	3	5	1	2	2	2	18
73A	Textile, apparel, and furnishings machine operators	6	1	5	1	1	1	3	18
80B	Motor vehicle operators	3	1	1	4	2	5	2	18
34A	Duplicating, mail, and other office machine operators	7	1	2	1	2	2	2	17
40A	Launderers, cooks, housekeepers, and butlers	1	2	6	1	2	1	4	17
58A	Plumbers, pipefitters, and steamfitters	5	5	1	2	1	2	1	17
175	Recreation workers	1	3	2	1	1	7	1	16
36A	Material recording, scheduling, and distribution clerks	4	2	1	3	1	2	3	16

Group Number	Occupation	Net Replacement Demand 1990 - 2005	Spec. Voc. Prep. (Months)	Average Certifications per 100,000 Workers in Labor Force 1990 - 92	Average Annual Employment Change 1989 - 93	Average Annual Unemployment Rates 1992 - 93	Projected Job Growth 1992 - 2005	Average Annual Wage Change 1989 - 93	Sum of Indicators
44A	Cleaning and building service, except household	3	1	3	2	1	4	2	16
72A	Woodworking machine operators	6	1	2	1	1	1	4	16
75A	Machine operators, assorted material	6	1	2	2	1	1	3	16
78A	Fabricators, assemblers, and handworking occupations	4	1	4	2	1	2	2	16
79A	Production inspectors, testers, samplers, and weighers	4	2	2	2	1	1	3	15
82A	Rail transportation occupations	1	2	1	1	3	5	2	15
316	Interviewers	4	1	1	1	1	5	1	14
61A	Extractive occupations	1	2	1	6	1	1	2	14
315	Typists	3	2	1	1	1	1	4	13
386	Statistical clerks	2	1	1	1	3	1	4	13
71A	Metalworking and plasticworking machine operators	3	2	3	1	1	1	2	13
85A	Material moving equipment operators	1	2	1	2	1	3	2	12
86A	Handlers, equipment cleaners, helpers, laborers	1	1	2	2	1	3	2	12

Source: Derived from data in tables 4.2, 4.5, 4.7, 4.9, 4.10, 4.12, 4.16.

public transportation attendants, and in 1993 there were 51,000. Thus, this occupation is at the margin of the bureau's criterion, and results may be suspect.

The list is ordered such that occupations most likely to have a shortage are at the top, those most likely to have a surplus at the bottom. The occupations at the bottom of the list are material moving equipment operators, metalworking and plastic machine operators, typists, handlers, equipment cleaners, helpers, laborers, and statistical clerks. Changes in technology and the decline of manufacturing in the United States most likely explain why these occupations rank so low. Computer technology is undoubtedly responsible for the decline in jobs for typists and statistical clerks, as word processing and spreadsheet programs eliminate clerical jobs.

In interpreting the results of the indicators, two important caveats should be kept in mind. First, the results may not capture policy changes not reflected in the various indicators, such as defense cutbacks. Second, there is no assurance that workers trained in a high-ranking occupation will find the type of job they desire. For example, small biotechnology firms may have difficulty finding biologists, while hundreds of biologists are applying unsuccessfully for academic positions.

There are several refinements that can be made to our analysis of the indicators. First, as our discussion in chapter 2 suggested, merely adding the indicators is not as useful as combining the indicators with a theoretical model or expert knowledge of the labor market. For example, in an occupation where the supply is inelastic, an increase in wages would not increase employment. Thus, in this instance the change in employment from 1989 to 1993 might not signal a shortage even though wages could be increasing rapidly.

Second, the statistical reliability of all our indicators is not equal. For example, indicators based on a small sample size would generally be less reliable than indicators based on a larger sample size.

Third, the inclusion of the skill index is a policy variable, not a shortage indicator, and an alternative summary of table 4.17 could delete it. Also, total replacement demand may be preferable to net replacement demand as an indicator for some occupations.

To take account of these various approaches, we tried several methods of constructing summary measures of shortage and surplus occupations. These approaches are shown in various columns of table 4.18.

Approach A: sum of indicators in table 4.17

Approach B: same as approach A, deleting skill

Approach C: same as approach A, excluding replacement demand, since this variable may not be as reliable as others and is consistently a poor indicator of occupations designated as a shortage by other indicators

Approach D: same as approach A, dropping both skill and replacement demand

Approach E: best six out of seven indicators

Approach F: same as approach A, using net replacement instead of total replacement

Approach G: same as approach A, deleting labor certification

Table 4.18 illustrates the value of the different indices, but it is difficult to interpret because of differences in the maximum scores of the various indices. To improve the ease of interpretation, we selected occupations ranked better than number 25 in any of the seven different approaches. Their relative position in table 4.18 is shown in table 4.19. A score of 1 is the best, and a score of 25 ranks it as twenty-fifth among the 193 occupations on the list.

To compare the approaches, in table 4.19 we highlighted the entries in every column in which the difference was plus or minus 10 from the rank shown in column A. The boxes in the table show these differences. The only occupation meeting the criteria for inclusion in the top ten is biological and life sciences, which is ranked eighth in table 4.17 and twenty-first when skill and net replacement are ignored. There is a great deal of uncertainty about the future of this occupation in any event. The cost containment in the drug industry that will likely result from health care reform could lead to sharp cutbacks in basic research and thus reduce opportunities for biologists.

When labor certifications are ignored, two occupations become more likely to be in excess demand: airplane pilots and police and detectives. To the extent that U.S. licensing requirements make it difficult to hire foreign workers for these two occupations, the approach ignoring certifications is probably more reliable as a measure in this case. It is interesting to note that in column G, in which labor certifications are deleted, the top eighteen occupations are essentially the same as the top eighteen in column A; the only occupation that appears in the top eighteen in column A but not in column G is college and university teachers. Yet even that occupation is not inconsistent in light of the fact that the Department of Labor uses a different set of rules for college and university teachers than for all other occupations. That occupation can be certified even if there is not a shortage of U.S. workers if it can be shown that a foreign teacher is better qualified for a given opening.

If the Department of Labor based labor certifications on political or other considerations besides labor market conditions, the labor certification indicator would falsely indicate an excess demand that may not exist in a given occupation. Occupations ranked lower by 15 or more include civil engineers, industrial engineers, and economists. However, in the absence of evidence that certification in these occupations is handled differently than for others in table 4.19, the analysis lends support to the belief that labor certification

TABLE 4.18. Alternative Ranking Systems

Group Number	Occupation	NR[a]	S[b]	L[c]	N[d]	U[e]	P[f]	W[g]	TR[h]	Approach[i] A	B	C	D	E	F	G
07A	Other natural scientists	6	7	7	7	7	5	3	2	42	35	36	29	39	38	35
086	Veterinarians	3	7	4	7	7	6	7	1	41	34	38	31	38	39	37
103	Physical therapists	2	4	7	7	6	7	7	3	40	36	38	34	38	41	33
084	Physicians	3	7	6	3	7	6	7	1	39	32	36	29	36	37	33
095	Registered nurses	2	6	7	5	7	7	5	2	39	33	37	31	37	39	32
104	Speech therapists	2	6	4	6	7	7	7	3	39	33	37	31	37	40	35
073	Chemists, except biochemists	4	6	7	6	6	5	4	2	38	32	34	28	34	36	31
078	Biological and life scientists	6	7	7	7	4	5	2	2	38	31	32	25	36	34	31
229	Computer programmers	5	6	6	4	5	6	6	3	38	32	33	27	34	36	32
064	Computer systems analysts and scientists	1	6	7	7	5	7	4	2	37	31	36	30	36	38	30
065	Operations and systems researchers and analysts	3	5	4	7	6	7	5	2	37	32	34	29	34	36	33
075	Geologists and geodesists	5	7	7	3	3	5	7	2	37	30	32	25	34	34	30
206	Radiological technicians	3	6	3	4	7	7	7	3	37	31	34	28	34	37	34
226	Airplane pilots and navigators	6	7	2	3	5	7	7	1	37	30	31	24	35	32	35
09A	Other therapists	2	6	5	5	6	7	5	3	36	30	34	28	34	37	31
15C	Teachers, college and university	6	7	7	4	5	5	2	4	36	29	30	23	34	34	29
176	Clergy	2	7	3	5	7	6	6	2	36	29	34	27	34	36	33
41A	Police and detectives	7	5	1	6	7	3	7	1	36	31	29	24	35	30	35
096	Pharmacists	2	6	6	2	7	6	6	1	35	29	33	27	33	34	29
053	Civil engineers	5	7	7	2	4	5	4	2	34	27	29	22	32	31	27
085	Dentists	5	7	5	1	7	2	7	1	34	27	29	22	33	30	29
678	Dental laboratory and medical appliance technicians	7	4	6	2	6	2	7	5	34	30	27	23	32	32	28
056	Industrial engineers	6	7	7	2	3	3	5	1	33	26	27	20	31	28	26
097	Dietitians	5	7	4	5	3	5	4	2	33	26	28	21	30	30	29
157	Teachers, secondary school	5	5	3	4	6	7	3	3	33	28	28	23	30	31	30
158	Teachers, special education	1	5	4	5	6	7	5	2	33	28	32	27	32	34	29
18A	Other editors, reporters, authors, and technical writers	1	7	5	5	4	5	6	4	33	26	32	25	32	36	28
014	Administrators, education and related fields	5	7	3	4	6	5	2	2	32	25	27	20	30	29	29
026	Management analysts	1	6	5	7	4	7	2	5	32	26	31	25	31	36	27
048	Chemical engineers	4	7	7	1	3	4	6	1	32	25	28	21	31	29	25
055	Electrical and electronic engineers	4	7	7	2	3	5	4	1	32	25	28	21	30	29	25
087	Optometrists	3	5	3	4	7	3	7	1	32	27	29	24	29	30	29
098	Inhalation therapists	2	3	2	7	7	7	4	3	32	29	30	27	30	33	30
15A	Teachers, NEC	1	6	6	7	4	6	2	4	32	26	31	25	31	35	26
166	Economists	6	7	7	1	3	5	3	6	32	25	26	19	31	32	25

Group Number	Occupation	NR[a]	S[b]	L[c]	N[d]	U[e]	P[f]	W[g]	TR[h]	Approach[i] A	B	C	D	E	F	G
167	Psychologists	1	7	4	6	5	7	2	1	32	25	31	24	31	32	28
178	Lawyers	2	7	3	3	7	6	4	1	32	25	30	23	30	31	29
65B	Precision woodworking occupations	6	5	7	7	1	5	1	6	32	27	26	21	31	32	25
013	Managers, marketing, advertising, and public relations	3	7	6	2	3	7	3	3	31	24	28	21	29	31	25
023	Accountants and auditors	2	7	5	3	4	6	4	4	31	24	29	22	29	33	26
044	Aerospace engineers	5	7	6	1	3	3	6	1	31	24	26	19	30	27	25
057	Mechanical engineers	4	7	7	2	3	4	4	1	31	24	27	20	29	28	24
16B	Librarians, archivists, and curators	4	6	4	5	5	2	5	4	31	25	27	21	29	31	27
43A	Cooks, including short-order	5	3	6	5	1	7	4	7	31	28	26	23	30	33	25
465	Public transportation attendants	4	1	1	7	4	7	7	6	31	30	27	26	30	33	30
007	Financial managers	2	7	4	4	4	5	4	2	30	23	28	21	28	30	26
05A	Other engineers	2	7	7	2	3	5	4	2	30	23	28	21	28	30	23
06A	Statisticians, actuaries, and other mathematical scientists	1	7	7	2	6	3	4	2	30	23	29	22	29	31	23
16A	Other social scientists	3	6	7	3	4	5	2	4	30	24	27	21	28	31	23
189	Photographers	5	4	2	5	2	5	7	4	30	26	25	21	28	29	28
18B	Professional specialty occupations	3	5	6	3	2	7	4	5	30	25	27	22	28	32	24
208	Health technologists and technicians, NEC	1	4	4	7	3	7	4	4	30	26	29	25	29	33	26
314	Stenographers	4	3	1	7	7	1	7	6	30	27	26	23	29	32	29
509	Small-engine repairers	7	3	3	7	3	3	4	4	30	27	23	20	27	27	27
179	Judges	2	7	1	6	7	2	4	1	29	22	27	20	28	28	28
203	Clinical laboratory technologists and technicians	2	4	5	3	4	5	6	2	29	25	27	23	27	29	24
255	Securities and financial services sales occupations	1	5	2	6	4	6	5	4	29	24	28	23	28	32	27
438	Food counter, fountain, and related occupations	7	1	5	6	1	4	5	7	29	28	22	21	28	29	24
457	Barbers	7	3	3	3	6	1	6	2	29	26	22	19	28	24	26
577	Electrical power installers and repairers	6	6	1	4	4	2	6	2	29	23	23	17	28	25	28
016	Managers, properties and real estate	1	6	2	5	3	6	5	3	28	22	27	21	27	30	26
01A	Other executive, administrative, and managerial	3	7	3	3	4	5	3	2	28	21	25	18	25	27	25
03A	Other management-related occupations	1	6	3	5	3	6	4	3	28	22	27	21	27	30	25
106	Physician's assistants	2	5	3	1	6	6	5	3	28	23	26	21	27	29	25
15B	Teachers, prekindergarten, kindergarten, and elementary	2	5	3	4	6	6	2	4	28	23	26	21	26	30	25
174	Social workers	1	6	3	3	4	7	4	3	28	22	27	21	27	30	25
177	Religious workers, NEC	1	6	4	3	7	6	1	5	28	22	27	21	27	32	24
188	Painters, sculptors, craft artists, and artist printmakers	3	6	5	2	3	5	4	5	28	22	25	19	26	30	23
204	Dental hygienists	1	3	2	3	7	7	5	3	28	25	27	24	27	30	26
234	Legal assistants	1	5	3	6	3	7	3	4	28	23	27	22	27	31	25
41C	Firefighting and fire prevention occupations	7	4	1	3	6	3	4	1	28	24	21	17	27	22	27

TABLE 4.18 - *Continued*

Group Number	Occupation	NR[a]	S[b]	L[c]	N[d]	U[e]	P[f]	W[g]	TR[h]	Approach[i] A	B	C	D	E	F	G
445	Dental assistants	5	3	3	3	3	7	4	6	28	25	23	20	25	29	25
46A	Personal service occupations, residual	1	2	5	6	2	7	5	7	28	26	27	25	27	34	23
507	Bus, truck, and stationary-engine mechanics	6	5	3	4	3	5	2	1	28	23	22	17	26	23	25
566	Carpet installers	6	5	2	1	2	5	7	3	28	23	22	17	27	25	26
033	Purchasing agents and buyers, NEC	4	6	5	6	3	1	2	3	27	21	23	17	26	26	22
186	Musicians and composers	2	7	5	1	3	5	4	5	27	20	25	18	26	30	22
22A	Other science technicians	4	4	4	6	3	5	1	3	27	23	23	19	26	26	23
30A	Supervisors, administrative support	5	4	1	3	4	5	5	3	27	23	22	18	26	25	26
424	Correctional institution officers	1	2	1	5	7	7	4	3	27	25	26	24	26	29	26
593	Insulation workers	7	4	1	3	1	7	4	7	27	23	20	16	26	27	26
008	Personnel and labor relations managers	6	6	3	1	3	5	2	2	26	20	20	14	25	22	23
009	Purchasing managers	3	6	3	2	4	3	5	1	26	20	23	17	24	24	23
163	Counselors, educational and vocational	3	7	3	2	4	6	1	4	26	19	23	16	25	27	23
185	Designers	2	6	4	3	3	4	4	4	26	20	24	18	24	28	22
207	Licensed practical nurses	2	2	1	2	6	7	6	3	26	24	24	22	25	27	25
43B	Food preparation and service occupations	6	1	6	4	1	7	1	7	26	25	20	19	25	27	20
458	Hairdressers and cosmetologists	2	2	3	3	4	7	5	5	26	24	24	22	24	29	23
534	Heating, air conditioning, and refrigeration mechanics	3	5	2	4	3	6	3	2	26	21	23	18	24	25	24
687	Bakers	3	4	6	3	2	2	6	6	26	22	23	19	24	29	20
82B	Water transportation occupations	1	4	4	7	1	2	7	4	26	22	25	21	25	29	22
029	Buyers, wholesale and retail trade, except farm products	6	3	4	5	3	3	1	4	25	22	19	16	24	23	21
04A	Architects, surveyors, and mapping scientists	3	6	7	1	3	4	1	3	25	19	22	16	24	25	18
406	Child care workers, private household	7	1	7	2	2	1	5	7	25	24	18	17	24	25	18
50A	Automobile mechanics, including apprentices	7	3	5	1	2	5	2	5	25	22	18	15	24	23	20
544	Millwrights	7	6	4	1	1	2	4	4	25	19	18	12	24	22	21
573	Drywall installers	7	3	1	5	1	7	1	6	25	22	18	15	24	24	24
198	Announcers	7	3	3	1	1	5	4	5	24	21	17	14	23	22	21
21A	Other technicians and related support occupations	4	5	3	2	3	3	4	4	24	19	20	15	22	24	21
317	Hotel clerks	7	1	2	3	1	7	3	7	24	23	17	16	23	24	22
318	Transportation ticket and reservation agents	3	2	1	7	3	7	1	4	24	22	21	19	23	25	23
433	Supervisors, food preparation and service occupations	2	5	2	2	2	7	4	6	24	19	22	17	22	28	22
447	Nursing aides, orderlies, and attendants	1	1	5	6	1	7	3	6	24	23	23	22	23	29	19
468	Child care workers, except private household	1	1	1	4	3	7	7	7	24	23	23	22	23	30	23
533	Miscellaneous electrical and electronic equipment repairers	5	4	5	1	1	2	6	3	24	20	19	15	23	22	19
55A	Supervisors, blue-collar	6	6	3	3	3	2	1	2	24	18	18	12	23	20	21
56A	Brickmasons and stonemasons, including apprentices	5	5	5	2	1	5	1	6	24	19	19	14	23	25	19

Group Number	Occupation	NR[a]	S[b]	L[c]	N[d]	U[e]	P[f]	W[g]	TR[h]	Approach[i]						
										A	B	C	D	E	F	G
63A	Tool and die makers, including apprentices	6	6	4	2	4	1	1	1	24	18	18	12	23	19	20
205	Health record technologists and technicians	1	4	1	3	5	7	2	3	23	19	22	18	22	25	22
275	Sales counter clerks	3	1	1	3	1	7	7	7	23	22	20	19	22	27	22
42A	Guards	4	2	1	3	1	7	5	7	23	21	19	17	22	26	22
435	Waiters and waitresses	7	1	1	3	1	7	3	7	23	22	16	15	22	23	22
514	Automobile body and related repairers	5	3	5	2	1	6	1	4	23	20	18	15	22	22	18
51A	Aircraft mechanics	4	4	2	3	1	2	7	1	23	19	19	15	22	20	21
523	Electronic repairers, communications and industrial equipment	4	5	4	4	2	2	2	5	23	18	19	14	21	24	19
527	Telephone line installers and repairers	6	5	1	1	6	1	3	1	23	18	17	12	22	18	22
538	Office machine repairers	7	4	2	1	4	2	3	1	23	19	16	12	22	17	21
53A	Mechanics and repairers, except supervisors	4	3	3	3	3	4	3	3	23	20	19	16	20	22	20
57B	Painters, construction and maintenance, paperhangers, plasterers	5	4	2	3	1	5	3	5	23	19	18	14	22	23	21
69A	Plant and system operators	6	3	1	3	5	2	3	1	23	20	17	14	22	18	22
035	Construction inspectors	3	5	1	2	3	6	2	2	22	17	19	14	21	21	21
254	Real estate sales occupations	3	3	1	2	5	3	5	5	22	19	19	16	21	24	21
274	Sales workers, other commodities	7	2	1	2	2	4	4	7	22	20	15	13	21	22	21
31A	Receptionists and information clerks, NEC	2	2	1	4	1	6	6	7	22	20	20	18	21	27	21
37A	Adjusters and investigators	1	2	1	6	3	6	3	5	22	20	21	19	21	26	21
387	Teacher's aides	1	1	1	5	4	7	3	6	22	21	21	20	21	27	21
443	Waiter's/waitress's assistants	7	1	3	3	1	6	1	7	22	21	15	14	21	22	19
529	Telephone installers and repairers	3	5	1	4	5	1	3	1	22	17	19	14	21	20	21
588	Concrete and terrazzo finishers	6	4	1	7	1	2	1	1	22	18	16	12	21	17	21
589	Glaziers	5	4	2	1	1	6	3	5	22	18	17	13	21	22	20
677	Optical goods workers	2	4	2	1	3	6	4	5	22	18	20	16	21	25	20
73B	Printing machine operators	6	4	3	1	2	5	1	4	22	18	16	12	21	20	19
027	Personnel, training, and labor relations specialists	2	6	1	1	3	6	2	3	21	15	19	13	20	22	20
197	Public relations specialists	3	4	3	2	3	5	1	6	21	17	18	14	20	24	18
213	Electrical and electronic technicians	1	5	3	1	2	5	4	3	21	16	20	15	20	23	18
23A	Other technicians, except health engineering and science	3	5	1	1	3	7	1	4	21	16	18	13	20	22	20
25A	Other sales occupations	3	3	2	1	3	4	5	6	21	18	18	15	20	24	19
32A	Records processing occupations, except financial	5	2	1	3	2	3	5	7	21	19	16	14	20	23	20
35C	Mail and message distributing operators	5	1	1	4	3	2	5	4	21	20	16	15	20	20	20
363	Production coordinators	4	2	2	3	3	3	4	5	21	19	17	15	19	22	19
38A	Miscellaneous administrative support	1	2	1	5	3	2	7	5	21	19	20	18	20	25	20
434	Bartenders	7	1	1	5	1	1	5	7	21	20	14	13	20	21	20
44B	Supervisors, cleaning and building service workers	5	3	1	1	3	6	2	3	21	18	16	13	20	19	20

TABLE 4.18 - *Continued*

Group Number	Occupation	NR[a]	S[b]	L[c]	N[d]	U[e]	P[f]	W[g]	TR[h]	Approach[i] A	B	C	D	E	F	G
565	Tile setters, hard and soft	5	4	4	1	1	5	1	1	21	17	16	12	20	17	17
595	Roofers	2	4	1	7	1	5	1	7	21	17	19	15	20	26	20
68A	Precision workers, assorted materials	6	4	5	2	1	2	1	5	21	17	15	11	20	20	16
21B	Drafting occupations and surveying and mapping technicians	6	5	3	1	2	2	1	5	20	15	14	9	19	19	17
253	Insurance sales occupations	4	2	1	4	4	3	2	2	20	18	16	14	19	18	19
276	Cashiers	7	1	1	3	1	5	2	7	20	19	13	12	19	20	19
407	Private household cleaners and servants	1	1	7	6	2	1	2	6	20	19	19	18	19	25	13
446	Health aides, except nursing	2	2	3	1	3	7	2	6	20	18	18	16	19	24	17
526	Household appliance and power tool repairers	6	4	4	1	3	1	1	2	20	16	14	10	19	16	16
65C	Sheet metal workers, including apprentices	6	5	2	1	1	3	2	6	20	15	14	9	19	20	18
686	Butchers and meat cutters	6	3	3	2	1	1	4	5	20	17	14	11	19	19	17
30B	Computer equipment operators	5	2	1	1	3	1	6	5	19	17	14	12	18	19	18
313	Secretaries	4	3	2	1	3	2	4	5	19	16	15	12	18	20	17
33A	Financial records processing	4	2	1	2	3	2	5	6	19	17	15	13	18	21	18
385	Data-entry keyers	1	2	1	7	1	4	3	7	19	17	18	16	18	25	18
467	Welfare service aides	1	1	1	1	2	7	6	5	19	18	18	17	18	23	18
47A	Farming, forestry, and fishing occupations	6	3	3	2	1	2	2	6	19	16	13	10	18	19	16
516	Heavy equipment mechanics	7	4	2	2	1	2	1	4	19	15	12	8	18	16	17
525	Data processing equipment repairers	1	3	1	3	3	7	1	2	19	16	18	15	18	20	18
56B	Carpenters and apprentices	4	4	2	2	1	4	2	5	19	15	15	11	18	20	17
59A	Other construction trades	2	2	3	2	1	6	3	4	19	17	17	15	18	21	16
63B	Machinists, including apprentices	4	6	3	1	2	1	2	2	19	13	15	9	18	17	16
65A	Other precision production occupations	4	4	5	3	1	1	1	4	19	15	15	11	18	19	14
66A	Other precision textile, apparel, and furnishings machine workers	3	3	7	1	2	1	2	4	19	16	16	13	18	20	12
72B	Metal and plastic processing machine operators	6	2	4	1	1	2	3	4	19	17	13	11	18	17	15
35A	Communication equipment operators	6	1	1	1	2	1	6	5	18	17	12	11	17	17	17
379	General office clerks	3	2	1	2	2	5	3	6	18	16	15	13	17	21	17
383	Bank tellers	7	2	1	1	4	1	2	7	18	16	11	9	17	18	17
57A	Electricians and apprentices	3	5	1	2	1	4	2	2	18	13	15	10	17	17	17
668	Upholsterers	3	3	5	1	2	2	2	3	18	15	15	12	17	18	13
73A	Textile, apparel, and furnishings machine operators	6	1	5	1	1	1	3	6	18	17	12	11	17	18	13
80B	Motor vehicle operators	3	1	1	4	2	5	2	6	18	17	15	14	17	21	17
34A	Duplicating, mail, and other office machine operators	7	1	2	1	2	2	2	5	17	16	10	9	16	15	15
40A	Launderers, cooks, housekeepers, and butlers	1	2	6	1	2	1	4	6	17	15	16	14	16	22	11
58A	Plumbers, pipefitters, and steamfitters	5	5	1	2	1	2	1	4	17	12	12	7	16	16	16
175	Recreation workers	1	3	2	1	1	7	1	6	16	13	15	12	15	21	14

Group Number	Occupation	NR[a]	S[b]	L[c]	N[d]	U[e]	P[f]	W[g]	TR[h]	Approach[i]						
										A	B	C	D	E	F	G
36A	Material recording, scheduling, and distribution clerks	4	2	1	3	1	2	3	6	16	14	12	10	15	18	15
44A	Cleaning and building service, except household	3	1	3	2	1	4	2	7	16	15	13	12	15	20	13
72A	Woodworking machine operators	6	1	2	1	1	1	4	6	16	15	10	9	15	16	14
75A	Machine operators, assorted material	6	1	2	2	1	1	3	6	16	15	10	9	15	16	14
78A	Fabricators, assemblers, and handworking occupations	4	1	4	2	1	2	2	5	16	15	12	11	15	17	12
79A	Production inspectors, testers, samplers, and weighers	4	2	2	2	1	1	3	4	15	13	11	9	14	15	13
82A	Rail transportation occupations	1	2	1	1	3	5	2	1	15	13	14	12	14	15	14
316	Interviewers	4	1	1	1	1	5	1	7	14	13	10	9	13	17	13
61A	Extractive occupations	1	2	1	6	1	1	2	6	14	12	13	11	13	19	13
315	Typists	3	2	1	1	1	1	4	7	13	11	10	8	12	17	12
386	Statistical clerks	2	1	1	1	3	1	4	2	13	12	11	10	12	13	12
71A	Metalworking and plasticworking machine operators	3	2	3	1	1	1	2	4	13	11	10	8	12	14	10
85A	Material moving equipment operators	1	2	1	2	1	3	2	4	12	10	11	9	11	15	11
86A	Handlers, equipment cleaners, helpers, laborers	1	1	2	2	1	3	2	7	12	11	11	10	11	18	10

Source: Derived from data in tables 4.17 and 4.10.

[a]NR = Net replacement demand 1992 - 2005
[b]S = Specific vocational preparation (months)
[c]L = Average certifications per 100,000 workers in labor force 1990 - 92
[d]N = Average annual employment change 1989 - 93
[e]U = Average annual unemployment rates 1992 - 93
[f]P = Projected job growth 1992 - 2005
[g]W = Average annual wage change 1989 - 93
[h]TR = Total replacement demand 1990 - 91
[i]Approaches: A = Sum of Indicators from table 4.17; B = Same as A, deleting skill; C = Same as A, deleting net replacement demand; D = Same as A, deleting skill and net replacement demand; E = Best six out of seven indicators; F = Same as A, using total instead of net replacement demand; G = same as A, deleting labor certifications

information assists in analyzing shortages. Another possibility is that since information on labor certifications wasn't updated in 1993, these occupations may have improved by then. This explanation seems more plausible, but it cannot be tested because the author did not have the latest labor certification information.

TABLE 4.19. Leading Occupations Ranked by Relative Position in Table 4.18

Group Number	Occupation	A[a]	B[b]	C[c]	D[d]	E[e]	F[f]	G[g]
07A	Other natural scientists	1	2	6	7	1	6	4
086	Veterinarians	2	3	2	3	3	4	1
103	Physical therapists	3	1	2	1	3	1	9
084	Physicians	5	8	6	7	7	8	9
095	Registered nurses	5	5	4	3	5	4	12
104	Speech therapists	5	5	4	3	5	2	4
073	Chemists, except biochemists	8	8	10	10	15	13	14
078	Biological and life scientists	8	12	17	21	7	20	14
229	Computer programmers	8	8	14	14	15	13	12
064	Computer systems analysts and scientists	10	12	6	5	7	6	18
065	Operations and systems researchers and analysts	11	8	10	7	15	13	9
075	Geologists and geodesists	12	16	17	21	15	20	18
206	Radiological technicians	13	12	10	10	15	8	6
226	Airplane pilots and navigators	14	16	21	28	10	32	4
09A	Other therapists	17	16	10	10	15	8	14
15C	Teachers, college and university	17	21	24	35	15	20	25
176	Clergy	17	21	10	14	15	13	9
41A	Police and detectives	17	12	29	28	10	50	4
096	Pharmacists	19	21	14	14	20	20	25
053	Civil engineers	21	30	29	44	23	40	39
085	Dentists	21	30	29	44	20	50	25
678	Dental laboratory and medical appliance technicians	21	16	49	35	23	32	33
056	Industrial engineers	25	37	49	20	28	>60	47
097	Dietitians	25	16	37	58	36	50	18
157	Teachers, secondary school	25	25	37	35	36	40	18
158	Teachers, special education	25	25	17	14	23	20	25
18A	Other editors, reporters, authors, and technical writers	25	37	17	21	23	13	33
014	Administrators, education and related fields	33	48	49	20	36	>60	25
026	Management analysts	33	37	21	21	28	13	39
098	Inhalation therapists	33	21	24	14	36	25	18
15A	Teachers, NEC	33	37	21	21	28	16	47
166	Economists	33	48	62	19	28	32	62
167	Psychologists	33	48	21	28	28	32	33
178	Lawyers	33	48	24	35	36	40	25
465	Public transportation attendants	42	16	49	>60	36	25	18
208	Health technologists and technicians, NEC	49	37	29	21	45	25	25

Source: Derived from data in table 4.18.

[a]A = Sum of Indicators from table 4.17
[b]B = Same as A, deleting skill
[c]C = Same as A, deleting net replacement demand
[d]D = Same as A, deleting skill and net replacement demand
[e]E = Best six out of seven indicators
[f]F = Same as A, using total instead of net replacement demand
[g]G = same as A, deleting labor certifications

Other occupations ranking 25 or lower in table 4.17 that rank in the top 15 in table 4.18 by some method are:

1. Special education teachers, ranking 25 in table 4.17 and 14 when skill and net replacement are ignored.
2. Other editors and reporters, ranking 25 in table 4.17 and 13 when total instead of net replacement is used.
3. Management analysts, ranking 33 in table 4.17 and 13 when total instead of net replacement is used.
4. Inhalation therapists, ranking 33 in table 4.17 and 14 when skill and net replacement are ignored.

While there is variability in the different indices, the story is consistent. The robustness of the methods lends further confidence to this approach for selecting occupations likely to have the greatest excess demand.

Although there are differences in the individual indicators, these differences are largely understandable when interpreted in the context of the theory discussed in chapter 2. For example, wages would be expected to increase above average in a shortage occupation, while employment may be constrained from increasing if the supply is inelastic. A good example of this may be primary care physicians.

CHAPTER 5

Identifying Shortages

Short Run versus Long Run

Recessions and Shortages

The U.S. economy has been characterized by cyclical fluctuations throughout its history. Just since World War II, there have been nine recessions: 1948–49, 1953–54, 1957–58, 1960–61, 1969–70, 1973–75, 1980, 1981–82, and 1990–91. Since 1854, there have been thirty-one recessions or depressions in the United States (U.S. Dept. of Commerce 1992). There is no reason to believe that these trends will not continue. There are likely to be more recessions, and we are likely to recover from them as well.

During recessions, occupations that might have a shortage of labor at other times may come into equilibrium or even have surplus labor. Recession periods, however, do not define the norm; they occupy a much smaller portion of the overall business cycle than do recovery and boom periods. For most purposes, therefore, an occupation that has a surplus of labor only during recessions would not be categorized in general as having a long-run surplus. By the same token, an occupation having a shortage of labor only during the peak of business cycles would not be considered to have a long-run shortage.

A long period of slow economic growth could result in there being a lot of workers in the pipeline available for work when the economy recovers, effectively eliminating a shortage and creating a surplus. It could also discourage students from choosing the surplus occupations, and in occupations that require long training times, a shortage could develop once the economy recovers. Thus, a recession might ease a shortage in the short run, but exacerbate it in the long run.

While cyclical fluctuations can temporarily reduce occupational demand and create hardship for displaced workers, they should not be allowed to influence long-term employment policy affecting education, training, or immigration. This is not to say that short-term labor shortages or surpluses should be ignored, only that long-term policy decisions should be carefully considered to take into account their effect on all phases of the business cycle. When an economic recovery is very slow, however, and workers face long periods of unemployment, a prediction of long-term recovery ought not to be an excuse to do nothing about unemployment, either.

During the 1990–91 recession, there was a 50 percent increase in the level of unemployment for managerial and professional specialty workers, from 2 percent to 3 percent, and slow economic growth after the recession failed to lower the rate significantly in 1992. According to an article in the *New York Times* (12 May 1992), surveys by university placement offices indicated that 1992 was the worst labor market in two decades for graduates in these fields. Nevertheless, most of the occupations ranked high by my shortage indicators are in the managerial and professional specialty category.

When economic growth revives, labor shortages are not likely to develop in professional occupations until the backlog of unemployed or underemployed college graduates are placed. Some occupations, however, have more jobs than graduates even during the worst job market in twenty years. These include, according to a Michigan State study cited in the *New York Times* (12 May 1992), business and management, engineering, health professions, computer, information sciences, engineering technologies, and physical sciences.

A current policy issue is whether the slowdown in the economy is a short-term problem related to the business cycle, or a long-term problem attributable to factors such as the loss of competitiveness in the United States. This issue is discussed in more detail in the section of this chapter dealing with factors affecting future shortages.

Training Time and the Cobweb Theory

The supply of labor in some occupations may depend on labor market conditions at the time of enrollment in training for these occupations. For occupations requiring long training times, such as engineering, a "cobweb" theory has been used to describe equilibrium, as shown in figure 5.1 (Ehrenberg and Smith 1982; Freeman 1976).

In this figure, supply and demand are initially in equilibrium (N_1,W_1). Demand shifts upward, but in the short run, with a fixed supply of labor, employers must pay a higher wage (W_2) to attract enough engineers to meet their needs. Engineering school enrollments increase as more students, perceiving an income advantage, choose that field of study. Four years later, however, the number of engineering graduates (N_2) exceeds the demand, and wages fall to W_3. But at wage W_3, fewer students decide to become engineers, and in time the supply of engineers decreases. The adjustment path in this model resembles a cobweb, which grows with progressively smaller adjustments until equilibrium is finally achieved.

The availability of foreign labor and the possibility of shifts from engi-

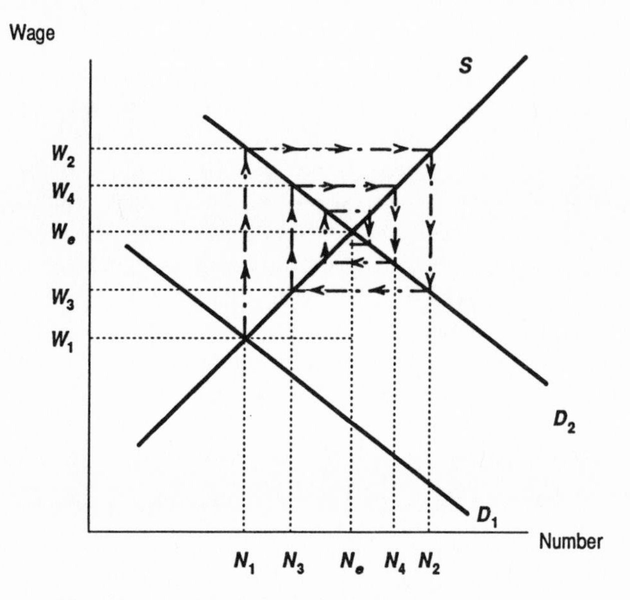

Fig. 5.1. A cobweb model of supply and demand

neering into sales or administration offer more flexibility than might be suggested by the simple cobweb theory. The underlying concept does apply, however, to those occupations where large numbers of students either avoid or enter training for an occupation based on their expectations about job prospects.

An ironic twist in forecasting labor shortages is that the forecasts themselves can have an effect on the labor market, resulting in what we might call a self-nullifying prophecy. For instance, if large numbers of students decide to prepare for certain occupations based on forecast information to the effect that those occupations will have a shortage of labor, the result could be an overabundance of labor in those occupations by the time the forecast period becomes actual.

Approaches to Forecasting Future Shortages

Differences in the mode of analysis can lead to different conclusions regarding future or even current shortages, with differing degrees of reliability and value for different time periods. The following discussion concerns the advantages and disadvantages of various methods that have been used to probe the labor market for signs of shortage or surplus: job vacancy surveys, employer skill surveys, labor demand and supply matrices, and indicators.

Job Vacancy Surveys

As discussed in chapter 2, job vacancy surveys can yield information on the average amount of time needed to fill a job opening, the number of job openings, the number of openings per employed worker, and the fill rate. Such data can give policymakers a perspective on current shortages, and in occupations that consistently have high vacancy rates, the information can also be used to infer future labor market conditions.

The main disadvantage of job vacancy surveys is the cost, but even if such a survey were conducted, it would still be only one shortage indicator, albeit an important one. As mentioned in chapter 2, many other factors need to be considered in conjunction with job vacancy rates to understand the dynamics of the labor market.

Employer Skill Surveys

Employer skill surveys have been used to determine what requirements businesses foresee for different types of labor. These surveys typically consist of a mail questionnaire sent to companies, asking businesspeople to predict their perceived hiring plans in the future.

The main problem with these surveys is that businesses generally disregard actions by other firms when making their forecasts. For example, during a recession, firms rarely plan on expanding their own output, yet some firms can and do expand during a recession simply because, with so many other firms decreasing production, total output may fall below demand. Another difficulty with employer surveys is that different assumptions are being made by the survey respondents, and the survey analysis may not take into account the assumptions underlying the responses. For example, if a significant technology is just over the horizon, some respondents may be aware of it while others are not, so that some of the responses will reflect the expected impact of the technology on employment and some will not.

On the other hand, employer skill surveys can be a useful tool in the analysis of future staffing needs when they are used to gather information about the nature of an industry, expected technological changes, current market conditions, or organizational factors that affect staffing.

Labor Demand and Supply Matrices

BLS Model. One of the most widely known projections of future labor market demand is made every other year by the Bureau of Labor Statistics (U.S. Dept. of Labor 1992b, 1992c). The BLS projections cover 174 final demand industry sectors and 228 commodity sectors. Within these sectors, BLS identifies staffing patterns from a survey it conducts every three years, making adjustments for anticipated changes in future relationships based on special studies of occupations and industries. (The Occupational Employment Statistics survey is conducted over a three-year period in each of three sectors, so that a different sector is surveyed each year.) For example, a small decrease is predicted in the employment coefficient for credit analysts due to increased computerization between 1990 and 2005.

The BLS prediction is based on a large occupation-by-employment matrix, which contains detailed projections for each occupational group within each industry group. Most state employment agencies use the matrix program to project demand by occupation for the state and subareas within the state. Some state agencies collect data on labor supply sources, such as graduates from various training institutions within the state, and compare the number of persons entering various occupations with future demand.

Projections from the BLS matrix are included for 193 occupational groups in the discussion in chapter 4. The actual matrix identifies 507 detailed occupations.

Bishop model. An evaluation of the BLS matrix approach by John Bishop found a faster rate of growth in the higher-level occupations than that forecast by BLS (Bishop and Carter 1990; Bishop 1992a). According to Bishop, BLS predicted a 1.8 percent decline in the employment share of managerial occupations from 1978 to 1990; the share actually grew by 21.3 percent. BLS predicted a 2.3 percent growth in the employment share of professionals; the share actually increased by 17.8 percent. Similarly, BLS overpredicted the growth in employment share of lower-skilled nonfarm occupations.

Bishop argues that the source of the bias in the BLS method is the use of a fixed coefficient occupational matrix, which assumes the constancy of staffing patterns with an industry sector. Even though BLS does limited studies that permit minor adjustment to staffing pattern changes, they fail to catch major trends within industry groups, such as the significant increase in the share of professionals and managers.

Using a model based on indicators, such as the wage premium paid to college majors, Bishop predicts a 2.5 percent annual growth rate in professional, technical, managerial, and sales representative occupations from 1988 to 2000, compared with a BLS prediction of 1.7 percent annual growth. The calculations by Bishop indicate a 2.8 percent increase in the supply of college graduates for the 1990s. While this still indicates that the growth in supply of college graduates exceeds demand by 0.3 percent per year, it is no different from the 1980–88 period, and far better than the 1972–80 period, when supply grew at a rate 2.3 percent greater than demand. Since wage premiums for college graduates grew substantially during the 1980–88 period, Bishop

TABLE 5.1. Labor Shortage Statistics, by Detailed Occupation, All Eight Industries, Six-Month Averages

Cohen 1990 Indicator Score	Occupation	Percentage of Job Openings Longer than 4 Weeks	Ratio of New Hires to Job Openings
	Total	37.3	1.87
[a]	General managers	75.7	1.30
28	Licensed practical nurses	57.6	0.39
25	Medical and clinical laboratory technicians	41.2	0.69
25	Medical and clinical laboratory technologists	62.2	0.36
[a]	Medical secretaries	58.6	0.55
31	Nursing aides, orderlies, and attendants	43.1	1.29
30	Radiologic technologists	71.3	0.49
39	Registered nurses	72.3	0.28
25	Secretaries	44.5	1.35
38	Systems analysts	61.4	0.99

Source: Employee Turnover and Job Opening Survey: Results of a Pilot Study on the Feasibility of Collecting Measures of Imbalances of Supply and Demand for Labor in an Establishment Survey, U.S. Department of Labor, Bureau of Labor Statistics 1991.

[a]This group was not comparable to any in the Cohen study.

argues that the 1990s will continue to be a period of strong demand for college graduates.

Indicators

The theoretical model developed in chapter 2, along with the arguments made in chapters 3 and 4, supports the approach of using indicators and past trends to project potential future shortages or surpluses. Bishop's arguments and analysis offer further validity to our argument. We rely on trends in wages, employment, BLS projections, and unemployment rates to establish the relative demand and supply of various occupations. We argue that this analysis provides an excellent way to identify potential shortages and surpluses. The method does not tell us where to draw the line, nor does it tell us by how much supply and demand are out of balance. It does not guarantee that every occupation on the top of the list has a labor shortage. When combined with reasonable analysis and interpretation, however, it can be a useful tool for policymakers.

As part of its pilot job vacancy survey, BLS selected occupations with the highest proportion of openings with a duration of more than four weeks and a low fill rate (U.S. Dept. of Labor 1991a). Only occupations with statistically reliable measures were selected. BLS then compared these occupations to the indicators used in my earlier study (Cohen 1990). The ten occupations selected by BLS, along with my 1990 indicator scores, are shown in table 5.1. None of the occupations selected by BLS fell in the bottom third of our occupational groups as ranked by the indicators. All but two were above the average, and half were in the top third. Because of the preliminary nature of the BLS pilot, exact correlations between our indicators and the pilot study would not be expected, even if the two approaches produced the same theoretical result.

The next section discusses various factors likely to have an effect on whether there will be future shortages or surpluses in various occupations.

Factors Affecting Future Shortages

Contingent Workers

According to Belous (1989), temporary workers increased by 175 percent from 1980 to 1988, and business services employment increased by 70 percent, while the overall labor force increased by only 14 percent. Part-timers also increased by 21 percent, and the self-employed increased by 19 percent.

Business service companies offer many alternative arrangements for meeting contingent employer demands. Employers may lease their own employees from a leasing company in a coemployment arrangement. A business service company may provide specific services to a firm, or it may subcontract an entire department of a company, such as legal services, shipping and receiving, the employee cafeteria, or computer services. These arrangements offer more flexibility to employers in dealing with shortages.

As mentioned previously, contingent workers can be used for staffing peak capacity needs during business booms without the need for more permanent employees. Retired workers may be available for contingent work assignments. Belous (1989) cites examples of hospitals that meet shortages by hiring part-time workers. Certain groups in the population, such as mothers with young children, might want part-time work rather than waiting to reenter the labor force full time. The demand for contingent workers could be dampened in the future if changes in payment for health care require employers to pay a premium for them.

Demographic Trends

Demographic factors can be of critical importance in explaining future occupational shortages or surpluses. The baby boomers born in 1946 will turn sixty in 2006. As more of the population is aged and not working, different

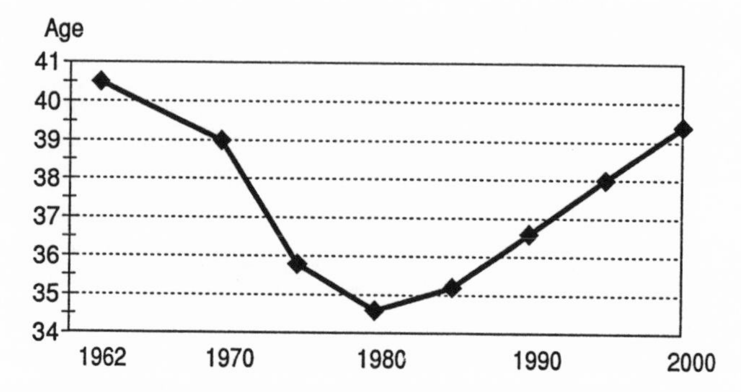

Fig. 5.2. Median age of the labor force. (Data from BLS *Outlook 2000,* 9.)

kinds of services will be demanded. The need for medical services increases with age. The need for college faculty has declined recently because the college-age population shrank by 25 percent from its peak size. By the year 2000, however, the college-age population will have increased significantly.

Older Workers. The major demographic story is the aging of the baby boomers. By the year 2005, the baby boomers born after World War II will be approaching their sixties.

Figure 5.2 shows the decreasing median age of the labor force from 1962 through 1980, as the baby boomers began to finish school and go to work. The trend has reversed over the last dozen years, however, and is expected to continue moving upward until the year 2005, when the median labor force age will be almost the same as it was in 1962.

The labor force of older workers is being shaped by two trends, the increasing proportion of older people in the population and the decline in the labor force participation rate of older men. As a result of advances in medical science, the percentage of the population over age sixty-five is markedly greater than it was a hundred years ago. Figure 5.3 illustrates the significant increase in importance of the population age sixty-five and older. The percentage of this population doubled from 1900 to 1950, then increased fourfold from 1950 to 1990. By 2005, more than 36 percent of the population is projected to be over age sixty-five—a ninefold increase in just under a century.

While the proportion of older workers in the labor force has increased steadily over the past century, the labor force participation rate of this group has declined sharply. Figure 5.4 traces the decline of labor force participation rates by sex. As the figure shows, the trends are entirely different for men and women. The labor force participation rate of women decreased over the fifty-year period from 1890 to 1940, increased sharply from 1940 to 1960, declined through 1988, rose in 1991, and declined in 1992. For men the rate has fallen constantly, from 68.3 percent in 1890 to 33.1 percent in 1960 to 13.6 percent

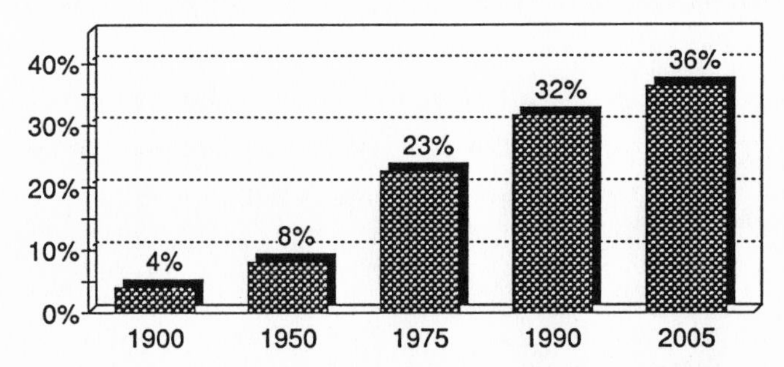

Fig. 5.3. Percentage of the U.S. population age 65 and older. (Date from Saunders 1993; U.S. Department of Labor, Bureau of Labor Statistics 1992g, 13; and U.S. Department of Commerce, Bureau of the Census, *Historical Statistics of the United States,* pt. 1, 15.)

in 1991, until 1992, when the rate rose slightly. Some of the recent decline may be due to the recent slow economic growth, but even so, that would not account for the great disparity in participation rates between men and women.

There is considerable disagreement among experts regarding future labor force participation rates of older workers. The Bureau of Labor Statistics projects the rate for men to fall from 16.4 percent in 1990 to 16 percent in 2005. Since the rate actually fell to 13.6 percent in 1991, the BLS projection could be interpreted as a rise in the labor force participation rate of older men. BLS actually had projected a drop in the participation rate of one percentage point, to 15.4 percent, then a rise to 16 percent by 2005 (Fullerton 1992). The fall in the rate from 1988 to 1991 and the rise in 1992 could be explained as cyclical. The rate fell more than its secular trend as workers became discouraged with fewer job opportunities during the 1991 recession.

One of the most difficult factors in projecting future shortages or surpluses will be the extent to which older workers will be willing to reenter the labor force or postpone retirement as shortages develop. In a period when firms are finding that they are paying for excess labor, they will attempt to reduce costs by providing incentives to workers to retire early. It is more difficult to predict whether, in times when excess labor is not as common, firms will actually offer incentives for older workers to stay.

In a study of factors affecting retirement, Phillip Levine and Olivia Mitchell (1991) note that government policies encouraging early retirement are being reversed. They also cite several factors that could lead to smaller or fewer pensions in the future. These factors would indicate a tendency toward longer participation in the labor force. The increasing use of contingent workers could also reduce pension availability and make later retirement more attractive to older workers. A major new research study by the Survey Re-

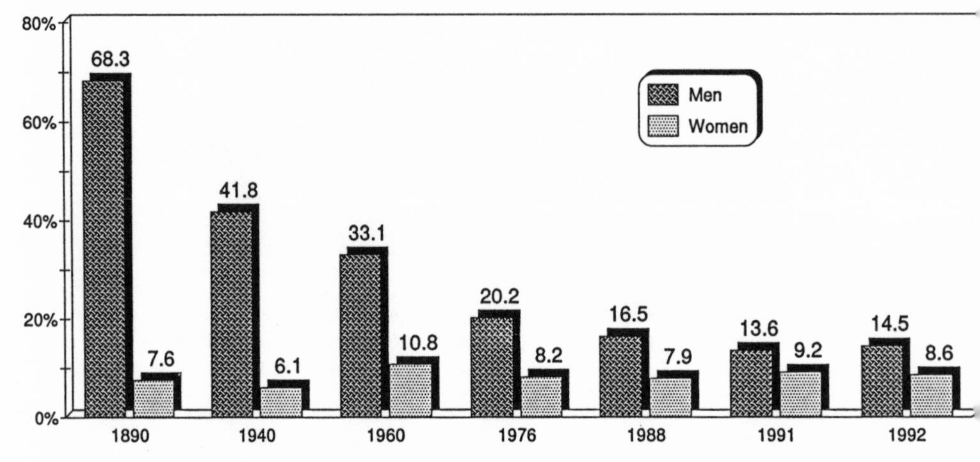

Fig. 5.4. Labor force participation rates, men and women over 65. (Based on Fullerton 1992; U.S. Department of Commerce, Bureau of the Census, *Historical Statistics of the United States Employment and Earnings.*)

search Center at the University of Michigan is looking in depth at factors affecting retirement and should be the source of many new insights on the retirement plans of older workers.

Changes in how health care is paid for could also influence early retirement. For example, if the government pays a significant proportion of the cost of retiree health care, employers might be more interested in offering incentives for early retirement.

Youth Labor Force. Figure 5.5 shows the fluctuating size of the civilian youth labor force (age 16–24) since 1948.

The dramatic growth of the youth labor force from 1955 to 1980 led to the reliance on youth for many minimum-wage jobs. In 1980, not only did that growth stop, but it began a decline which has only just reversed itself. The declining population of youth resulted in employers having difficulty finding enough workers at the minimum wage. It also reduced the demand for high school and college teachers. Although the size of this age group has begun to grow again, by 2005 it will still be well below the peak level attained in 1980, and its rate of growth will be much slower than what it was in the 1970s.

Minorities. Figure 5.6 illustrates the projected growth of various population segments by race and Hispanic origin from 1990 to 2005, according to BLS projections. While the total labor force is projected to grow by 21 percent from 1990 to 2005, the number of people of Asian and Hispanic origin in the labor force is projected to grow by 75 percent for each group during this period. This dramatic growth is due largely to projected increases in immigration; immigration trends are discussed in greater depth in a later

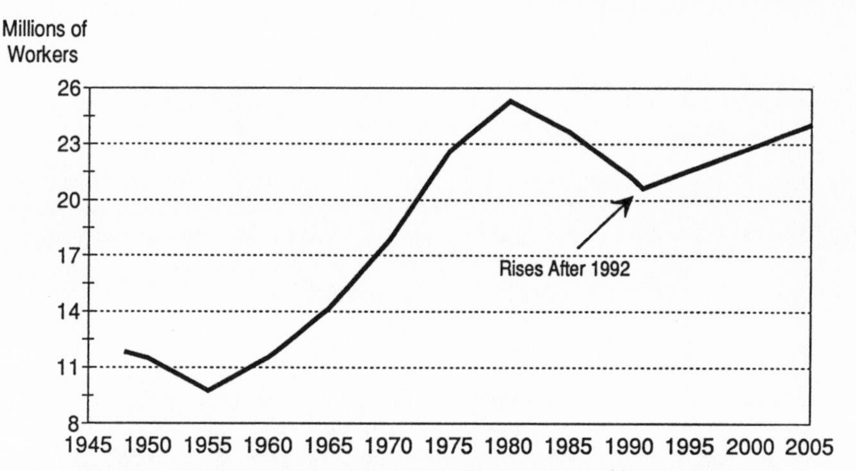

Fig. 5.5. Civilian labor force for the 16-to-24 age group, 1948–2005. (Data from U.S. Department of Labor, Bureau of Labor Statistics 1992g; Fullerton 1992; U.S. Department of Labor, Bureau of Labor Statistics, *Labor Force Statistics Derived from the Current Population Survey, 1948–87,* Bulletin 2307, August 1988, 75.)

section. The black labor force is also expected to grow at a rate significantly greater than the overall rate. From 1990 to 2005, the black labor force rate is expected to grow by 32 percent.

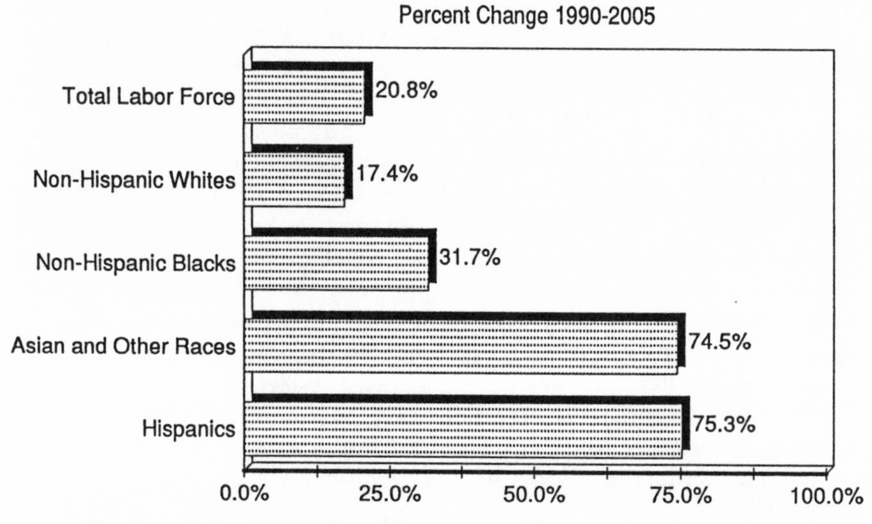

Fig. 5.6. Labor force growth by race and Hispanic origin, projected 1990–2005. (Data from U.S. Department of Labor, Bureau of Labor Statistics, *Occupational Outlook Quarterly,* Fall 1991.)

Two of the three fastest-growing segments of the population, Hispanics and blacks, occupy a disproportionate number of the jobs scheduled to grow at the slowest rate from 1900 to 2005. As the discussion earlier in the chapter suggested, the fastest-growing jobs will be those requiring a college degree. While 24 percent of all workers completed four or more years of college in 1990, only 15 percent of all blacks and only 10 percent of all Hispanics completed four or more years of college. These disparities could lead to a situation in which both unemployment and labor shortages will increase in the decade ahead (Silvestri and Lukasiewicz 1992).

Education and Productivity

Productivity growth in manufacturing in the United States in the last thirty years has been the lowest among industrial countries, as figure 5.7 illustrates. In interpreting productivity comparisons, two factors should be kept in mind: First, productivity growth in less-developed countries may be larger as the countries convert labor-intensive manufacturing processes to a more efficient and automated form of production. The level of productivity in the United States may be higher even if the rate of change is lower. (Of course, this will not be true forever.) Second, overall productivity in the United States is much lower than the rate of growth in manufacturing. For example, from 1979 to 1990, productivity in manufacturing grew by an annual rate of 3.1 percent, while output per hour of all persons in private business grew by only 1.2 percent. Productivity during that period for nonfarm private business grew at an annual rate of only 1 percent. From 1991 to 1992, nonfarm business sector productivity grew by 2.7 percent (U.S. Dept. of Labor, Bureau of Labor Statistics 1993).

It has been suggested that a way to increase productivity is to move toward a system of work organization in which workers play a more significant part in work decisions. (National Center on Education and the Economy, 1990). Implementing such a system would require providing workers with the tools to make decisions on complex work issues, both through the educational system and through increased worker training programs. To the extent that more work organization moves toward cooperative labor-management models, a greater demand will be generated for workers with analytic skills, increasing the potential for shortages unless the educational system is improved.

Most American students currently have little incentive to choose a curriculum emphasizing math and science. The reason for this lack of incentive has much to do with the typical American industry's organizational structure. The most common form of work organization in America is the Taylor model (U.S. Congress 1990), named after scientific management pioneer Frederick W. Taylor. In the Taylor (1911) model, managers and supervisors make deci-

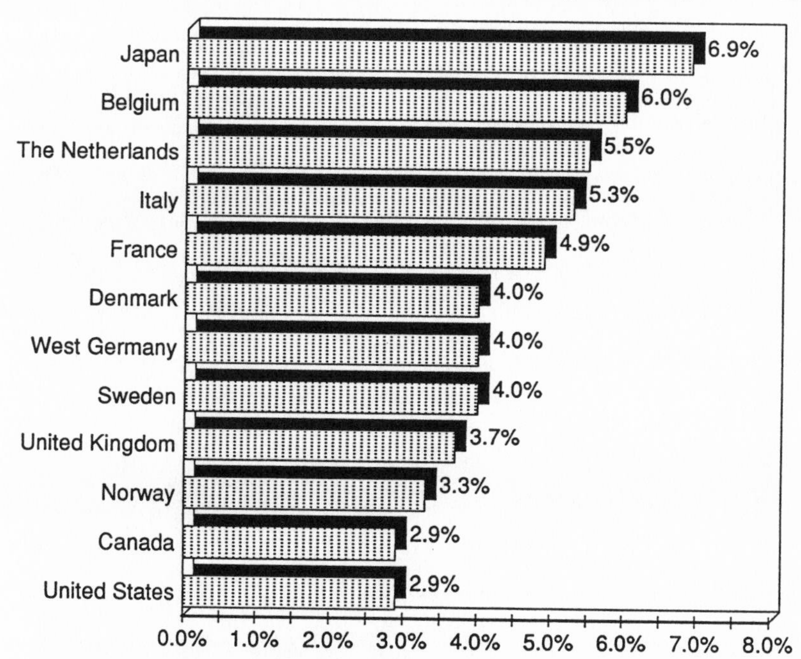

Fig. 5.7. Annual rate of productivity growth in selected countries, 1960–90. (Data from U.S. Department of Labor, Bureau of Labor Statistics, *News Release*, August 20, 1991.)

sions and tell workers what to do. Since most U.S. companies rely on the Taylor model, educational achievement in math and science has not been an important factor in explaining wage growth or hiring success among American workers. According to Bishop (1992b), "for the 80 percent of youth who are not planning to pursue a career in medicine, science or engineering there are no immediate labor market rewards for developing competencies in science and mathematics. For the great bulk of students, therefore, the incentives to devote time and energy to the often difficult task of learning these subjects are very weak and significantly delayed."

Contrast the Taylor model to the system used in Japan, where a prevalent form of work organization is quality circles, with management and labor working together to make decisions on how to carry out work tasks. For labor-management cooperation to work, however, the workers must be sufficiently educated to be able to make the necessary decisions. This creates a strong incentive for Japanese students to work toward mastering math and science skills.

Solving the work-preparedness problem in the United States recalls the age-old question of which came first, the chicken or the egg: Each side of the problem must be solved first before the other side can be solved. The structure of work organization must be changed to provide incentive for students to focus their efforts on math and science, but the work structure can't be changed until there are workers prepared to cope with the new structure. The ideal solution here would seem to be a business-education alliance, already being tried in some communities, in which business leaders meet with education planners to design a curriculum based on where students will be able to find jobs in the future.

Factors such as the productivity of the U.S. work force play an important role in determining the competitiveness of U.S. products. In a talk delivered at the Ninth World Congress of the International Industrial Relations Association in Sydney, Australia, 1 September 1992, Norbert Von Kunitzki, director general of the Belgian conglomerate Sidmar, indicated that when looking for a country to do business in, the company is far more interested in the skills and education of the work force than in finding the location with the lowest labor costs.

According to Lester Thurow (1992), former dean of the MIT Sloan School of Management, "skilled people become the only sustainable competitive advantage." He indicated that the education of the smartest 25 percent of the labor force is critical in inventing new products, and the education of the bottom 50 percent is critical in starting the new processes required to produce the new products.

U.S. Secretary of Labor Robert Reich, in a talk before the National Press Club in Washington, D.C., 18 October 1993, suggested the need for technicians to play a much greater role in the manufacturing process, as they do in other countries. This change in work cooperation could improve manufacturing productivity.

American Business Strategies

Differences in business strategies between the United States and Japan have led to significant differences in economic growth in the United States versus Japan over the past few decades, according to Lester Thurow (1992). U.S. firms, says Thurow, attempt to maximize profits and seek out a rate of return as high as 15 percent on investment. As the rate of return declines, U.S. firms drop out of markets. Japanese firms, on the other hand, seek to build an empire. The firm is willing to expand even if the return on investment falls below what U.S. firms might feel is necessary to stay in the market. In the long run, this leads to more jobs for Japanese-controlled firms and fewer jobs for U.S. workers.

The Japanese government cooperates with firms by setting up national strategies, as they did in the mainframe computer industry. These strategies helped the Japanese capture a significant portion of the mainframe computer market. Similar strategies were used by European countries to assist Airbus in achieving competitiveness in the production of commercial airplanes—and a 20 percent market share (Thurow 1992).

The advantages that foreign firms have over American firms with respect to government cooperation could be overcome if the U.S. government were to take a more active role in supporting strategic industries. Closing the advantage gap between profit maximization and empire building, however, would require a fundamental change of attitude on the part of corporate America. The tendency to sacrifice long-run benefits to short-term gains is a time-honored tradition in this country.

Finally, the formation of the European Free Trade Association could make it more difficult for U.S. manufacturers to export to Europe. The United States, on the other hand, can form its own trading bloc with Canada and Mexico. Such a bloc could serve to expand U.S. trade opportunities, but it could also have adverse economic impacts on some portions of the population. The net impact over the next decade, however, is likely to be small. Some observers believe that the North American Free Trade Agreement (NAFTA) may have an impact on demand for U.S. workers during the rest of the decade. According to a study by Stern, Deardorff, and Brown (1992), there would be at most 76,620 U.S. workers displaced over a ten-year period as a result of NAFTA. The study also concluded that an upper bound on U.S. workers' wage loss would be at most $80 million per year as a result of NAFTA. The impact of current trends in investment in Mexico and the continual shifting of jobs from the United States to Mexico is much larger than the impact of NAFTA. These trends will continue regardless of NAFTA.

The Stern, Deardorff, and Brown model simulated the results of NAFTA, removal of nontariff barriers, and a relaxation by Mexico of foreign direct investment restrictions. Under all these scenarios, holding total employment change at zero, 11,162 jobs would be created for U.S. agricultural workers, 1,510 jobs would be created for marketing and sales workers, and all other major occupational groups would lose jobs. The groups suffering the biggest losses would be skilled workers (4,418 jobs), semi-unskilled workers (1,958 jobs), administrative and clerical (1,922 jobs), and professional (1,806 jobs). If only NAFTA tariffs were effected, only four of the nine occupational groups would lose jobs (assuming constant employment): professional, service, agriculture, and skilled labor. In this scenario, agricultural workers would lose the most jobs—1,296. Market and sales would gain the most—1,992.

A study by DRI/McGraw-Hill (1992) found a small positive impact on U.S. employment with NAFTA in place. A report by the Office of Technology

Assessment also states that NAFTA is "not likely to have large impacts on job opportunity for U.S. workers over the next five years" (U.S. Congress, Office of Technology Assessment 1992).

Thus, NAFTA and related North American tariff investment policy changes are not expected to have a major impact on whether or not there are shortages of labor later in the decade. Our analysis was not intended to investigate the benefits and costs of NAFTA, only to consider whether it will make much difference in whether shortages develop over the next decade. We concluded that it was not likely to make much difference in either direction.

Immigration

Immigration policy has served many different functions during the course of U.S. history. Prior to 1920, immigration was used to build a country needing inhabitants. Immigration policy was to allow nearly anyone into the United States who wanted to come. The first restrictions on immigration were enacted in 1875, barring convicts and prostitutes, then paupers. In 1882, Congress passed the Chinese Exclusion Act, the first legislation restricting immigration based on national origin. Laws to protect U.S. workers from lower-paid foreign labor were also enacted in the 1880s (U.S. House 1992).

Beginning in the 1920s, Congress enacted laws setting quotas on the number of immigrants allowed in from different countries. These quotas have undergone various changes, first to restrict Asians, then to limit immigrants to reflect the ethnic mix of the United States, then to a variety of other complex country quotas.

Congress enacted a major revision of immigration policy in 1952. This was the beginning of a preference system allocating slots to immigrants based on their education, exceptional abilities, or presence of relatives with legal status in the United States (U.S. House 1992). The law did not restrict immigrants from Western Hemisphere countries. In addition, refugees were admitted who did not count against any quota. Laws since 1952 have dealt with imposing limits on Western Hemisphere immigrations, control of illegal immigrations, and refugees.

The latest major immigration reform was the Immigration and Nationality Act of 1990, signed on November 29, 1990 (U.S. House 1992). In 1990, the law increased the number of employment-based certifications from 54,000 to 140,000 out of a total of 700,000 immigrants. Prior to the passage of the new bill, approximately 50,000 certifications were requested every year. It was feared that when the 1990 law went into effect, the number of certification requests would double because of the additional certifications allowed under the new law. This didn't happen, however, because the new law's initial period coincided with a U.S. recession.

Immigration law distinguishes between permanent immigrants, temporary immigrants, and nonimmigrants. A permanent immigrant becomes a U.S. citizen and is issued a green card. A temporary immigrant may work in the United States for a limited period of time to alleviate a labor shortage. A nonimmigrant is a foreign national with permission to stay in the country for a specified reason, such as someone working for a foreign corporation doing business in the United States.

A discussion of the laws and regulations regarding each of the aforementioned groups extends beyond the scope of this book. The major focus of our discussion is on permanent immigrants, who are admitted according to a certification process whereby an employer must prove to the government that there is an insufficient number of U.S. workers who can perform the job for which the employer wants to hire an immigrant. The process of labor certification was initiated to protect U.S. workers from losing out to cheap labor from abroad. The employer applies to the U.S. Employment Service for a labor certification. The job is listed at the Employment Service and advertised in the newspaper. If no qualified U.S. applicants appear, the government makes a determination that there are insufficient U.S. workers available to perform the job. In addition to determining that there are insufficient workers, the job offer must be at or above prevailing wages.

The Immigration and Nationality Act of 1990 established five classes of employment-based immigrants: (1) priority workers; (2) aliens who are members of the professions holding advanced degrees, or who have exceptional ability; (3) skilled workers, professionals, and other workers; (4) special immigrants; and (5) entrepreneurs who create jobs (U.S. House 1992). A specified number of slots are allocated each year to each of these categories. Immigrants' family members are also included in the number of slots allocated to each category.

Priority workers include: (1) aliens of "extraordinary abilities" whose accomplishments in science, arts, education, business, or athletics are internationally recognized; (2) outstanding professors and researchers; and (3) multinational executives and managers. Approximately 40,000 slots have been allocated each year to priority workers. Aliens who are professionals and those of exceptional ability are allocated another 40,000 slots. Skilled workers, professionals, and other workers are also allocated approximately 40,000 slots. Skilled workers are defined as those in occupations requiring at least two or more years of training. "Other workers" includes unskilled workers, but this category is limited to 10,000 workers. Special immigrants are allocated about 10,000 slots. These include occupations such as certain ministers. Finally, entrepreneurs who invest in the United States in a new enterprise are allocated approximately 10,000 slots. Entrepreneurs must meet certain requirements, however, such as a minimum investment of $1 million (unless the investment is made in targeted areas facing high unemployment, in which case the requirement is lowered). The total of 140,000 slots allocated for employment-based preferences is 20 percent of the total allocated for all visas in 1992. Assuming half the visas go to applicants and half go to family members, 70,000 workers a year will be admitted for employment-based immigration.

According to Bureau of Labor Statistics projections, 1,730,000 new jobs will be created on the average each year from 1990 to 2005 (Fullerton 1992). Thus, only about 5 percent of the new jobs over the next fifteen years will be filled by employment-based immigrants.

Foreign labor is not entirely a bad thing for the United States. Immigrants add diversity to our work force and bring connections to a world economy. Even if our educational system could produce all the needed workers, there may be benefits derived from increasing our connections with foreign business through employment-based immigration. In addition, immigrants are consumers of other U.S. goods and services.

While there remains the possibility that immigration could lower earnings of nonimmigrant U.S. workers, most studies have found otherwise. Butcher and Card (1991) analyzed the relationship between immigration and wage changes in twenty-four cities from 1979 to 1989 and found that "the relative size of immigrant inflows bears little or no relation to changes in wages for the least-skilled workers in different cities."

In a survey of the literature, Greenwood and McDowell (1986) concluded that "substantive empirical evidence regarding the effects of immigration is generally scarce. . . . Little direct evidence is available on immigrants' impact on the employment opportunities and wages of domestic workers." According to Borjas (1990), "Recent econometric evidence has not been able to establish a single instance in which the increase in the supply of immigrants had a significant adverse impact on the earnings of natives."

A recent study analyzed the impact of immigrants on native workers' earnings and employment (Sorensen et al. 1992). The study analyzed employment-preference immigrants separately from family-preference immigrants. Changes in earnings as a function of increases in immigrant population were estimated for thirty-three Metropolitan Statistical Areas (MSAs) by immigrant preference category. A two-stage least squares model was used, which included demographic and human capital variables. The study found a 1.8 percent loss in white native male pay for a 10 percent increase in number of naturalized foreign-born immigrants, and a 3.8 percent loss in black male native pay for a 10 percent increase in naturalized foreign-born immigrants. The study also found a 3 percent loss of earnings among Hispanic native-born males for a 10 percent increase in naturalized foreign-born immigrants. The effects on native employment of worker-preference and family-preference immigrants, on the other hand, were found to be very small or insignificant. A 10 percent increase in worker-preference immigrants had no significant effect on black or Hispanic native male wages, but a 1 percent negative impact on white native male wages. Family-preference immigrants were found to have a positive impact on white and black male native earnings.

If worker-preference immigrants were concentrated in particular occupations, it is possible that the negative impact on earnings could be greater. However, if worker-preference immigrants are admitted for occupations in specific labor markets in which there are shortages, the impact may be merely to prevent wages from growing faster than they would have in the absence of the immigrants. Alternatively, a policy of shifting the number of immigrants admitted from family-preference categories to worker-preference categories, without increasing the total number of immigrants, may have a different impact than suggested by the coefficients in the study by Sorensen et al. (1992). It seems implausible that we can continually improve the earnings of white and black natives by reducing worker-preference immigrants and increasing family-preference immigrants. A consideration that could explain the finding, however, is that family-preference immigrants are less likely to enter employment (Sorensen et al. 1992). When they do enter employment, they require a greater investment in training than do worker-preference immigrants. If highly skilled workers are brought in as worker-preference immigrants, they can be productive with little extra training. Less-skilled immigrants, on the other hand, might require considerable extra training to make them equally productive. Investment in training for family-preference immigrants who do not have the skills to qualify for the worker preference may not be cost effective.

A lack of good data makes it difficult to come up with conclusive proof that immigrants either do or do not adversely affect the earnings of domestic workers. As we move into the twenty-first century, we will be competing in a world economy to determine which country can produce the best products for the lowest prices. Immigration policy can be used to improve the standard of living for Americans if the immigrants are skilled workers whose contribution to the economy will create job opportunities for other workers.

If, on the other hand, immigration policy is such as to allow an influx of low-skilled workers who require large amounts of government aid before they become productive citizens, the result could be a decline in per capita income over the next few decades. Lester Thurow (1992) has calculated the cost as follows: "If a new American is to have an average amount of space, a $20,000 investment has to be made in his or her housing. Until that new American is old enough to begin work, he or she will require feeding - another $20,000. To get to the average American educational level, he or she will require $100,000 in public and private expenditures. For that individual to attain the average American productivity at work, another $80,000 investment will have to be made in plant and equipment. Yet another $10,000 will be necessary to build the public infrastructure. . . . Basically, each new American will require an investment of $240,000 before he or she is capable of fitting into the American economy." Thurow argues that for the United States to increase its population growth to 4 percent, 40 percent of gross national product (GNP) would have to be devoted to new Americans, and U.S. citizens would have to take a sharp cut in their standard of living.

Bringing in immigrants who have skills that are in demand in the world economy makes sense as part of U.S. immigration policy. At the same time, however, humanitarian concerns and family reunification should remain important considerations in overall immigration policy.

Another provision of the Immigration and Nationality Act of 1990 (Section 122) was to provide for a pilot project to use labor market information to determine whether certain occupations are facing shortages or surpluses. Labor certification is currently handled on a case-by-case basis, and it is a long and costly process. Using labor market information to identify shortages, entire occupations could be certified automatically. Because the economy was growing so slowly at the time the pilot was scheduled to be carried out, the pilot was not conducted, even though ten potential occupations were identified.

The one exception to the current case-by-case procedure is that registered nurses and physical therapists are automatically certified by the Department of Labor (Schedule A). This determination predates our research on labor shortages, but it coincides with our findings on occupations most likely to be in short supply (see chapter 4). That this one instance of automatic certification has been working well argues in favor of using the methodology developed through our research.

Automatic certification does not totally supplant the case-by-case procedure, however. Although no advertising of the job is required to prove no U.S. workers are available, each admission still requires verification by the Immigration and Naturalization Service to determine that the applicant meets the qualifications for the position. There is another list of occupations (Schedule B) considered likely to be in surplus, but the determination is less definite. Immigrants applying for jobs in the occupations on this list could still be certified, but the presumption would be against certification and the evidence would have to be more convincing.

Labor Shortages and the Rest of the World

There are other methods firms can use to tap foreign labor without hiring immigrant workers. In today's economy, many firms are international and can shift portions of their business activity to low-cost areas such as Taiwan,

Korea, or Mexico. For example, Prudential Insurance was faced with an insufficient supply of clerical workers to enter policy information. The company developed a way information could be shipped to Ireland, entered into computers there, then transferred back to the United States by telecommunications. Several computer software companies have also made arrangements to contract with lower-paid computer programmers in Ireland. Another company has recently made arrangements with companies in the Soviet Union to contract out fiber optic research.

Use of subcontracted foreign labor is feasible in some situations and extremely difficult in others. Software development may be readily accomplished in this manner, but customer support or sales involving the need for customer contact would be difficult. Even customer contact, however, could be accomplished through telephone and fax. In the future, video telephones may even permit significant use of remote personnel to support U.S. operations and could even further increase the potential of foreign contracts.

In analyzing future shortages, it would be useful to know about the supply in other countries of workers in an occupation being studied and how easily work can be subcontracted abroad. Even the work of the two high-demand occupations, registered nurses and physical therapists, could be affected by foreign contracting. Suppose a hospital center were opened in another country, where U.S. citizens with medical problems could make use of extensive testing or treatment facilities at prices so much lower than domestic rates that even the cost of the trip would not be a deterrent. It may seem farfetched, but there is potential for such a development, if foreign medical personnel are available for significantly lower wage rates than their American counterparts.

Government Priorities and Labor Shortages

Because the federal government is a major purchaser of goods and services, shifts in government spending can make a major difference in the need for particular occupations. In addition to direct government purchasing, government regulations can also affect job markets. For instance, standards on pollution can affect the demand for, among others, natural resource graduates, automotive engineers, and chemists. No-fault insurance or limits on liability can affect the demand for lawyers. State and local spending is also a significant factor affecting total demand.

To illustrate the impact of government spending, we will examine two areas: defense and health.

Defense Spending. Reductions in defense spending are likely to lessen the probability of shortages in the short run but could well contribute to them in the longer run. A study by the Congressional Budget Office (U.S. Congress, Congressional Budget Office 1992) projects that if the defense budget is cut by 29 percent by 1997, and if the reductions are used to reduce the federal deficit, 500,000 jobs would be lost by 1996. The effect of reducing the federal deficit, however, would have very beneficial long-term effects. In the beginning of the twenty-first century, real GNP could rise by more than 1.5 percent above the base level.

If the peace dividend resulting from the defense cuts is used in productive investments such as human capital or improving roads, ports, or other public facilities, the short-run negative impact can be lessened and a long-term positive impact will be retained. If the peace dividend is used for consumption that does not enhance long-term productivity, no long-term benefits will accrue to the economy, but the short-term negative impacts can be minimized.

In 1993, further cuts in defense spending were proposed. According to a Bureau of Labor Statistics study, 1.8 million private-sector jobs would be lost between 1987 and 1997 as a result of the revised cuts, in addition to 950,000 government jobs (including military). Of the 1.8 million civilian jobs lost, about 25 percent would be in executive, managerial, and professional specialty occupations, according to the BLS study (Saunders 1993).

When the economy is sluggish, the additive impact of defense cuts would certainly take pressure off any shortages in the short run. However, the Bureau of Labor Statistics predicts an average annual growth of employment of 1.5 million workers a year from 1990 through 2005 (U.S. Congress, Congressional Budget Office 1992). Thus, the short-term impact of defense cuts would be a loss of employment equivalent to two years of average employment growth. Over the long run, if the peace dividend is invested, the net impact will be to increase employment permanently.

National Health Insurance and Medical Inflation. Medical costs have increased significantly in the last decade. From 1983 to 1991, medical costs rose 90 percent, compared to a 40 percent rise in all items (U.S. Dept. of Labor, Bureau of Labor Statistics 1993). Medical costs as a percentage of gross national product have increased from 8.6 percent in 1979 to 12–14 percent in 1992 (Burke 1991, Shapiro 1992).

The increases in health care will put downward pressure on costs. Health maintenance organizations (HMOs) will increase in importance and traditional fee-for-service health care will decline. In the arena of employer-provided health care, 2 percent of employees were covered by HMOs and preferred provider organizations (PPOs) in 1979; by 1989 the percentage had grown to 27 percent of all employees (Burke 1991).

It is inevitable that some kind of national health care program will evolve as the government gets more and more involved in the effort to provide health care to all citizens. Projecting the demand for future workers in an area where the role of government could increase so dramatically is especially difficult. It is almost certain that more health care personnel will be required. The only question seems to be how much demand will increase with government as a major provider. To the extent that the government limits increases in wages and costs that can be charged by medical care providers, incentives to enter health professions will be reduced, increasing the likelihood of shortages. This would be mitigated somewhat if the government could achieve significant increases in medical productivity which reduced the need for medical personnel.

One casualty of medical care reform could be expenditures on medical research. As drug companies and other biotechnology concerns find their profits reduced, they may reduce their research budgets, which in turn will reduce the demand for medical and biotechnology scientists (Shapiro 1992). On the other hand, government may invest more directly in biotechnology research, reducing the impact of lower drug prices.

Even in the absence of national health insurance, however, government spending on Medicare and Medicaid is projected to triple, from $198 billion in 1992 to $605 billion by the year 2002, according to the Congressional Budget Office, as cited in a *New York Times* article, 14 August 1992). If national health insurance were adopted, a Congressional Budget Office analysis suggests that while demand for billing staff would decrease, the demand for health care personnel would increase. If medical coverage is expanded, the demand for medical services will increase (U.S. Congress 1991).

President Clinton proposed a health care plan that would reduce the enormous amount of clerical work necessary to process claims, give coverage to more than 30 million additional people, give primary care physicians more control over what services Americans receive, and shift more care to the home. The net results of such a plan would be to reduce the demand for clerical workers and increase demand for primary care physicians and home care workers.

Technological Change

The pace of technological change and the rate of infusion of new technologies can have a major impact on future demand. New innovations can create the need for new occupations that do not exist today.

Typically, in the framework of a ten-year forecast, technological innovations will have a minimal impact on future demand, largely because it takes a long time from when an innovation is first developed until it is mass produced and used. Recently developed innovations, however, could certainly have an impact within the ten-year time frame. For example, videophones and teleconferencing have been around for several years, but few people today have videophones. The telephone industry has begun an aggressive marketing campaign to encourage the use of videophones; within the next ten years, this technology may cut back significantly on the need for salespeople, executives, and technicians to travel. The obvious implications of such a development would be an increase in demand for producing and marketing videophones and a decrease in the transportation and hotel industries. In a similar vein, as the price of computing is constantly being reduced, it becomes economically more desirable to automate certain functions currently being done manually. CD-ROM technology, for example, is revolutionizing the storage of books, data, and pictures, thereby changing libraries.

In its forecasts for the year 2005, the Bureau of Labor Statistics is already taking into account projected technological changes. Both industry assumptions and occupational assumptions are made. For example, for central office and private branch exchange (PBX) installers and repairers, the forecast reflects a "significant decrease reflecting improvements which permit more telephone signals per wire, and advances in switching technology which increases capacity and reliability" (U.S. Dept. of Labor 1992c).

Industrial Restructuring

In recent years, large corporations have announced layoffs and permanent staff cuts. Newspaper reports of these cuts can be a misleading indicator of future employment trends. First, they represent only one aspect of the employment decision; second, they do not reflect what is happening in small and midsize firms; and finally, they do not tell us whether these cuts differ historically from cuts that have taken place at a similar point in the business cycle.

A somewhat better approach to measuring displacement is the survey conducted by the Bureau of Labor Statistics, which measures worker displacement (Herz 1991). These data indicate that there were 5 million displaced workers from 1979 to 1983 and 4.3 million during the 1985–89 expansion. The survey counts only workers with three or more years of tenure with the employer. Displacement of workers in managerial and professional specialty occupations increased from 703,000 in 1979–83 to 869,000 in 1985–89, but this increase was about the same as the growth in employment for this group.

When the growth of the overall labor force is taken into account, displacement rates declined from 8.3 percent in 1979–83 to 6.4 percent in 1985–89. As might be expected, the displacement rate increased during the 1990–91 recession period, more even than during the 1979–83 period. From January 1991 to January 1992, 5.6 million workers were displaced (U.S. Dept. of Labor 1992e). Displacement of managerial and professional specialty occupations increased from 869,000 in 1985–89 to 1,210,000 in 1991–92. It is too early to tell whether the displacement rate will soon fall back to prerecession levels or whether the increase reflects structural difficulties that cannot be readily resolved.

Retraining Policies and Worker Quality

Labor shortages can be minimized if companies, unions, government, and public and private schools offer needed training in occupations in which future excess demand is anticipated. Tax policy can be used to offer incentives for increased retraining.

Investments in human capital today are treated less favorably than are other forms of investment. It is more difficult to get a loan against future human earnings than earnings of a building or other productive asset. Firms can depreciate or expense investments in plant and equipment, but they may be restricted in expensing certain retraining costs. Also, firms may be reluctant to invest in individuals for fear that they will leave after the firm makes the investment. Policies that recognize the inherent differences between human and physical capital are needed to encourage additional training that will increase the productivity of the U.S. work force.

As the work force ages and more time elapses between formal school and the individual workers' ages, the need for retraining becomes even more important. The increasing percentage of jobs requiring training also points to the need for increased training. Apprenticeship, traditionally a popular alternative to college, has not increased since the early 1980s. Only 16 percent of U.S. civilian workers are trained as apprentices (U.S. Congress 1990).

To reverse the virtual standstill in real wages American workers have experienced since 1978, productivity growth must be encouraged. Worker retraining is a means to this end. As was discussed earlier, changing production methods to provide more worker involvement will also require extensive retraining. One out of every five adults reads at only the eighth-grade level (U.S. Congress 1986).

The emphasis of government programs has been on training the economically disadvantaged rather than providing support for broader-based programs which could avert labor shortages. In part, this policy could be effective in the short run in times of slow economic growth, but it neglects future needs if not enough skilled workers are available toward the end of the 1990s. Worker training could be more effective if done in conjunction with the needs of firms, rather than by government alone. Tax incentives to firms to train their workers could mitigate some of the fear that workers could leave after training.

Myth or Reality?

The evidence presented in this chapter does not conclusively prove labor shortages will be prevalent in the years to come. For example, trends in early retirement could be reversed; retirees could return to the labor force, either as full-time or contingent workers. The economy could remain stagnant for the balance of the decade. The United States could be entering a period of peace, during which significant budget cuts are made to the defense budgets, resulting in a significant drop in the demand for engineers and scientists. Any of these factors could mitigate labor shortages in some or all occupations. The evidence for labor shortages being likely during the 1990s, however, appears much stronger. Following is a summary of the factors that indicate labor shortages for this decade.

1. The labor force of 16- to 24-year-olds will be smaller than in the 1980s and its rate of growth slower than in the 1970s.
2. For U.S. companies to compete with foreign companies, they will have to have a better-educated work force, more automated processes, better labor-management relations, or lower pay. Lower pay seems unlikely, but the other alternatives appear to be plausible. A likely innovation to make America more competitive is to involve workers more in decision making. Since only 5 percent of U.S. workers in manufacturing are currently in worker-involvement efforts, there is considerable room for these efforts to take hold. The net result would be a significant increase in demand for skilled workers.
3. Apprenticeship systems have been largely ignored in the early 1990s, due at least in part to the weakness of the economy. As older workers retire, there may not be enough new workers in the pipeline to meet future needs.
4. Before the 1990–91 recession, there were labor shortages in a number of industries. Wages in professional specialty areas increased 5.4 percent from 1983–90, compared with an overall increase of 4.1 percent. History would suggest continued patterns of recessions followed by recovery. Under such a scenario, labor shortages will not fully return but will become more acute, given the other factors mentioned.
5. The population is aging, and older people demand more health care. Millions of Americans are uncovered by health care. Government intervention to increase availability to uncovered Americans would again only increase demand. Cost-containment efforts could discourage potential health care providers from entering the occupation or discourage existing personnel from staying in, thus reducing the sup-

ply. Fear among health workers of contracting communicable diseases may also be a factor-limiting supply.

By the turn of the century, the major impact of military cutbacks is likely to be over, and the dividends of peacetime spending are likely to be under way. Labor shortages are likely to reemerge. While government policies can help the economy grow rapidly, they can also assure training, education, and immigration policies to manage or prevent upcoming labor shortages.

CHAPTER 6

Measuring Shortages for Subnational Areas or More Detailed Occupational Levels

Shortage Indicators for Subnational Areas

The indicators discussed in chapters 3 and 4 relied heavily on data collected monthly in the Current Population Survey, published by the U.S. Bureau of Labor Statistics, which is based on an approximately 1:1,500 sample of U.S. households. CPS data on employment and unemployment are published for seventeen cities and fifty metropolitan areas, but only for aggregate occupational groups. While it is possible to obtain geographic data on the current population at the state level, in most states the data for most of the occupational groups are not sufficiently reliable.

In chapter 4 we constructed seven indicators for each of 193 occupational groups at the national level. Since chapter 4 indicated that the occupations most likely to be in short supply in the future were in the professional specialties and the executive, administrative, and managerial categories, we first examine differences in these broad occupational groups by state. Two of the seven indicators—unemployment rate and rate of change of employment—can be computed for these two groups by state.

We chose not to include the Department of Labor's measure of specific vocational preparedness because it is the same across areas and therefore not of much interest to a study comparing differences across areas. The 1990–2005 BLS projection by state by occupation was not available as of this writing. The number of labor certifications by occupation has been computed for all 193 groups. We also computed the average annual number of labor certifications per 100,000 workers in the labor force for 1990–92. Labor force by occupation and state was taken from the 1990 census.

Occupational wage changes from the CPS are not as reliable at the state level; in fact, the Bureau of Labor Statistics doesn't even publish these data. Measurement of replacement demand variations would certainly not be reliable at the state level.

Analysis of Employment Change and Unemployment Rates across States

We constructed measures of employment change from 1989 to 1992, and the average unemployment rate from 1990 to 1992, for two broad occupational groups: executive, administrative and managerial; and professional specialty. Our findings are summarized in figures 6.1 through 6.6.

Figure 6.1 shows differences in average unemployment among the states for executives. Nebraska, South Dakota, and Wyoming had the lowest average unemployment rates for executives, and the next lowest rates were in eleven other, mostly small, states.

Figure 6.2 shows employment growth for executives. No states had employment growth for executives high enough to make the top growth category in 1989–92. Only one state, Minnesota, was in the next-highest category. Eleven other, mostly small, states were in the above-average category. All the other states were below average. The ranks were based on all occupations, and the ranges were determined based on 1986–89 conditions.

Figure 6.3 combines the two index values for the two indicators. The maximum possible score was 14, but no state had a score greater than 11. Eight small states had scores of 10 or 11. The data would argue against a current overall shortage of executives in any state.

Figures 6.4 and 6.5 present similar comparisons for average unemployment rates and employment change for professional specialty occupations, and figure 6.6 combines the indices for those two indicators. As shown in figure 6.6, the states with the highest indicator scores for professional specialty occupations were Colorado, Delaware, Georgia, Nebraska, Nevada, New Mexico, Tennessee, and Washington. Current Population Survey data are of little additional value because these states have such low populations, and the professional specialty group is so broad, that the sample size is not sufficient to yield further insights.

Analysis of Differences in Labor Certifications across States

The certification of permanent workers involves a determination by the Department of Labor whether a particular employer can find U.S. workers to do the job for which the employer wants to hire an alien. Differences in the number of certifications by state can give some indication of where shortages exist within the country, adding further detail to the overall picture. All other factors being equal, however, larger states will have more certifications than small states. To adjust for this disparity, we normalized certifications by measuring them per 1,000 workers in the labor force.

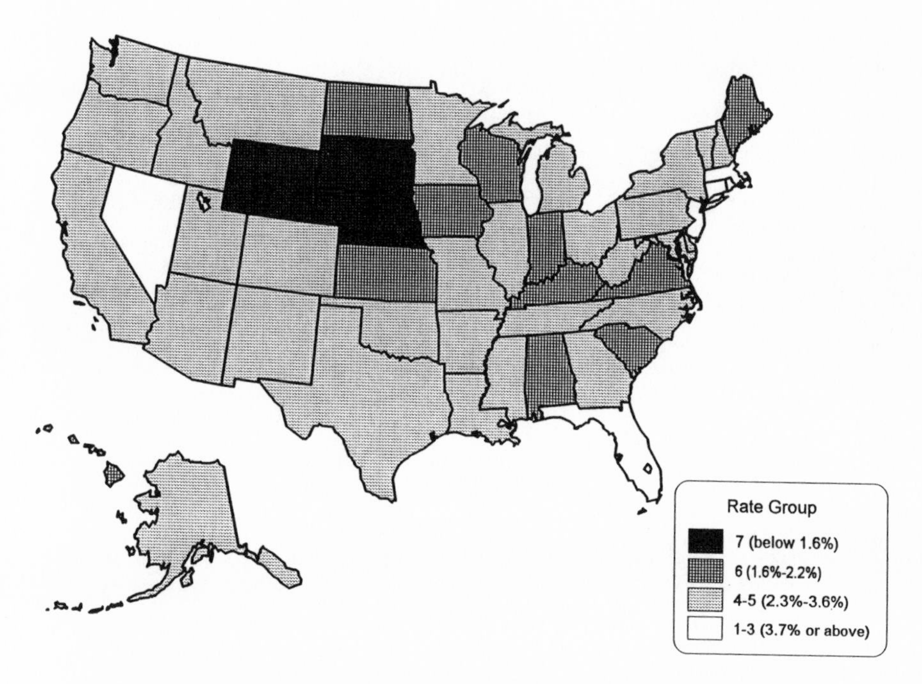

Fig. 6.1. Executive occupations, average unemployment rate, 1990–92

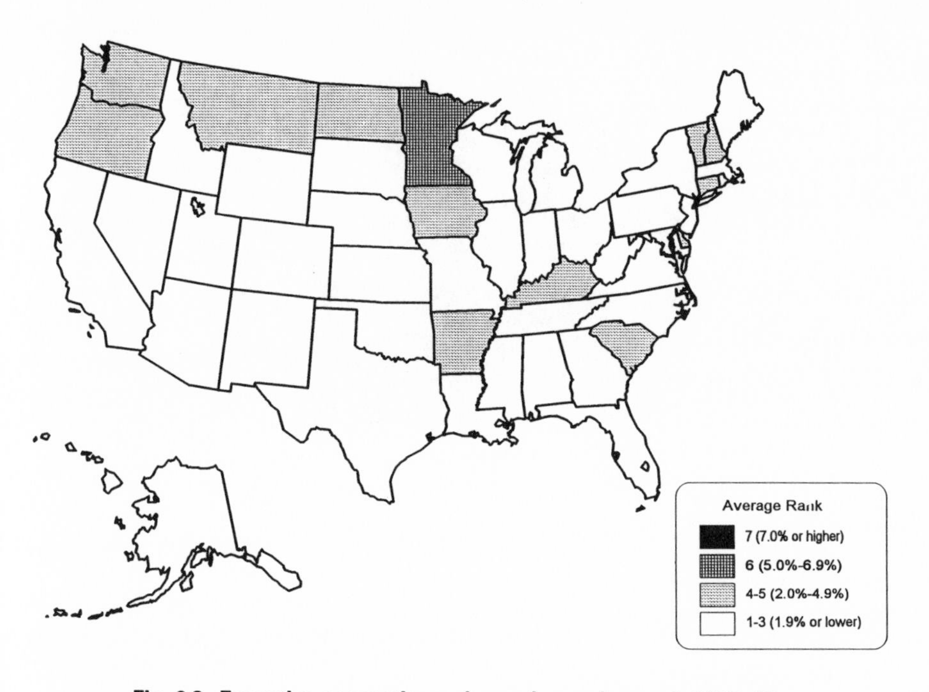

Fig. 6.2. Executive occupations, change in employment, 1989–92

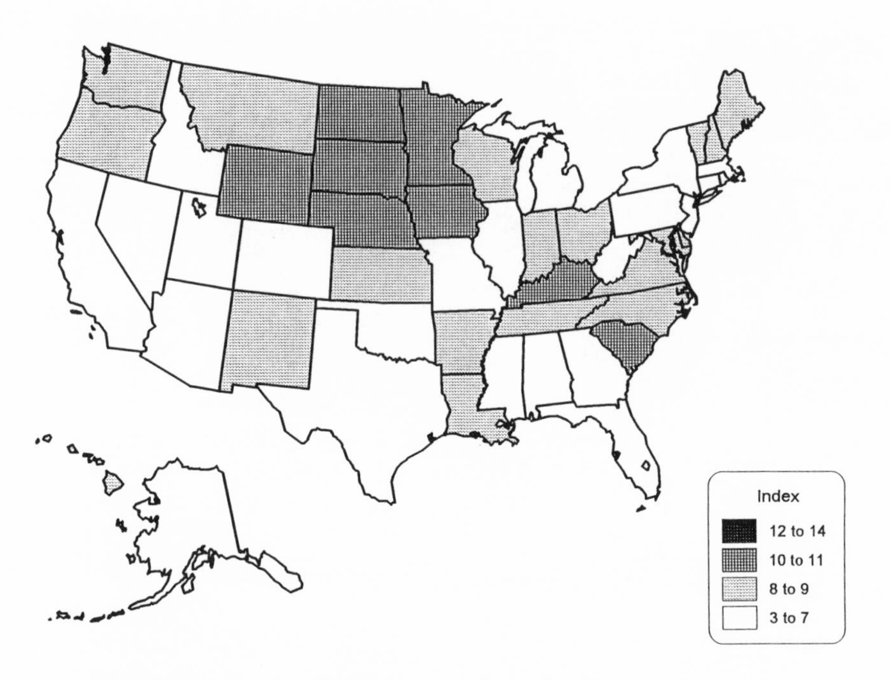

Fig. 6.3. Executive occupations, employment change and average unemployment rate, 1989–92

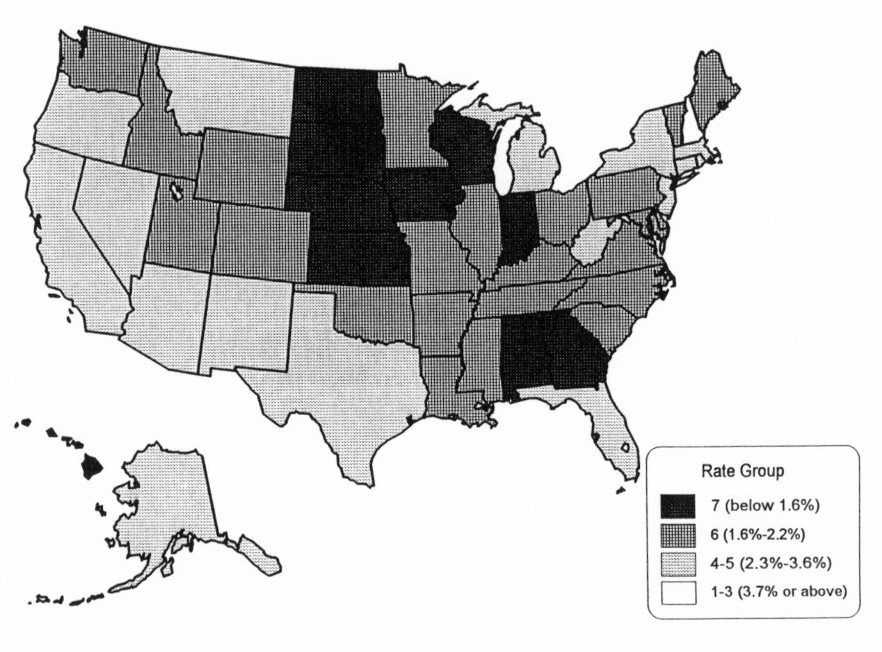

Fig. 6.4. Professional specialty occupations, average unemployment rate, 1990–92

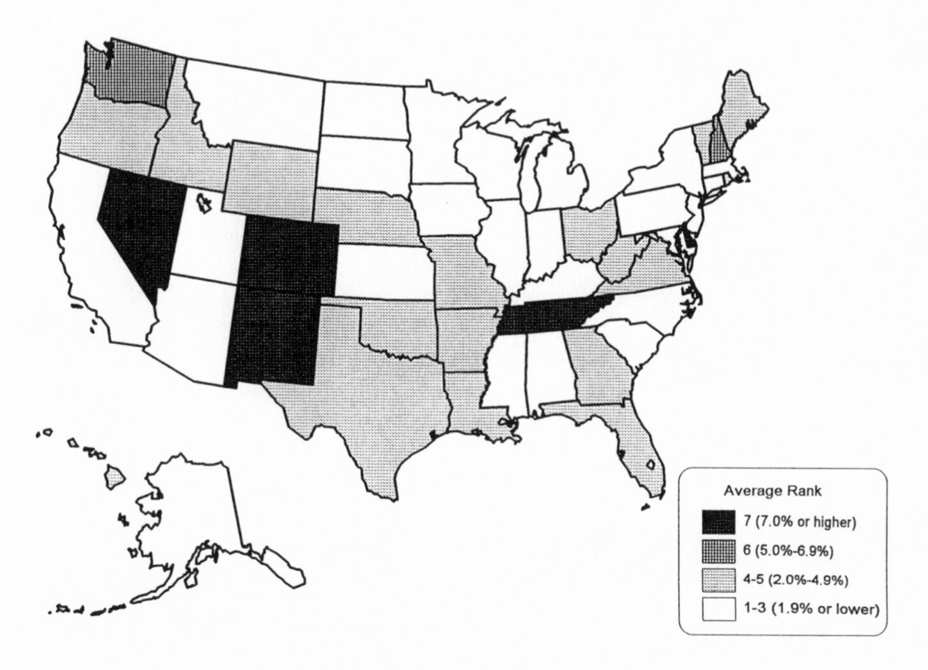

Fig. 6.5. Professional specialty occupations, change in employment, 1989–92

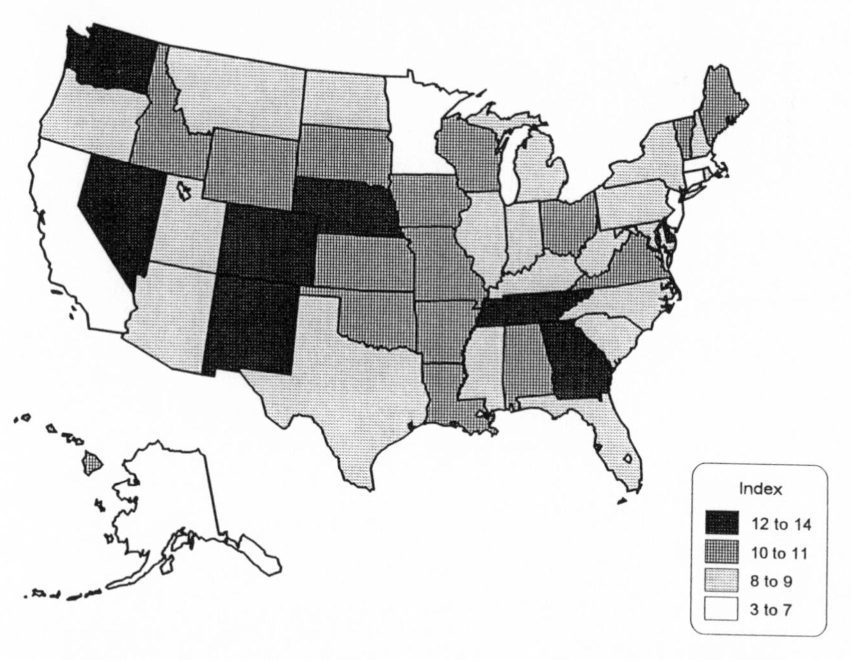

Fig. 6.6. Professional specialty occupations, employment change and average unemployment rate, 1989–92

The average annual number of approved permanent labor certifications from 1990 to 1992 in an occupational group was normalized by the 1990 labor force. On the average, there were 0.3 labor certifications per 1,000 workers in the labor force.

Some limitations of these data as a regional indicator are:

1. The current process does not consider overall labor market conditions, or even labor market conditions in a particular occupation in a particular labor market; it considers only a particular employer and a particular job. One certification request that I happened to notice was for a systems analyst who could speak Farsi. The Department of Labor examiner is supposed to disallow qualifications that are more specific than the job reasonably should require.
2. There are differences in the time required to process certifications by region. For instance, the New York region has a greater backlog than does the San Francisco region. Thus, New York certifications in 1992 may have been initiated in 1990, whereas the certifications for 1992 in San Francisco may have been initiated in 1991.
3. Immigrants want to work in certain states where other immigrants have already settled. Ports of entry such as New York, Texas, and California are more likely to hire immigrants than are states in the middle of the country.
4. Some occupations are unsuitable for immigrants because they require training or licensing not readily available outside the United States. Requirements could vary by state as well.

Table 6.1 shows differences across states and occupational groups in certifications per 1,000 workers in the labor force, based on average annual labor certifications from 1990 to 1992. Only approvals for permanent workers were counted. Ranks shown correspond to those derived in table 4.17. The higher the rank, the more favorable the labor market conditions in an occupation.

Occupations with a score of 1 for a particular state have three to six times the average number of labor certifications per 1,000 workers in the labor force. Some occupations, such as physical therapists and nurses, were not measured because the Department of Labor has automatically designated them as shortage occupations.

There are distinct differences in labor certifications across states and across occupations. Of the thirty-seven states represented in table 6.1, eleven had scores of 1 or higher in more than twelve occupations: California, District of Columbia, Illinois, Maryland, Massachusetts, Michigan, New Jersey, New York, Pennsylvania, Texas, and Virginia. Certain occupations had a score of 1

TABLE 6.1. Groups Having One or More Certifications per 1,000 Labor Force in Selected Occupations and States

Occupation	Rank	Alabama	Arizona	California	Colorado	Connecticut	D.C.	Delaware	Florida	Georgia	Hawaii	Idaho	Illinois	Iowa	Kansas	Kentucky	Louisiana	Maryland	Massachusetts	Michigan	Minnesota	Missouri	Nebraska	New Jersey	New York	North Carolina	North Dakota	Ohio	Oregon	Pennsylvania	South Carolina	Tennessee	Texas	Utah	Virginia	Washington	West Virginia	Wisconsin
Biological and life scientists	45			9		9			1				5	7	9		9	9	9	5	4	9	9	9	9	2		4		4	9	9	9	9	3	4		
Other natural scientists	44	1	1	4	1	3	4		1				2		3		1	1	4	2	1	2		3	7			1		1		1	4		1			
Physicians	43	1														2			1								3										7	
Chemists, except biochemists	38	2	3	4		2		4					2	6	5		3	2	5	1		3		3	4	1		1		1			4					2
Chemical engineers	37	4		9	7			2	3				4				2	3	7	2				4	3			2		3			6		2			
Pharmacists	37			2														2	1																1			
Teachers, college and university	37	2	2	1	3	1	9	3	2	4	1		4	2	2	2	4	3	2	4	1	3	3	3	2	2	3	3	1	4	1	2	2	3	3	2	5	2
Geologists and geodesists	37			4																										2			1					
Other therapists	37																							1	1													
Computer systems analysts and scientists	36	8	3	9	1	2	9	3	2	3	4		6	3	1		3	4	1	9	1	3	2	9	9	2		3	6	3		1	7	2	4	4	4	2
Other engineers	36		1	1			9		1		1		1						1	3				2	1			1	1	1			1	1				1
Dentists	35			1															1																			
Dental laboratory and medical appliance techicians	34			1																				1	1													
Electrical and electronic engineers	33		3	9		1	4		1			4	2					1	6	1				1	1				3	1			2					1
Editors, reporters, authors, and technical writers	33						2																															
Mechanical engineers	33	2	3	6	1	1			1	1			2	3			2	4	1	5	1	1		4	2	1		2		2			4		2			2
Civil engineers	33		1	4			9		1	1	5		2					2	1	1				2	2			1		1			1		1	1		
Aerospace engineers	33																											2							3			
Other social scientists	33			1															3						3													
Industrial engineers	32		1	4									1							2				3	2					1			1		1			
Managers, marketing, advertising, and public relations	32			1																					1													
Precision woodworking occupations	32			1														2						3	9										1			
Accountants and auditors	31			1			2																															
Statisticians, actuaries, and other math. scientists	31			7									2					1		2		4		2	3			4		2			2					
Teachers NEC	31			1			5											3						1	1										1			
Computer programmers	31			3			1																							1								
Cooks, including short-order	30			1			9											2						2	4										1			
Clinical laboratory technologists and technicians	30						6																															
Professional specialty occupations	29			1			4																		1													
Food preparation and service occupations	29						9											7							1										9			
Economists	29			7			3		1				1							1				2	3					1			1					
Teachers, special education	28			2																					5													
Social workers	28						2																															
Food counter, fountain, and related occupations	28						9											9																	9			

Source: Derived from unpublished labor certification data from the U.S. Department of Labor, Employment and Training Administration; and unpublished data from the 1990 Census of Population and Housing, Equal Employment Opportunity File, U.S. Department of Commerce, Economic and Statistics Administration, Bureau of the Census.

Note: Code corresponds to number of certifications per 1,000 workers. Code number 1 = 1.0 - 1.9 certifications, 2 = 2.0 - 2.9, 3 = 3.0 - 3.9, 4 = 4.0 - 4.9, 5 = 5.0 - 5.9, 6 = 6.0 - 6.9, 7 = 7.0 - 7.9, 8 = 8.0 - 8.0, 9 = 9.0 or more.

or more in the majority of states shown on the table: biological and life scientists, other natural scientists, chemists except biochemists, college and university teachers, and mechanical engineers. College and university teachers had a score of 1 or more in thirty-six of the thirty-seven states. The requirement for certification in this category, however, is different from that for other occupations. Employers need show only that the alien selected is the best, not the only, qualified candidate.

Despite the number of states with a score of 1 or more for college and university teachers, only in the District of Columbia were there nine or more labor certifications per 1,000 workers in the labor force. In the biological and life sciences group, on the other hand, fourteen states had nine or more labor certifications per 1,000 workers in the labor force.

Occupational Analysis at the Detailed Occupational Level

More than 12,500 occupational codes are listed in the *Dictionary of Occupational Titles* (*DOT*) and 503 detailed occupational categories listed in the 1980 Census Bureau occupational classification system. There are 664 Standard Occupational Codes (SOCs), 800 Occupational Employment Statistics (OES) survey codes, and 642 Bureau of Labor Statistics matrix codes.

While it is possible to analyze some occupations at a level of detail finer than the occupational group level, several problems occur. For example, some occupations may map into the same BLS matrix occupation but different census categories, or the same census categories but different matrix categories. The same census code may map into several different occupations. At the occupational group level, the categories are more consistent across the various systems.

Statistical reliability of the various measures depends upon the sample size for the occupation. As smaller occupational units are selected, the coefficients of variation become larger. For example, many occupations have fewer than 45,000 people employed nationally. Using the Current Population Survey, which is approximately a 1:1,500 sample, we would be constructing indicators on thirty or fewer people nationally for these occupations each month. In this instance, reliability can be increased by taking yearly averages, or by estimating two- to three-year averages.

Occupational data are available from the census on a 1:7 sample basis, but census data are collected only once every ten years. Furthermore, the occupational classification errors are likely to be far more serious in the census than in the Current Population Survey, in which trained enumerators are used, or in establishment surveys, in which firms classify what their employees do. In the census, one family member who acts as respondent may not even know the detailed occupation of other family members. The CPS interviews are conducted eight times in a sixteen-month period, so a respondent who gives a "don't know" reply in one interview may then get the information from the family member in question and supply it correctly in the next interview.

Table 6.2 illustrates some of the differences between census and CPS labor force counts for occupations in which the differences are significant. For example, the census reports 3 million elementary school teachers, whereas the CPS reports only 1.5 million. A further investigation of census methods revealed that census coders automatically code a respondent as "elementary school teacher" if the occupation indicated by the respondent is "teacher." CPS enumerators ask further questions to qualify the type of teacher. That

TABLE 6.2. 1990 Census and CPS 1990 Annual Average Labor Force Comparison, where Difference > 40% and Base of Both Titles over 50,000 (Omitting Miscellaneous, NEC, and Not Specified)

Census	Group	Title	CPS Labor Force 1990	Census Labor Force Apr. '90	Percent Difference
008	008	Personnel and labor relations managers	125,000	275,495	-55%
057	057	Mechanical engineers	322,000	185,872	73%
106	106	Physician's assistants	68,000	25,569	166%
155	15B	Teachers, prekindergarten and kindergarten	472,000	269,330	75%
156	15B	Teachers, elementary school	1,527,000	3,024,189	-50%
157	157	Teachers, secondary school	1,228,000	624,400	97%
158	158	Teachers, special education	275,000	62,216	342%
175	175	Recreation workers	108,000	50,779	113%
277	25A	Street and door-to-door sales workers	385,000	230,927	67%
373	36A	Expediters	131,000	238,789	-45%
377	37A	Eligibility clerks, social welfare	91,000	49,506	84%
379	379	General office clerks	813,000	1,491,116	-45%
387	387	Teacher's aides	508,000	275,543	84%
406	406	Child care workers, private household	334,000	164,252	103%
438	438	Food counter, fountain, and related occupations	359,000	236,480	52%
446	446	Health aides, except nursing	469,000	222,977	110%
467	467	Welfare service aides	100,000	48,190	108%
518	53A	Industrial machinery repairers	517,000	332,779	55%
525	525	Data processing equipment repair	161,000	91,657	76%
534	534	Heating, air conditioning, and refrigeration mechanics	277,000	192,983	44%
538	538	Office machine repairers	77,000	41,888	84%
549	53A	Not specified mechanics and repairers	233,000	492,093	-53%
555	55A	Supervisors, electricians, and power transmission installers	40,000	73,556	-46%
704	71A	Lathe and turning machine operators	62,000	36,530	70%
754	75A	Packaging and filling machine operators	514,000	281,245	83%
759	75A	Painting and paint-spraying machine operators	213,000	136,177	56%
806	80B	Driver-sales workers	206,000	143,353	44%
855	85A	Grader, dozer, and scraper operators	111,000	64,880	71%
865	86A	Helpers, construction trades	152,000	85,604	78%
873	86A	Production helpers	87,000	37,983	129%

Source: Derived from *Employment and Earnings*, January 1991, U.S. Department of Labor, Bureau of Labor Statistics; and unpublished data from the 1990 Census of Population and Housing, Equal Employment Opportunity File, U.S. Department of Commerce, Economic and Statistics Administration, Bureau of the Census.

would also explain why the CPS reports 275,000 special education teachers while the census reports only 62,216. Overall, the differences between CPS and census counts are small for most occupations. Only the most troublesome ones are shown in the table.

Among other obvious problems in the comparison, not shown in the table, are differences between occupational classifications such as not elsewhere classified (NEC) and occupation not specified. Such miscellaneous categories tend to differ between the two surveys, but the differences are meaningless because they occur within generally comparable categories. Other differences occur because we are comparing average 1990 employment to April 1990 census employment, but these differences appear to be small.

Employment and wage data are not even collected for some classification systems, such as the *DOT* and the SOC system. Even if this information were available, it is not clear how useful it would be for some occupations. For example, car wash attendants and parking lot attendants are separate classifications, but an unemployed car wash attendant could easily switch occupations to take a job as a parking lot attendant. Since workers in such occupations are substitutable, it would be meaningless to measure shortages at this level of aggregation. For some occupations, however, particularly those requiring higher skills, it may be useful to make such distinctions. For example, French and Japanese chefs would probably not consider themselves substitutable for one another.

A key factor in determining which occupations require more detailed analysis may be the amount of specialized training involved. Once it is determined whether more detailed occupational information would assist in the analysis, the next question is where to get the information and whether it is worth the cost. It may be possible to determine the specialty of recent graduates with Ph.D.s in a given field from data collected by the Department of Education. The Department of Health and Human Services conducts a sample survey of nurses every four years, which would yield useful information about that profession. Some professional associations, such as those for engineers and dentists, collect information about their members. When the information is already collected, there would be no cost, but collecting the information from a special survey could be prohibitively expensive.

Labor certification data are collected by *DOT* classification. Table 6.3 shows all detailed *DOT* occupations for which twenty-five or more certifications were made over the three-year period 1990–92. There are many inconsistencies in the use of this classification across states, and there have also been changes in some *DOT* codes from 1990 to 1992. Nevertheless, table 6.3 provides some insights into more detailed occupational classifications. For example, it is possible to divide the occupational group biological and life scientists into more detailed occupations. Table 6.3 shows that by far the

TABLE 6.3. Certifications by *DOT* in Rank Order, with at Least 25 Certifications over Three Years

DOT Title	*DOT* Code	Group	1990	1991	1992	Total	Rank
Aquatic biologist	0041061022	078	57	2	10	69	45
Biochemist	0041061026	078	148	270	369	787	45
Biologist	0041061030	078	40	116	197	353	45
Biophysicist	0041061034	078	22	25	26	73	45
Geneticist	0041061050	078	5	32	42	79	45
Microbiologist	0041061058	078	39	75	102	216	45
Physiologist	0041061078	078	31	45	73	149	45
Electro-optical engineer	0023061010	07A	50	19	23	92	44
Physicist	0023061014	07A	96	146	208	450	44
Environmental analyst	0029081010	07A	34	53	79	166	44
Materials scientist	0029081014	07A	16	16	23	55	44
Agronomist	0040061010	07A	16	8	5	29	44
Horticulturist	0040061038	07A	7	7	14	28	44
Histopathologist	0041061054	07A	23	13	13	49	44
Pharmacologist	0041061074	07A	20	44	52	116	44
Food technologist	0041081010	07A	19	11	24	54	44
Pathologist	0070061010	084	14	22	25	61	43
Anesthesiologist	0070101010	084	13	9	21	43	43
Cardiologist	0070101014	084	22	15	28	65	43
General practitioner	0070101022	084	34	49	73	156	43
Family practitioner	0070101026	084	5	7	29	41	43
Internist	0070101042	084	32	62	84	178	43
Neurologist	0070101050	084	8	8	18	34	43
Obstetrician	0070101054	084	9	8	11	28	43
Pediatrician	0070101066	084	10	22	26	58	43
Radiologist	0070101090	084	6	11	16	33	43
Surgeon	0070101094	084	21	18	48	87	43
Psychiatrist	0070107014	084	8	15	16	39	43
Chemist	0022061010	073	277	330	485	1,092	38
Absorption and adsorption engineer	0008061010	048	42	2	1	45	37
Chemical design engineer, processes	0008061014	048	10	35	65	110	37
Chemical engineer	0008061018	048	72	156	222	450	37
Chemical research engineer	0008061022	048	34	52	59	145	37
Geologist	0024061018	075	17	32	22	71	37
Geophysicist	0024061030	075	8	23	22	53	37
Hydrologist	0024061034	075	16	14	17	47	37
Engineer, soils	0024161010	075	0	15	10	25	37
Pharmacist	0074161010	096	92	117	142	351	37
Occupational therapist	0076121010	09A	23	40	42	105	37
Faculty member, college or university	0090227010	15C	2,130	2,044	2,665	6,839	37
Engineering manager, electronics	0003167070	05A	3	13	11	27	36
Plant engineer	0007167014	05A	7	10	10	27	36
Petroleum engineer	0010061018	05A	6	11	16	33	36
Metallurgist, physical	0011061022	05A	35	25	43	103	36
Industrial health engineer	0012167034	05A	25	1	3	29	36
Nuclear engineer	0015061014	05A	10	5	15	30	36
Biomedical engineer	0019061010	05A	51	22	33	106	36
Materials engineer	0019061014	05A	22	31	50	103	36
Optical engineer	0019061018	05A	4	11	20	35	36
Pollution control engineer	0019081018	05A	8	24	18	50	36
Project engineer	0019167014	05A	132	135	189	456	36
Chemical laboratory chief	0022161010	05A	18	11	7	36	36
Software engineer	0030062010	05A	0	2	1,218	1,220	36
Manager, data processing	0169167030	05A	37	38	66	141	36
Director, research and development	0189117014	05A	94	102	133	329	36
Systems analyst, electronic data processing	0012167066	064	1,328	1,109	1,287	3,724	36
Software engineer	0020061640	064	0	72	40	112	36

(continued)

TABLE 6.3 - *Continued*

DOT Title	*DOT* Code	Group	1990	1991	1992	Total	Rank
Computer applications engineer	0020062010	064	219	1,203	151	1,573	36
Engineering analyst	J020067010	064	114	69	90	273	36
Programmer-analyst	0030162014	064	0	0	155	155	36
Systems programmer	0030162022	064	0	0	28	28	36
Systems analyst	0030167014	064	0	0	193	193	36
User support analyst	0032262010	064	0	0	28	28	36
Information scientist	0109067010	064	22	27	34	83	36
Clinical psychologist	0045107022	167	14	12	19	45	36
Psychologist, counseling	0045107026	167	9	15	12	36	36
Radiologic technologist	0078362026	206	3	7	22	32	36
Dentist	0072101010	085	28	52	44	124	35
Dental laboratory technician	0712381018	678	14	39	26	79	34
Management analyst	0161167010	026	33	65	88	186	33
Manager, records analysis	0161167018	026	26	1	1	28	33
Aerodynamicist	0002061010	044	20	5	0	25	33
Aeronautical engineer	0002061014	044	38	23	23	84	33
Aeronautical design engineer	0002061022	044	17	6	6	29	33
Civil engineer	0005061014	053	237	280	317	834	33
Sanitary engineer	0005061030	053	3	20	27	50	33
Structural engineer	0005061034	053	158	133	136	427	33
Transportation engineer	0005061038	053	16	54	34	104	33
Electrical engineer	0003061010	055	394	414	488	1,296	33
Electrical test engineer	0003061014	055	36	21	16	73	33
Electrical design engineer	0003061018	055	21	97	105	223	33
Electrical research engineer	0003061026	055	17	29	28	74	33
Electronics engineer	0003061030	055	525	514	577	1,616	33
Electronics design engineer	0003061034	055	44	255	222	521	33
Electronics research engineer	0003061038	055	17	32	32	81	33
Electronics test engineer	0003061042	055	11	69	38	118	33
Electrical engineer, power system	0003167018	055	3	11	21	35	33
Systems engineer, electronic data processing	0003167062	055	369	473	512	1,354	33
Transmission and protection engineer	0003167066	055	205	0	1	206	33
Automotive engineer	0007061010	057	62	20	90	172	33
Mechanical engineer	0007061014	057	317	367	487	1,171	33
Mechanical design engineer, facilities	0007061018	057	15	18	28	61	33
Mechanical design engineer, products	0007061022	057	93	66	81	240	33
Applications engineer, manufacturing	0007061038	057	8	13	24	45	33
Mechanical research engineer	0007161022	057	21	30	43	94	33
Sociologist	0054067014	16A	4	13	8	25	33
Urban planner	0199167014	16A	14	15	22	51	33
Newswriter	0131267014	18A	28	14	5	47	33
Reporter	0131267018	18A	11	29	21	61	33
Writer, technical publications	0131267026	18A	6	15	23	44	33
Editor, newspaper	0132017014	18A	2	13	10	25	33
Editor, technical and scientific publications	0132017018	18A	10	8	14	32	33
Editor, publications	0132037022	18A	16	15	11	42	33
Manager, export	0163117014	013	47	100	123	270	32
Manager, advertising	0163167010	013	51	5	2	58	32
Manager, sales	0163167018	013	78	148	175	401	32
Manager, advertising	0164117010	013	8	12	12	32	32
Account executive	0164167010	013	13	7	9	29	32
Manager, customer technical services	0189117018	013	15	35	38	88	32
Manager, quality control	0012167014	056	14	15	21	50	32
Industrial engineer	0012167030	056	41	81	84	206	32
Manufacturing engineer	0012167042	056	85	69	89	243	32
Production engineer	0012167046	056	2	20	16	38	32
Production planner	0012167050	056	7	19	14	40	32
Quality control engineer	0012167054	056	52	61	60	173	32

TABLE 6.3 - *Continued*

DOT Title	*DOT* Code	Group	1990	1991	1992	Total	Rank
Lawyer	0110107010	178	64	78	79	221	32
Lawyer, corporation	0110117022	178	14	21	16	51	32
Cabinetmaker	0660280010	65B	129	79	48	256	32
Carver, hand	0761281010	65B	7	11	12	30	32
Furniture finisher	0763381010	65B	49	35	18	102	32
Controller	0186117014	007	52	101	70	223	31
Manager, financial institution	0186117038	007	18	18	14	50	31
Vice president, financial institution	0186117078	007	20	30	40	90	31
Director, preschool	0092137010	014	10	10	9	29	31
Director, educational program	0099117010	014	13	12	16	41	31
Business manager, college or university	0186117010	014	42	2	0	44	31
Accountant, tax	0160162010	023	49	33	37	119	31
Auditor	0160162014	023	38	59	40	137	31
Accountant	0160162018	023	469	394	310	1,173	31
Accountant, budget	0160167014	023	15	53	34	102	31
Accountant, cost	0160167018	023	21	41	43	105	31
Accountant, property	0160167022	023	30	7	4	41	31
Accountant, systems	0160167026	023	8	41	45	94	31
Auditor, internal	0160167034	023	17	21	17	55	31
Mathematician	0020067014	06A	17	17	39	73	31
Statistician, mathematical	0020067022	06A	7	8	19	34	31
Actuary	0020167010	06A	101	41	41	183	31
Statistician, applied	0020167026	06A	14	42	70	126	31
Instructor, vocational training	0097227014	15A	20	20	15	55	31
Instructor, physical education	0099224010	15A	14	5	11	30	31
Children's tutor	0099227010	15A	139	139	66	344	31
Teacher, adult education	0099227030	15A	18	28	30	76	31
Tutor	0099227034	15A	12	15	24	51	31
Instructor, dancing	0151027014	15A	8	9	10	27	31
Teacher, music	0152021010	15A	16	23	19	58	31
Instructor, sports	0153227018	15A	26	40	44	110	31
Training representative	0166227010	15A	27	19	18	64	31
Consultant	0189167010	15A	78	77	115	270	31
Acupuncturist	0079271010	208	14	18	13	45	31
Programmer, business	0020162014	229	772	78	60	910	31
Programmer, chief, business	0020167018	229	5	17	20	42	31
Programmer, engineering and scientific	0020167022	229	77	50	85	212	31
Programmer, information system	0020187010	229	38	50	53	141	31
Programmer, process control	0020187014	229	25	12	11	48	31
Software technician	0020262010	229	22	10	22	54	31
Computer programmer	0030162010	229	0	0	29	29	31
Teacher, secondary school	0091227010	157	138	139	120	397	30
Teacher, elementary school	0092227010	15B	206	192	189	587	30
Teacher, kindergarten	0092227014	15B	14	12	16	42	30
Teacher, preschool	0092227018	15B	33	55	71	159	30
Clergy member	0120007010	176	55	43	36	134	30
Medical technologist	0078361014	203	52	71	128	251	30
Baker, second	0313361010	43A	28	3	9	40	30
Cook	0313361014	43A	283	207	152	642	30
Cook, short-order	0313361022	43A	42	30	13	85	30
Cook, specialty	0313361026	43A	19	30	18	67	30
Cook, specialty, foreign food	0313361030	43A	1,661	1,027	994	3,682	30
Baker	0313381010	43A	18	23	15	56	30
Baker, pizza	0313381014	43A	19	21	19	59	30
Cook, pastry	0313381026	43A	23	25	28	76	30
Cook	0315361010	43A	10	12	8	30	30
Dietitian, clinical	0077127014	097	7	10	13	30	29
Economist	0050067010	166	45	90	104	239	29

(continued)

TABLE 6.3 - *Continued*

DOT Title	*DOT* Code	Group	1990	1991	1992	Total	Rank
Market-research analyst I	0050067014	166	225	204	246	675	29
Librarian	0100127014	16B	8	14	20	42	29
Curator	0102017010	16B	9	12	12	33	29
Pastoral assistant	0129107026	18B	5	13	9	27	29
Translator	0137267018	18B	11	22	31	64	29
Dancer	0151047010	18B	17	3	8	28	29
Coach, professional athletes	0153227010	18B	20	14	13	47	29
Producer	0159117010	18B	8	8	15	31	29
Administrative assistant	0169167010	18B	29	41	50	120	29
Research assistant II	0199267034	18B	5	12	19	36	29
Gemologist	0199281010	18B	15	18	13	46	29
Financial planner	0251257022	255	13	21	15	49	29
Salad maker	0317384010	43B	19	1	5	25	29
Pantry goods maker	0317684014	43B	101	86	29	216	29
Cook helper	0317687010	43B	177	168	88	433	29
Kitchen helper	0318687010	43B	286	403	240	929	29
Operations research analyst	0020067018	065	31	52	58	141	28
Teacher, emotionally impaired	0094227010	158	18	6	9	33	28
Teacher, handicapped students	0094227018	158	28	42	44	114	28
Teacher, mentally impaired	0094227022	158	7	8	15	30	28
Counselor	0045107010	163	19	25	32	76	28
Caseworker	0195107010	174	24	11	14	49	28
Social worker, psychiatric	0195107034	174	14	14	12	40	28
Interior designer	0142051014	185	14	31	14	59	28
Cloth designer	0142061014	185	35	12	22	69	28
Fashion designer	0142061018	185	16	40	48	104	28
Furniture designer	0142061022	185	22	9	3	34	28
Industrial designer	0142061026	185	13	25	33	71	28
Floral designer	0142081010	185	16	17	8	41	28
Nurse, licensed practical	0079374014	207	6	20	20	46	28
Fast food worker	0311472010	438	116	83	112	311	28
Counter attendant, lunchroom or coffee shop	0311477014	438	27	8	11	46	28
Counter attendant, cafeteria	0311677014	438	17	21	12	50	28
Dental assistant	0079371010	445	34	39	26	99	28
Contract administrator	0162117014	01A	7	20	20	47	27
Manager, office	0169167034	01A	25	25	35	85	27
Superintendent, construction	0182167026	01A	15	25	21	61	27
Manager, branch	0183117010	01A	38	19	20	77	27
Production superintendent	0183117014	01A	43	60	73	176	27
General supervisor	0183167018	01A	5	25	26	56	27
Import-export agent	0184117022	01A	32	28	36	96	27
Manager, operations	0184117050	01A	10	18	28	56	27
Manager, fast food services	0185137010	01A	11	14	12	37	27
Executive chef	0187161010	01A	14	15	14	43	27
Manager, fish-and-game club	0187167102	01A	28	0	0	28	27
Manager, food service	0187167106	01A	100	139	134	373	27
Manager, travel agency	0187167158	01A	13	30	37	80	27
Association executive	0189117010	01A	22	6	3	31	27
Manager, industrial organization	0189117022	01A	45	45	62	152	27
President	0189117026	01A	23	38	49	110	27
Project director	0189117030	01A	50	90	87	227	27
Vice president	0189117034	01A	126	98	130	354	27
Manager, department	0189167022	01A	18	26	22	66	27
Program manager	0189167030	01A	9	20	34	63	27
Financial analyst	0020167014	03A	116	197	172	485	27
Broker and market operator, grain	0162157010	03A	47	0	1	48	27
Foreign exchange trader	0186167014	03A	2	18	5	25	27
Loan officer	0186267018	03A	14	16	12	42	27

TABLE 6.3 - *Continued*

DOT Title	*DOT* Code	Group	1990	1991	1992	Total	Rank
Credit analyst	0191267014	03A	12	10	9	31	27
Electronics technician	0003161014	213	7	21	22	50	27
Technician, semiconductor development	0003161018	213	27	0	0	27	27
Child monitor	0301677010	406	1,282	1,111	590	2,983	27
Electrician, automotive	0825281022	533	18	14	16	48	27
Director, religious education	0129107022	177	20	18	17	55	26
Estimator	0160267018	363	16	11	9	36	26
Barber	0330371010	457	6	18	7	31	26
Nursery school attendant	0359677018	468	5	12	8	25	26
Baker, head	0313131010	46A	51	2	2	55	26
Chef	0313131014	46A	92	106	110	308	26
Pastry chef	0313131022	46A	26	7	17	50	26
Sous chef	0313131026	46A	23	18	14	55	26
Guide, travel	0353167010	46A	22	35	21	78	26
Supervisor, janitorial services	0381137010	46A	16	20	25	61	26
Musician, instrumental	0152041010	186	10	16	16	42	25
Choral director	0152047010	186	31	17	19	67	25
Art director	0141031010	188	17	15	17	49	25
Graphic designer	0141061018	188	23	35	43	101	25
Painter	0144061010	188	10	14	10	34	25
Public relations representative	0165067010	197	21	21	31	73	25
Mechanical engineering technician	0007161026	21A	3	8	15	26	25
Mathematical technician	0020162010	22A	50	1	5	56	25
Automobile mechanic	0620261010	50A	300	211	181	692	25
Automobile service station mechanic	0620261030	50A	51	17	2	70	25
Transmission mechanic	0620281062	50A	10	6	9	25	25
Tool maker	0601280042	63A	10	9	7	26	25
Tool and die maker	0601280046	63A	21	16	11	48	25
Paralegal	0119267026	234	11	22	30	63	24
Diesel mechanic	0625281010	507	40	26	17	83	24
Architect	0001061010	04A	199	186	150	535	23
Landscape architect	0001061018	04A	2	20	13	35	23
Physician assistant	0079364018	106	3	4	18	25	23
Receptionist	0237367038	31A	25	15	3	43	23
Dining room attendant	0311677018	443	65	52	27	144	23
Automobile body repairer	0807381010	514	136	78	54	268	23
Manufacturer's service representative	0638261018	544	18	13	24	55	23
Tile setter	0861381054	565	16	16	12	44	23
Shoe repairer	0365361014	66A	18	20	18	56	23
Patternmaker	0781381026	66A	7	19	18	44	23
Alteration tailor	0785261010	66A	83	63	66	212	23
Custom tailor	0785261014	66A	36	45	39	120	23
Dressmaker	0785361010	66A	78	14	30	122	23
Sample stitcher	0785361018	66A	52	70	64	186	23
Shop tailor	0785361022	66A	8	29	16	53	23
Orthopedic boot and shoe designer and maker	0788261010	66A	12	12	5	29	23
Buyer	0162157018	029	29	73	58	160	22
Travel agent	0252157010	274	78	55	44	177	22
Nurse, practical	0354374010	447	114	38	13	165	22
Birth attendant	0354377010	447	46	0	0	46	22
Home attendant	0354377014	447	813	574	246	1,633	22
Nurse assistant	0355674014	447	39	26	36	101	22
Cosmetologist	0332271010	458	78	47	44	169	22
Hair stylist	0332271018	458	33	44	14	91	22
Bakery supervisor	0526131010	55A	15	13	17	45	22
Supervisor, garage	0620131014	55A	4	14	14	32	22
Cabinetmaker, supervisor	0660130010	55A	19	9	9	37	22
Supervisor, garment manufacturing	0786132010	55A	52	38	38	128	22

(*continued*)

TABLE 6.3 - *Continued*

DOT Title	*DOT* Code	Group	1990	1991	1992	Total	Rank
Maintenance supervisor	0891137010	55A	10	7	10	27	22
Automobile upholsterer	0780381010	668	22	6	3	31	22
Furniture upholsterer	0780381018	668	16	14	11	41	22
Baker	0526381010	687	125	104	69	298	22
Drafter, architectural	0001261010	21B	10	8	11	29	21
Supervisor, estimator and drafter	0019161010	21B	31	0	0	31	21
Sales engineer, electrical products	0003151010	25A	6	14	9	29	21
Sales engineer, electronics products and systems	0003151014	25A	16	65	46	127	21
Sales engineer, mechanical equipment	0007151010	25A	13	18	26	57	21
Wholesaler II	0185157018	25A	96	175	156	427	21
Commissary manager	0185167010	25A	47	0	2	49	21
Manager, retail store	0185167046	25A	71	58	100	229	21
Wholesaler I	0185167070	25A	17	17	18	52	21
Manager, insurance office	0186167034	25A	6	11	8	25	21
Traffic agent	0252257010	25A	9	9	17	35	21
Sales clerk, food	0290477018	25A	14	6	5	25	21
Model, photographer's	0961367010	25A	33	38	25	96	21
Medical assistant	0079367010	446	34	30	12	76	21
Maintenance mechanic	0638281014	53A	32	47	42	121	21
Sewing machine repairer	0639281018	53A	16	22	11	49	21
Watch repairer	0715281010	53A	15	10	16	41	21
Bricklayer	0861381018	53A	28	14	3	45	21
Maintenance repairer, building	0899381010	53A	29	39	19	87	21
Electrician	0824261010	57A	16	26	10	52	21
Procurement engineer	0162157034	033	19	3	3	25	20
Purchasing agent	0162157038	033	24	51	63	138	20
Manager, contracts	0163117010	033	50	2	1	53	20
Legal secretary	0201362010	313	7	12	9	28	20
Medical secretary	0201362014	313	4	14	21	39	20
Secretary	0201362030	313	246	176	171	593	20
Audit clerk	0210382010	33A	23	5	3	31	20
Bookkeeper	0210382014	33A	19	47	57	123	20
Foreign clerk	0214467010	33A	27	21	9	57	20
Host/hostess, restaurant	0310137010	433	62	20	14	96	20
Waiter/waitress, formal	0311477026	435	32	74	21	127	20
Construction equipment mechanic	0620261022	516	12	16	9	37	20
Roofer	0866381010	595	15	8	7	30	20
Machinist	0600280022	63B	61	26	29	116	20
Machinist, automotive	0600280034	63B	10	11	6	27	20
Maintenance machinist	0600280042	63B	10	19	13	42	20
Jeweler	0700281010	65A	143	105	86	334	20
Stone setter	0700381054	65A	44	42	24	110	20
Model maker II	0709381018	65A	7	9	9	25	20
Diamond selector	0770281010	65A	22	28	19	69	20
Gem cutter	0770281014	65A	8	13	7	28	20
Butcher, meat	0316681010	686	17	7	3	27	19
Meat cutter	0316684018	686	14	26	21	61	19
Shipping and receiving clerk	0222387050	36A	16	14	7	37	18
Administrative clerk	0219362010	379	17	20	11	48	18
Heating and air conditioning installer/servicer	0637261014	534	7	12	13	32	18
Cement mason	0844364010	56A	37	36	22	95	18
Marble setter	0861381030	56A	10	9	10	29	18
Stonemason	0861381038	56A	74	36	33	143	18
Painter	0840381010	57B	53	16	17	86	18
Cook	0305281010	40A	22	36	49	107	17
Construction worker I	0869664014	59A	40	43	15	98	17
House worker, general	0301474010	407	8,025	5,127	2,004	15,156	16
Caretaker	0301687010	407	23	41	22	86	16

TABLE 6.3 - *Continued*

DOT Title	*DOT* Code	Group	1990	1991	1992	Total	Rank
Day worker	0301687014	407	32	69	46	147	16
Companion	0309677010	407	4	12	10	26	16
Farmworker, fruit II	0403687010	47A	262	0	1	263	16
Groundskeeper, industrial-commercial	0406684014	47A	10	12	12	34	16
Landscape gardener	0408161010	47A	81	68	33	182	16
Lawn-service worker	0408684010	47A	33	6	1	40	16
Laborer, landscape	0408687014	47A	30	82	27	139	16
Stable attendant	0410674022	47A	132	70	32	234	16
Horse trainer	0419224010	47A	10	14	24	48	16
Electronics mechanic	0828281010	523	17	19	16	52	16
Plumber	0862381030	58A	7	25	5	37	16
Cleaner, hospital	0323687010	44A	23	2	3	28	15
Cleaner, housekeeping	0323687014	44A	91	92	41	224	15
Housecleaner	0323687018	44A	37	30	14	81	15
Cleaner, commercial or institutional	0381687014	44A	209	530	222	961	15
Cleaner, industrial	0381687018	44A	8	15	3	26	15
Janitor	0382664010	44A	40	46	23	109	15
Sexton	0389667010	44A	8	14	5	27	15
Cleaner, window	0389687014	44A	40	95	39	174	15
Presser, machine	0363682018	73A	33	17	8	58	15
Knitting machine operator	0685665014	73A	19	5	1	25	15
Oriental rug repairer	0782381014	73A	24	34	34	92	15
Binder, chainstitch	0786682034	73A	59	0	0	59	15
Lockstitch machine operator	0786682170	73A	140	135	28	303	15
Overlock machine operator, complete garment	0786682198	73A	22	2	1	25	15
Sewing machine operator, semiautomatic	0786685030	73A	150	233	176	559	15
Sewing machine operator	0787682046	73A	113	196	46	355	15
Painter, transportation equipment	0845381014	75A	14	8	6	28	15
Carpenter	0860381022	56B	63	93	23	179	14
Rug cleaner, hand	0369384014	78A	0	22	7	29	14
Turkey-roll maker	0525684058	78A	25	0	0	25	14
Animal eviscerator	0525687010	78A	21	24	2	47	14
Poultry dresser	0525687070	78A	26	253	358	637	14
Poultry eviscerator	0525687074	78A	50	53	163	266	14
Doughnut maker	0526684010	78A	22	11	9	42	14
Welder, combination	0819384010	78A	32	15	11	58	14
Poultry hanger	0525687078	86A	18	0	10	28	13
Poultry-dressing worker	0525687082	86A	135	47	41	223	13
Laborer, shellfish processing	0529686058	86A	28	16	1	45	13
Construction worker II	0869687026	86A	139	61	36	236	13
Car wash attendant, automatic	0915667010	86A	24	9	1	34	13
Packager, hand	0920587018	86A	32	25	24	81	13
Laborer, stores	0922687058	86A	3	42	4	49	13
Automobile service station attendant	0915467010	85A	20	10	5	35	12

Source: Unpublished data from the U.S. Department of Labor, Employment and Training Administration.

largest biological and life science group receiving certifications is biochemist, with 787 certifications. Biologists come in second, with 353 certifications.

It is also possible to examine the certifications by year. Both of the aforementioned subcategories of biological and life scientists grew substantially each year from 1990 to 1992. Biochemists grew from 148 in 1990 to 270 in 1991 to 369 in 1992. Biologists grew from 40 to 116 to 197 over the same period. The trend is not always upward. Accountants declined over the period 1990–92, from 469 to 394 to 310. It should be noted that two different

DOT codes were used for accountants. It was necessary to sum them before making a comparison.

The level of occupational detail reflected in table 6.3 is not sufficient to enable policymakers to designate shortage and surplus occupations. The educational and experience level of the population is also important.

Various college placement services collect data on the relationship between job openings and candidates, by occupation and level of degree. Michigan State University, for example, has an institute that collects data from other institutes in Michigan. It classifies occupations by level of degree and shortage level, as "limited supply," meaning far more openings than applicants; "possible shortage," meaning more jobs than applicants; "approximate balance"; or "surplus," meaning more applicants than jobs. Table 6.4 shows occupations classified as limited supply or possible shortage from the 1992–93 Michigan State survey (Scheetz and Klefstad 1992). Some occupations, such as physical chemistry, have shortages at the Ph.D. level but not at other levels. Others, such as computer engineering, have possible shortages at all levels, from associate's degree to Ph.D.

Other possible sources of data on supply and demand include private computerized placement services, such as Jobnet, and the public Employment Service. The problem with using such sources is that they may not be typical of the universe, or their penetration may be low. For example, Employment Service placements accounted for less than 5 percent of the new hires in 1991 (based on a comparison of administrative data received from the U.S. Employment Service for 1991, and data estimated as shown in table 2.3). The Employment Service can provide some useful information, however. For example, a large number of enrolled applicants in an occupation would be evidence of a surplus, and a large number of unfilled job openings would be evidence of a shortage. Sometimes, too, it is possible to run special tabulations by education and experience to get more detailed information about the application pool or job order requirements.

Another source used in our research was the actual certification files maintained by the regional offices of the U.S. Department of Labor. Employers are required to advertise the jobs for which they want to hire aliens, to show a good faith effort at offering the job to U.S. workers. The job requirements listed in the ads are recorded in the certification files, including type and number of years of experience, education, and any other special qualifications. The files also contain similar information about applicants for the jobs.

For purposes of a pilot study, information was collected in five regional offices of the Employment Service for occupations selected as being most likely to have a shortage of labor. Not all the information was collected systematically, using the same methodology. In some instances, interviews with staff were sufficient to establish shortage categories; in other instances,

TABLE 6.4. Supply and Demand for Michigan's College and University Graduates 1992 - 93, by Degree for Occupations with Limited Supply (L) or Possible Shortage (P)

Occupation	Degrees			
	Associate's	Bachelor's	Master's	Ph.D.
Accounting		P	P	P
Adult education administration	P			
Allied health, other			L	
Analytical chemistry			P	L
Anatomy				L
Anesthesiology			L	
Applied mathematics				L
Architectural design and construction		P		
Banking and finance		P	P	P
Bilingual/bicultural education		P	P	
Biochemistry/biophysics		P		P
Building construction management		P		
Business administration and management				P
Business and office, general	L			
Business data processing	P	P		
Chemical engineering		P	P	P
Chemical technology		L		
Chemistry, general			P	P
Clothing production	P			
Community services		P		
Composition			P	
Computer applications	P			
Computer engineering	P	P	P	P
Computer programming	P			
Computer science	P	P	P	L
Computer technology	P			
Corrections	P	P		
Court reporting	P	P		
Data processing	P	P		
Dental hygiene	P			
Dentistry				P
Education for deaf/hearing impaired		P		
Education for mentally handicapped		P		
Education for physically handicapped		P		
Education of emotionally handicapped		L		
Education, foreign languages	P			
Education, reading		P		
Education for visually handicapped			P	
Educational media			P	P
Educational statistics and research				P
Educational testing/evaluation			P	P
Electrical engineering	P	P	P	L
Electrical engineering technology		P		
Electrical/electronic technology		P		
Engineering mechanics			P	P
Engineering science		P		
Environmental and health engineering		P		
Experimental psychology				P
Food sciences				P
Forestry and related sciences				L
Funeral services		P		
Geography				L

(*continued*)

TABLE 6.4 - *Continued*

Occupation	Degrees			
	Associate's	Bachelor's	Master's	Ph.D.
Geological engineering			L	
Geriatrics		P		
Hotel/motel management	P	L	P	
Immunology				L
Industrial arts		P		
Industrial engineering	P	L		L
Industrial production technology		L		
Industrial sales		P		
Industrial technology		P		
Industrial/organizational psychology				L
Information sciences and systems	P	P		
Inorganic chemistry			P	L
Insurance marketing		P		
Labor/industrial relations			P	
Landscape architecture	P			
Law				P
Legal assisting		L		
Legal secretarial		P		
Library science			P	
Library/archival sciences			P	P
Management information systems		P		
Management science		P	L	
Manufacturing science			P	
Manufacturing technology		P		
Marketing		P		
Marketing management			P	
Materials engineering		P	P	P
Maternal/child health			L	
Mathematics education		P	P	P
Mathematics, general			P	P
Mechanical engineering		P	P	P
Mechanical/related technologies		P		
Medical assisting		P		
Medical laboratory technology		P		
Medical surgical			L	
Medical technology			P	
Medicine, human				L
Mental health/human services		P		
Metallurgical engineering		P	L	L
Microbiology			P	P
Music education			P	
Music education, vocal		P		
Nuclear engineering		P	P	
Nursing, general		L	P	P
Occupational therapy		P	P	
Office supervision and management	P	P		
Operations research		P	P	P
Organic chemistry			P	L
Osteopathic medicine				L
Pathology				L
Petroleum engineering		P		
Petroleum technology	P			
Pharmacology, human and animal			P	L

TABLE 6.4 - *Continued*

Occupation	Degrees			
	Associate's	Bachelor's	Master's	Ph.D.
Pharmacy			L	L
Physical chemistry				P
Physical sciences	P			
Physical therapy		P		
Physical therapy assisting	P			
Physics			P	P
Physiological psychology				P
Physiology, human and animal				P
Plastics technology	P	P		
Practical nursing	P			
Product management		P		
Psychiatric/mental health			L	
Psychology, clinical				L
Public health			P	
Quality control technology	P			
Radiograph medical technology		L		
Reading education				P
Recreation therapy		P		
Respiratory therapy	P			
Respiratory therapy technology	P			
School psychology				P
Science education		P	P	P
Secretarial, executive	P			
Secretarial, legal	P			
Secretarial, medical	P			
Social psychology				P
Social work, general			P	P
Special education, general		P	P	P
Special learning disabilities		P	L	
Speech pathology/audiology			L	L
Statistics				P
Stenographic	P			
Surgical technology	P			
Systems engineering		P	L	P
Taxation			P	
Teacher's aide	P			
Technical education		P		P
Technology		P		
Tool and die making	P			
Toxicology		P		
Trade and industrial education				L
Trade and industrial supervision management		L		
Transportation management			P	P
Water and wastewater management	P			
Word processing	P	P		
Zoology				P

Source: Estimated Supply and Demand for Michigan's College and University Graduates of 1992 - 93, Collegiate Employment Research Institute, Michigan State University.

data were collected more systematically. Table 6.5 illustrates the differences in data collection methods by focusing on one occupation, chemist. For example, line 6 shows that there were thirty-seven applicants for a job in Michigan requiring a master's degree and nine months of experience in chemistry. At the same time, there was an opening for a job in theoretical and organic chemistry requiring a Ph.D. and two years' experience, and no one applied for it. It may be that not all the applicants are qualified, but the numbers of people applying for various jobs do tell us something about the labor market. In any case, table 6.5 is presented only as an illustration of the type of analysis undertaken to further refine the occupational groups.

Employment Service job applicant and job order data were also used to make more precise selections of occupational groups in which shortages may exist. Because of the limited coverage of the public Employment Service for most jobs, these data may not be representative of labor market activity. Nevertheless, a large imbalance one way or the other would be consistent with either a shortage or a surplus. Table 6.6 shows total applicants during 1992, active applicants at the end of the fiscal year, and unfilled openings. There was a close match between active applicants and unfilled openings for biological, systems analyst, and chemical engineer positions. There were many

TABLE 6.5. Applicants for Chemistry Jobs, *DOT* 022.061.010, Region V

	Degree	Experience	Subfield	Wage	Applicants
Michigan					
	Ph.D.	2 years	Chemical engineering	$57,000	3
	Ph.D.	2 years	Theoretical organic chemistry	$56,000	0
	Ph.D.	2 years	Physical chemistry	$48,506	1
	Ph.D.		Atmospheric chemistry	$50,350	0
	B.S.	2 years	Mechanical/chemical engineering	$43,500	0
	M.S.	9 months	Chemistry	$38,000	37
	M.S.	1 year	Industrial pharmacy	$34,320	24
	Ph.D.	2 years	Chemistry	$52,000	0
	Ph.D.		Chemistry	$44,000	3
	Ph.D.	3 years	Polymer chemistry	$42,000	17
Ohio					
	Ph.D.	2 years	Chemistry	$42,370	20
	Ph.D.	4 years	Polymer chemistry	$65,100	18
	Ph.D.	2 years	Chemistry	$45,000	23
	Ph.D.	2 years	Chemistry	$48,408	33
	Ph.D.	1 year	Chemistry	$39,520	15
	Ph.D.	2 years	Chemistry	$42,370	37
	Ph.D.	2 years	Chemistry	$23,180	8
	Ph.D.	2 years	Chemistry	$42,000	26

Source: Derived from data collected from U.S. Department of Labor, Employment and Training Administration, Region V.

more openings than active applicants for specialty cooks. The ratio of active applicants to unfilled openings for accountants, on the other hand, was 381:47. For electrical engineers it was 182:17. These data do not distinguish years of experience or educational level.

Government agencies such as the Bureau of Labor Statistics, the National Science Foundation, Health and Human Services, and the Employment and Training Administration were interviewed. A division of Health and Human Services, for example, has a method of determining primary care physician shortages by area. Its methodology compares the ratio of physicians per population with standards for adequate medical care. Although the division makes determinations at areas below the state level, it said that if it were to choose one state in which shortages exist, it would be West Virginia—the same state identified by our methodology.

We identified ten occupations and areas that were likely to have shortages, according to the following procedure.

Approximately 12,700 occupational codes are listed in the *Dictionary of Occupational Titles*, 4th edition (U.S. Department of Labor, Employment and Training Administration 1991). In addition to these, approximately 500 old

TABLE 6.6. Massachusetts Employment Service Applicants and Unfilled Openings, Fiscal Year 1992

DOT Code	Title	Total Applicants	Active Applicants	Unfilled Openings
041061026	Biochemist	39	10	6
041061030	Biologist	53	13	8
041061058	Microbiologist	17	0	0
019167014	Project engineer	56	20	4
189117014	Director, research & development	111	28	7
003167062	Systems engineer, EDP	182	52	35
012167066	Systems analyst, EDP	377	109	90
030062010	Software engineer	22	16	29
070061010	Pathologist	6	1	3
003061010	Electrical engineer	650	182	17
161670010	Electronics engineer	205	48	21
160167010	Accountant	1,491	381	47
008061018	Chemical engineer	69	20	14
007061014	Mechanical engineer	451	107	20
005061014	Civil engineer	330	94	13
030167014	Systems analyst	10	5	5
005061034	Structural engineer	20	6	6
022061010	Chemist	127	31	20
023061014	Physicist	34	10	0
313361030	Cook, specialty, foreign	29	6	19

Source: Unpublished data from Massachusetts Employment and Training Department, November 1992.

and new codes were used by the Department of Labor from 1990 to 1992 in the labor certification process. All these occupations were aggregated into 193 groups, except for a few strictly military occupations.

Each of the seven indicators described in chapter 4 was ranked on a scale of 1 to 7. The higher the rank, the more favorable the prospects for the occupation. For example, occupations with the lowest unemployment rate and highest rate of growth in wages and in actual or projected employment were given a rank of 7. The ranks for each of the 193 occupational groups were computed based on conditions in 1992. Just as this book was being completed, revised national data became available and were incorporated in chapter 4. Therefore, chapter 4 reflects more current information on indicators than does this chapter.

Occupations with a total score of 35 to 49 for all indicators were selected as possible candidates for shortage (group A). In addition, three other occupations with a score of 28 to 34 were selected (group B). Group A occupations were initially determined to be those having an annual average during fiscal years 1990 to 1992 of three or more labor certifications per 1,000 members of the labor force in 1990 in a state. A list of the selected occupations was then presented to federal, regional, and state government experts for further scrutiny. State-occupation combinations were dropped from the list in instances in which the experts judged that sufficient numbers of U.S. workers were available. It was also decided that the list would be narrowed to only those occupations with ten or more labor certifications in 1992.

The number of labor certifications per 1,000 members of the labor force, by occupation and state, is shown in table 6.1. The occupations selected are listed in table 6.7, which also contains details on interviews conducted in the various states and regions.

Seven occupations were selected for group A: mechanical engineers, chemical engineers, chemists, biological scientists, computer systems analysts, physicians, and special education teachers. As table 6.4 indicates, however, shortages were identified in most occupations only at the advanced-degree levels, and only in a few states.

Three group B occupations were identified: medical technologists (a subset of the group clinical laboratory technologists and technicians); cooks from the subcategory specialty, foreign food, Chinese or Japanese; and materials engineers. Medical technologists were chosen because, according to the Bureau of Labor Statistics, "The number of new graduates entering the field in recent years has dropped off, prompting reports of shortages" (U.S. Department of Labor 1992a). Labor market information on cooks is available only for all cooks, but the Chinese-Japanese subcategory was selected because there have been a large number of labor certifications in that occupation. Materials engineers were selected for three reasons: (1) they were in the group ranked third highest out of the 193 occupational groups; (2) a survey by the Michigan State University Collegiate Employment Research Institute found possible shortages at the bachelor's, master's, and doctorate levels (Scheetz and Klefstad 1992); and (3) this occupation is one of the important areas designated by the National Science Foundation for additional support. States were selected for these three occupations based on the number of certifications issued. Some states were deleted when local interviews indicated no shortage

BLE 6.7. Designated Labor Shortages, by Area and Occupation

sis	Occupation	Alabama	Arizona	California	Connecticut	D.C.	Georgia	Illinois	Kansas	Louisiana	Maryland	Massachusetts	Michigan	Missouri	Nebraska	New Jersey	New York	Ohio	Pennsylvania	Tennessee	Texas	Virginia	Washington	West Virginia
A	Biological & life sciences, Ph.D.			X	X			X	X	X	X	X	X	X	X	X	X	X	X	X	X		X	
A	Chemistry, Ph.D.			X								X		X		X	X				X			
A	Chemical engineer, master's - 2 years experience or Ph.D.							X				X									X			
A	Computer scientist, software engineer, master's - 2 years experience or Ph.D.	X	X				X	X					X	X							X			
B	Cooks, specialty, foreign food, Chinese or Japanese cuisine - 2 years experience			X		X		X			X	X							X		X	X		
B	Materials engineering, master's or Ph.D.			X									X					X	X					
A	Mechanical engineer, master's - 2 years experience or Ph.D.		X																		X			
B	Medical technologists			X				X									X				X			
A	Primary care physicians																							X
A	Special education teachers																X							
	Interviewed regional office	N	P	P	N	P	N	P	N	P	P	N	P	N	N	P	P	P	P	N	P	P	T	P
	Reviewed SAMS information	N	N	J	N	N	N	Y	N	Y	N	Y	N	N	N	Y	Y	Y	N	N	Y	N	Y	N
	Interviewed State ES	N	N	P	N	N	N	N	N	N	N	P	T	N	N	T	P	N	N	N	N	N	N	N

rce: Malcolm S. Cohen, "The Use of Labor Market Indicators to Determine Labor Shortages," final report .S. Department of Labor, Employment and Training Administration, March 1993.

occupations with a score of 35 to 49, B = occupations with a score of 28 to 34, Y = yes, N = no, personal visit, J = job bank data only, T = telephone interview.

in the specialty cooks category, but no local interview information was obtained on medical technologists or materials engineers.

A list of ten possible shortage occupations was published in the Federal Register in March 1993 (U.S. Department of Labor, Employment and Training Administration 1993), and approximately five hundred comments were received in response. The comments were very negative on the inclusion of any science, engineering, or computer occupations on the shortage list but generally did not take serious exception to the inclusion of physicians, medical technologists, specialty cooks, or special education teachers. In many comments it was argued that various science and engineering occupations could be substituted for one another. For example, a laid-off aeronautical engineer could hold mechanical engineering jobs if they were in short supply. Many comments cited the number of candidates (hundreds) for faculty positions in science. Some also suggested that even though the unemployment rate was low for scientists and engineers, many of them might be underemployed and not working in their field. There may be dual labor markets for scientists and engineers, such that the supply of scientists and engineers available for academic positions may be plentiful while small firms face shortages. Further research in this area could be useful.

CHAPTER 7

Summary and Policy Implications

This book begins with a theory of labor shortages based on static and dynamic models of the labor market and integrates it with more recent theoretical considerations offered by Robert M. Solow, such as efficiency wage theory and insider-outsider theories, which could explain why wages may not clear labor markets. Because we have no direct measures of labor shortages, we developed a theoretical model to predict changes in vacancies, which we argued could be estimated by a model having the unemployment rate and rate of change of employment as explanatory variables. Without a dependent variable to estimate, we argued that the best we could do to estimate shortages would be to develop indicators to capture the variance in the independent variables.

If our objective had been to measure shortages in a particular occupation, it would have made sense to build an analytic model for that occupation and estimate parameters. Because the purpose of our research was to investigate comparative shortages and surpluses, however, that approach was not feasible. For example, hospitals collect data on vacancies for some occupations, such as nurses, so an analytical model of nursing shortages could be estimated. Even for an occupation as narrowly defined as nursing, however, this approach would be incomplete because nurses also work outside of hospitals. Furthermore, we showed that there is not an exact correspondence between shortages and vacancies.

We found by looking at data from indicators that, even in a period of slow growth, occupations could be identified in which there was a possibility of a labor shortage. The occupations identified were: biological and life scientists, chemists, chemical engineers, computer scientists, cooks, materials engineers, mechanical engineers, medical technologists, primary care physicians, and special education teachers. We found some evidence, however, that would argue against a current shortage in the science, engineering, and computer fields.

National data were analyzed through the end of 1993. Other occupations scoring very high when 1993 data were considered were veterinarians, computer programmers, and operations and systems researchers. As of this writing, however, there were too many unemployed computer programmers to consider theirs a shortage occupation.

A list of 12,741 occupations was first organized into 193 groups, then ranked according to a system of indicators developed for this study. Occupations with a high ranking were those with the greatest likelihood of shortage, but the indicators did not identify a shortage for all occupations within any one group. Occupations were also examined geographically, and no single occupation was determined to have a possible shortage in all states. The highest-ranking occupations overall were those requiring an advanced degree, those in technical or health-related fields, and those in new and emerging fields. We concluded that, on balance, significant shortages could be expected in many of the higher-ranking occupations by the turn of the century.

There are many factors that could change our forecast, however. Government policy is probably the single most important variable. One area where government policy can be very influential is in education and training. Armed with information about potential future shortages, school systems can plan their curricula to offer training and career counseling aimed at the jobs that will be available when students graduate. A policy of early identification of potential shortages, combined with sound training and immigration policy, can anticipate shortages before they occur and thus help balance labor market supply and demand.

From 1989 to 1992, the economy showed virtually no job growth. Small firms were unsuccessful in creating the jobs that normally come from this sector, and large firms have been in a long-term job decline that extends back for decades. If the economy is to recover, there has to be an environment in which both small and large firms can prosper. Government initiatives can have a great deal of influence in creating such an environment.

There has been virtually no shortage of executives since the late 1980s, largely as a result of extensive corporate restructuring and slow economic growth. This restructuring has taken the form of replacing regular employees with contractual employees or increasing the use of service firms. As the economy improves, there will be an increase in the demand for the services of such firms, which will lead in turn to an increase in demand for executives to manage these firms. This restructuring has also led to a decrease in demand for midlevel managers of large firms, but the growth of the service sector will lead to an increase in demand for top-level executives in small firms. It is possible that the former midlevel managers can step into top-level management at smaller firms. If not, there could be both a shortage and a surplus, at different levels, in the manager-executive job categories.

International considerations also play a much larger role than they have in the past. Foreign firms compete with U.S. firms in the product market, and immigration policy influences potential labor supply. Current immigration policy requires extensive federal resources to determine which foreign workers ought to be certified. Most of the applicants certified are already in the United States, and many are working under a temporary certification. The current procedure requires that a job be posted to give U.S. workers a chance to apply before a foreign worker is certified; applicants and employers must fill out numerous forms, which then have to be processed; and in many cases, employers incur extensive legal fees in their effort to hire the foreign workers they want. In addition, prevailing wage surveys are conducted to determine the minimum wage at which immigrants must be compensated so that the U.S. wage is not adversely affected.

Substitution of labor market indicators for case-by-case determination would save valuable resources in those instances where a shortage is strongly indicated for an occupation. Surely, the national interest would be better served by allocating immigration slots to occupations where there is a general shortage, rather than to specific jobs where an individual employer is having difficulty recruiting a particular worker with certain qualifications.

At a time of slow economic growth, labor shortages seem less important than does stimulating the economy so that unemployed workers can find jobs. Our ability to stimulate the economy, however, may depend in part on what bottlenecks occur as the economy improves. Workers who are unqualified for the jobs that become available will still be out of work, and if there are not enough workers to meet the demand, there will be a gap in the cycle that fuels the economy and keeps it strong.

Some positive steps that can be taken to minimize labor shortages in the future are:

1. Improve vocational education and apprenticeship programs and implement outreach programs to draw in that portion of high school graduates not going to college.
2. Publish annual shortage lists by detailed occupation, educational level, and geographic location. These lists can be used for counseling, immigration purposes, or training needs assessments.
3. Integrate shortage information as a criterion into the funding decisions of government agencies. For example, increased funding in the form of scholarships might be appropriate in academic fields designated as having worker shortages.
4. Tie immigration admissions to labor shortages by making it easier for workers in shortage occupations to be admitted to the United States. This goal can be accomplished by eliminating the need for labor certification in areas where labor shortages exist. Where country quotas might be exceeded by an automatic certification policy, either the quotas could be expanded to accommodate larger numbers of

immigrants in shortage occupations or adjustments could be made in other immigration preference areas.

5. Support efforts by U.S. employers to train workers in shortage occupations.

If these steps are taken, the economy can continue to expand without labor shortage bottlenecks which could add to inflationary pressures and slow down potential economic growth. The best outcome would be that our predictions never come to pass because sufficient investments are made in providing labor market information and training U.S. workers.

Appendix: Composition of Groups by 1990 Census Code

Group Code and Title	Census Code and Title
007 Financial managers	
	007 Financial managers
008 Personnel and labor relations managers	
	008 Personnel and labor relations managers
009 Purchasing managers	
	009 Purchasing managers
013 Managers, marketing, advertising, and public relations	
	013 Managers, marketing, advertising, and public relations
014 Administrators, education and related fields	
	014 Administrators, education and related fields
016 Managers, properties and real estate	
	018 Managers, properties and real estate
01A Other executives and managers	
	004 Chief executives and general administrators, public administration
	005 Administrators and officials, public administration
	006 Administrators, protective services
	015 Managers, medicine and health
	016 Postmasters and mail superintendents
	017 Managers, food serving and lodging establishments
	019 Funeral directors
	021 Managers, service organizations, not elsewhere classified (NEC)
	022 Managers and administrators, NEC, salaried and self-employed
023 Accountants and auditors	
	023 Accountants and auditors

(continued)

Group Code and Title	Census Code and Title
026 Management analysts	
	026 Management analysts
027 Personnel, training, and labor relations specialists	
	027 Personnel, training, and labor relations specialists
029 Buyers, wholesale and retail trade, except farm products	
	029 Buyers, wholesale and retail trade, except farm products
033 Purchasing agents and buyers, NEC	
	033 Purchasing agents and buyers, NEC
035 Construction inspectors	
	035 Construction inspectors
03A Other management-related occupations	
	024 Underwriters
	025 Other financial officers
	028 Purchasing agents and buyers, farm products
	034 Business and promotion agents
	036 Inspectors and compliance officers, except construction
	037 Management related occupations, NEC
044 Aerospace engineers	
	044 Aerospace engineers
048 Chemical engineers	
	048 Chemical engineers
04A Architects, surveyors, and mapping scientists	
	043 Architects
	063 Surveyors and mapping scientists
053 Civil engineers	
	053 Civil engineers
055 Electrical and electronic engineers	
	055 Electrical and electronic engineers
056 Industrial engineers	
	056 Industrial engineers
057 Mechanical engineers	
	057 Mechanical engineers
05A Other engineers	
	045 Metallurgical and materials engineers
	046 Mining engineers
	047 Petroleum engineers
	049 Nuclear engineers
	054 Agricultural engineers
	058 Marine and naval architects
	059 Engineers, NEC

Group Code and Title	Census Code and Title	
064 Computer systems analysts and scientists		
	064	Computer systems analysts and scientists
065 Operations and systems researchers and analysts		
	065	Operations and systems researchers and analysts
06A Statisticians, actuaries, and other mathematical scientists		
	066	Actuaries
	067	Statisticians
	068	Mathematical scientists, NEC
073 Chemists, except biochemists		
	073	Chemists, except biochemists
075 Geologists and geodesists		
	075	Geologists and geodesists
078 Biological and life scientists		
	078	Biological and life scientists
07A Other natural scientists		
	069	Physicists and astronomers
	074	Atmospheric and space scientists
	076	Physical scientists, NEC
	077	Agricultural and food scientists
	079	Forestry and conservation scientists
	083	Medical scientists
084 Physicians		
	084	Physicians
085 Dentists		
	085	Dentists
086 Veterinarians		
	086	Veterinarians
087 Optometrists		
	087	Optometrists
095 Registered nurses		
	095	Registered nurses
096 Pharmacists		
	096	Pharmacists
097 Dietitians		
	097	Dietitians
098 Inhalation therapists		
	098	Respiratory therapists
09A Other therapists		
	099	Occupational therapists
	105	Therapists, NEC
103 Physical therapists		
	103	Physical therapists

(*continued*)

Group Code and Title	Census Code and Title
104 Speech therapists	
	104 Speech therapists
106 Physician's assistants	
	106 Physician's assistants
157 Teachers, secondary school	
	157 Teachers, secondary school
158 Teachers, special education	
	158 Teachers, special education
15A Teachers, NEC	
	159 Teachers, NEC
15B Teachers, prekindergarten, kindergarten, elementary	
	155 Teachers, prekindergarten and kindergarten
	156 Teachers, elementary school
15C Teachers, college and university	
	113–154 Teachers, postsecondary
163 Counselors, educational and vocational	
	163 Counselors, educational and vocational
166 Economists	
	166 Economists
167 Psychologists	
	167 Psychologists
16A Other social scientists	
	168 Sociologists
	169 Social scientists, NEC
	173 Urban planners
16B Librarians, archivists, and curators	
	164 Librarians
	165 Archivists and curators
174 Social workers	
	174 Social workers
175 Recreation workers	
	175 Recreation workers
176 Clergy	
	176 Clergy
177 Religious workers, NEC	
	177 Religious workers, NEC
178 Lawyers	
	178 Lawyers
179 Judges	
	179 Judges
185 Designers	
	185 Designers

Group Code and Title		Census Code and Title	
186	Musicians and composers		
		186	Musicians and composers
188	Painters, sculptors, craft artists, and artist printmakers		
		188	Painters, sculptors, craft artists, and artist printmakers
189	Photographers		
		189	Photographers
18A	Editors, reporters, authors, and technical writers		
		183	Authors
		184	Technical writers
		195	Editors and reporters
18B	Other professional specialty occupations		
		088	Podiatrists
		089	Health diagnosing practitioners, NEC
		187	Actors and directors
		193	Dancers
		194	Artists, performers, and related workers, NEC
		199	Athletes
197	Public relations specialists		
		197	Public relations specialists
198	Announcers		
		198	Announcers
203	Clinical laboratory technologists and technicians		
		203	Clinical laboratory technologists and technicians
204	Dental hygienists		
		204	Dental hygienists
205	Health record technologists and technicians		
		205	Health record technologists and technicians
206	Radiologic technicians		
		206	Radiologic technicians
207	Licensed practical nurses		
		207	Licensed practical nurses
208	Health technologists and technicians, NEC		
		208	Health technologists and technicians, NEC
213	Electrical and electronic technicians		
		213	Electrical and electronic technicians
21A	Other technicians and related support occupations		
		214	Industrial engineering technicians
		215	Mechanical engineering technicians
		216	Engineering technicians, NEC
21B	Drafting occupations and surveying and mapping technicians		

(*continued*)

Group Code and Title		Census Code and Title	
		217	Drafting occupations
		218	Surveying and mapping technicians
226	Airplane pilots and navigators		
		226	Airplane pilots and navigators
229	Computer programmers		
		229	Computer programmers
22A	Other science technicians		
		223	Biological technicians
		224	Chemical technicians
		225	Science technicians, NEC
234	Legal assistants		
		234	Legal assistants
23A	Other technicians, except health, engineering, and science		
		227	Air traffic controllers
		228	Broadcast equipment operators
		233	Tool programmers, numerical control
		235	Technicians, NEC
253	Insurance sales occupations		
		253	Insurance sales occupations
254	Real estate sales occupations		
		254	Real estate sales occupations
255	Securities and financial services sales occupations		
		255	Securities and financial services sales occupations
25A	Other sales occupations		
		243	Supervisors and proprietors, sales occupations
		256	Advertising and related sales occupations
		257	Sales occupations, other business services
		258	Sales engineers
		259	Sales representatives, mining, manufacturing, and wholesale
		263	Sales workers, motor vehicles and boats
		264	Sales workers, apparel
		265	Sales workers, shoes
		266	Sales workers, furniture and home furnishings
		267	Sales workers, radio, TV, hi-fi, and appliances
		268	Sales workers, hardware and building supplies
		269	Sales workers, parts
		277	Street and door-to-door sales workers
		278	News vendors
		283	Demonstrators, promoters, and models, sales
		284	Auctioneers
		285	Sales support occupations, NEC

Group Code and Title	Census Code and Title	
274 Sales workers, other commodities		
	274	Sales workers, other commodities
275 Sales counter clerks		
	275	Sales counter clerks
276 Cashiers		
	276	Cashiers
30A Supervisors, administrative support		
	303	Supervisors, general office
	304	Supervisors, computer equipment operators
	305	Supervisors, financial records processing
	306	Chief communications operators
	307	Supervisors, distribution, scheduling, and adjusting clerks
30B Computer equipment operators		
	308	Computer operators
	309	Peripheral equipment operators
313 Secretaries		
	313	Secretaries
314 Stenographers		
	314	Stenographers
315 Typists		
	315	Typists
316 Interviewers		
	316	Interviewers
317 Hotel clerks		
	317	Hotel clerks
318 Transportation ticket and reservation agents		
	318	Transportation ticket and reservation agents
31A Receptionists and information clerks, NEC		
	319	Receptionists
	323	Information clerks, NEC
32A Records processing occupations, except financial		
	325	Classified-ad clerks
	326	Correspondence clerks
	327	Order clerks
	328	Personnel clerks, except payroll and timekeeping
	329	Library clerks
	335	File clerks
	336	Records clerks
33A Financial records processing		
	337	Bookkeepers, accounting and auditing clerks
	338	Payroll and timekeeping clerks

(*continued*)

Group Code and Title	Census Code and Title
	339 Billing clerks
	343 Cost and rate clerks
	344 Billing, posting, and calculating machine operators
34A Duplicating, mail, and other office machine operators	
	345 Duplicating machine operators
	346 Mail preparing and paper handling machine operators
	347 Office machine operators, NEC
35A Communication equipment operators	
	348 Telephone operators
	353 Communications equipment operators, NEC
35C Mail and message distributing operators	
	354 Postal clerks, except mail carriers
	355 Mail carriers, postal service
	356 Mail clerks, except postal service
	357 Messengers
363 Production coordinators	
	363 Production coordinators
36A Material recording, scheduling, and distribution clerks	
	359 Dispatchers
	364 Traffic, shipping, and receiving clerks
	365 Stock and inventory clerks
	366 Meter readers
	368 Weighers, measurers, checkers, and samplers
	373 Expediters
	374 Material recording, scheduling, and distributing clerks, NEC
379 General office clerks	
	379 General office clerks
37A Adjusters and investigators	
	375 Insurance adjusters, examiners, and investigators
	376 Investigators and adjusters, except insurance
	377 Eligibility clerks, social welfare
	378 Bill and account collectors
383 Bank tellers	
	383 Bank tellers
385 Data-entry keyers	
	385 Data-entry keyers
386 Statistical clerks	
	386 Statistical clerks

Group Code and Title	Census Code and Title
387 Teacher's aides	
	387 Teacher's aides
38A Miscellaneous administrative support	
	384 Proofreaders
	389 Administrative support occupations, NEC
406 Child care workers, private household	
	406 Child care workers, private household
407 Private household cleaners and servants	
	407 Private household cleaners and servants
40A Launderers, cooks, housekeepers, and butlers	
	403 Launderers and ironers
	404 Cooks, private household
	405 Housekeepers and butlers
41A Police and detectives	
	414 Supervisors, police and detectives
	418 Police and detectives, public service
	423 Sheriffs, bailiffs, and other law enforcement officers
41C Firefighting and fire prevention occupations	
	413 Supervisors, firefighting and fire prevention occupations
	416 Fire inspection and fire prevention occupations
	417 Firefighting occupations
424 Correctional institution officers	
	424 Correctional institution officers
42A Guards	
	415 Supervisors, guards
	425 Crossing guards
	426 Guards and police, except public service
	427 Protective service occupations, NEC
433 Supervisors, food preparation and service occupations	
	433 Supervisors, food preparation and service occupations
434 Bartenders	
	434 Bartenders
435 Waiters and waitresses	
	435 Waiters and waitresses
438 Food counter, fountain, and related occupations	
	438 Food counter, fountain, and related occupations
43A Cooks, including short-order	
	436 Cooks

(*continued*)

Group Code and Title		Census Code and Title	
43B	Miscellaneous food preparation and service occupations		
		439	Kitchen workers, food preparation
		444	Miscellaneous food preparation occupations
443	Waiters/waitresses' assistants		
		443	Waiters/waitresses' assistants
445	Dental assistants		
		445	Dental assistants
446	Health aides, except nursing		
		446	Health aides, except nursing
447	Nursing aides, orderlies, and attendants		
		447	Nursing aides, orderlies, and attendants
44A	Cleaning and building service, except household		
		449	Maids and housemen
		453	Janitors and cleaners
		454	Elevator operators
		455	Pest control occupations
44B	Supervisors, cleaning and building service workers		
		448	Supervisors, cleaning and building service workers
457	Barbers		
		457	Barbers
458	Hairdressers and cosmetologists		
		458	Hairdressers and cosmetologists
465	Public transportation attendants		
		463	Public transportation attendants
467	Welfare service aides		
		465	Welfare service aides
468	Child care workers, except private household		
		466	Family child care providers
		467	Early childhood teacher's assistants
		468	Child care workers, NEC
46A	Personal service occupations, residual		
		456	Supervisors, personal service occupations
		459	Attendants, amusement and recreation facilities
		461	Guides
		462	Ushers
		464	Baggage porters and bellhops
		469	Personal service occupations, NEC
47A	Farming, forestry, and fishing occupations		
		473–499	Farming, forestry, and fishing occupations
507	Bus, truck, and stationary-engine mechanics		
		507	Bus, truck, and stationary-engine mechanics
509	Small-engine repairers		

Group Code and Title	Census Code and Title
	509 Small-engine repairers
50A Automobile mechanics, including apprentices	
	505–506 Automobile mechanics, including apprentices
514 Automobile body and related repairers	
	514 Automobile body and related repairers
516 Heavy-equipment mechanics	
	516 Heavy-equipment mechanics
51A Aircraft mechanics	
	508 Aircraft engine mechanics
	515 Aircraft mechanics, except engine
523 Electronic repairers, communications and industrial equipment	
	523 Electronic repairers, communications and industrial equipment
525 Data processing equipment repair	
	525 Data processing equipment repair
526 Household appliance and power tool repairers	
	526 Household appliance and power tool repairers
527 Telephone line installers and repairers	
	527 Telephone line installers and repairers
529 Telephone installers and repairers	
	529 Telephone installers and repairers
533 Miscellaneous electrical and electronic equipment repairers	
	533 Miscellaneous electrical and electronic equipment repairers
534 Heating, air conditioning, and refrigeration mechanics	
	534 Heating, air conditioning, and refrigeration mechanics
538 Office machine repairers	
	538 Office machine repairers
53A Other mechanics and repairers, except supervisors	
	517 Farm equipment mechanics
	518 Industrial machinery repairers
	519 Machinery maintenance occupations
	535 Camera, watch, and musical instrument repairers
	536 Locksmiths and safe repairers
	539 Mechanical controls and valve repairers
	543 Elevator installers and repairers
	547 Specified mechanics and repairers, NEC
	549 Not specified mechanics and repairers
544 Millwrights	
	544 Millwrights
55A Supervisors, blue collar	

(*continued*)

Group Code and Title		Census Code and Title	
		503	Supervisors, mechanics and repairers
		553	Supervisors, brickmasons, stonemasons, and tile setters
		554	Supervisors, carpenters and related workers
		555	Supervisors, electricians and power transmission installers
		556	Supervisors, painters, paperhangers, and plasterers
		557	Supervisors, plumbers, pipefitters, and steamfitters
		558	Supervisors, NEC
		613	Supervisors, extractive occupations
		628	Supervisors, production occupations
		803	Supervisors, motor vehicle operators
		823	Railroad conductors and yardmasters
		843	Supervisors, material moving equipment operators
		864	Supervisors, handlers, equipment cleaners, and laborers
565	Tile setters, hard and soft		
		565	Tile setters, hard and soft
566	Carpet installers		
		566	Carpet installers
56A	Brickmasons and stonemasons, including apprentices		
		563–564	Brickmasons and stonemasons, including apprentices
56B	Carpenters and apprentices		
		567–569	Carpenters and apprentices
573	Drywall installers		
		573	Drywall installers
577	Electrical power installers and repairers		
		577	Electrical power installers and repairers
57A	Electricians and apprentices		
		575–576	Electricians and apprentices
57B	Painters, construction and maintenance, paperhangers, plasterers		
		579	Painters, construction and maintenance
		583	Paperhangers
		584	Plasterers
588	Concrete and terrazzo finishers		
		588	Concrete and terrazzo finishers
589	Glaziers		
		589	Glaziers

Group Code and Title		Census Code and Title	
58A	Plumbers, pipefitters, and steamfitters		
		585–587	Plumbers, pipefitters, and steamfitters, including apprentices
593	Insulation workers		
		593	Insulation workers
595	Roofers		
		595	Roofers
59A	Construction trades, NEC, residual		
		594	Paving, surfacing, and tamping equipment operators
		596	Sheet metal duct installers
		597	Structural metal workers
		599	Construction trades, NEC
61A	Extractive occupations		
		598	Drillers, earth
		614	Drillers, oil well
		615	Explosives workers
		616	Mining machine operators
		617	Mining occupations, NEC
63A	Tool and die makers, including apprentices		
		634–635	Tool and die makers, including apprentices
63B	Machinists, including apprentices		
		637–639	Machinists, including apprentices
65A	Other precision production occupations		
		636	Precision assemblers, metal
		643	Boilermakers
		644	Precision grinders, fitters, and tool sharpeners
		645	Patternmakers and model makers, metal
		646	Layout workers
		647	Precious stones and metals workers (jewelers)
		649	Engravers, metal
		655	Miscellaneous precision metal workers
		683	Electrical and electronic equipment assemblers
65B	Precision woodworking occupations		
		656	Patternmakers and model makers, wood
		657	Cabinetmakers and bench carpenters
		658	Furniture and wood finishers
		659	Miscellaneous precision woodworkers
65C	Sheet metal workers, including apprentices		
		653–654	Sheet metal workers, including apprentices
668	Upholsterers		
		668	Upholsterers

(*continued*)

Group Code and Title		Census Code and Title	
66A	Other precision textile, apparel, and furnishings machine workers		
		666	Dressmakers
		667	Tailors
		669	Shoe repairers
		674	Miscellaneous precision apparel and fabric workers
677	Optical goods workers		
		677	Optical goods workers
678	Dental laboratory and medical appliance technicians		
		678	Dental laboratory and medical appliance technicians
686	Butchers and meat cutters		
		686	Butchers and meat cutters
687	Bakers		
		687	Bakers
68A	Other precision workers, assorted materials		
		675	Hand molders and shapers, except jewelers
		676	Patternmakers, layout workers, and cutters
		679	Bookbinders
		684	Miscellaneous precision workers, NEC
		688	Food batchmakers
		693	Adjusters and calibrators
69A	Plant and system operators		
		694	Water and sewage treatment plant operators
		695	Power plant operators
		696	Stationary engineers
		699	Miscellaneous plant and system operators
71A	Metalworking and plasticworking machine operators		
		703	Lathe and turning machine setup operators
		704	Lathe and turning machine operators
		705	Milling and planing machine operators
		706	Punching and stamping press machine operators
		707	Rolling machine operators
		708	Drilling and boring machine operators
		709	Grinding, abrading, buffing, and polishing machine operators
		713	Forging machine operators
		714	Numerical control machine operators
		715	Miscellaneous metal, plastic, stone, and glassworking machine operators
		717	Fabricating machine operators, NEC

Group Code and Title	Census Code and Title	
72A Woodworking machine operators		
	726	Wood lathe, routing, and planing machine operators
	727	Sawing machine operators
	728	Shaping and joining machine operators
	729	Nailing and tacking machine operators
	733	Miscellaneous woodworking machine operators
72B Metal and plastic processing machine operators		
	719	Molding and casting machine operators
	723	Metal plating machine operators
	724	Heat treating equipment operators
	725	Miscellaneous metal and plastic processing machine operators
73A Textile apparel and furnishings machine operators		
	738	Winding and twisting machine operators
	739	Knitting, looping, taping, and weaving machine operators
	743	Textile cutting machine operators
	744	Textile sewing machine operators
	745	Shoe machine operators
	747	Pressing machine operators
	748	Laundering and dry cleaning machine operators
	749	Miscellaneous textile machine operators
73B Printing machine operators		
	734	Printing press operators
	735	Photoengravers and lithographers
	736	Typesetters and compositors
	737	Miscellaneous printing machine operators
75A Machine operators, assorted material		
	753	Cementing and gluing machine operators
	754	Packaging and filling machine operators
	755	Extruding and forming machine operators
	756	Mixing and blending machine operators
	757	Separating, filtering, and clarifying machine operators
	758	Compressing and compacting machine operators
	759	Painting and paint spraying machine operators
	763	Roasting and baking machine operators, food
	764	Washing, cleaning, and pickling machine operators

(*continued*)

Group Code and Title	Census Code and Title
	765 Folding machine operators
	766 Furnace, kiln, and oven operators, except food
	768 Crushing and grinding machine operators
	769 Slicing and cutting machine operators
	773 Motion picture projectionists
	774 Photographic process machine operators
	777 Miscellaneous machine operators, NEC
	779 Machine operators, not specified
78A Fabricators, assemblers, and handworking occupations	
	783 Welders and cutters
	784 Solderers and brazers
	785 Assemblers
	786 Hand cutting and trimming occupations
	787 Hand molding, casting, and forming occupations
	789 Hand printing, coating, and decorating occupations
	793 Hand engraving and printing occupations
	795 Miscellaneous handworking occupations
79A Production inspectors, testers, samplers, and weighers	
	689 Inspectors, testers, and graders
	796 Production inspectors, checkers, and examiners
	797 Production testers
	798 Production samplers and weighers
	799 Graders and sorters, except agricultural
80B Motor vehicle operators	
	804 Truck drivers
	806 Driver–sales workers
	808 Bus drivers
	809 Taxicab drivers and chauffeurs
	814 Motor transportation occupations, NEC
82A Rail transportation occupations	
	824 Locomotive operating occupations
	825 Railroad brake, signal, and switch operators
	826 Rail vehicle operators, NEC
82B Water transportation occupations	
	828 Ship captains and mates, except fishing boats
	829 Sailors and deckhands
	833 Marine engineers
	834 Bridge, lock, and lighthouse tenders

Group Code and Title	Census Code and Title	
85A Material moving equipment operators		
	844	Operating engineers
	845	Longshore equipment operators
	848	Hoist and winch operators
	849	Crane and tower operators
	853	Excavating and loading machine operators
	855	Grader, dozer, and scraper operators
	856	Industrial truck and tractor equipment operators
	859	Miscellaneous material moving equipment operators
86A Handlers, equipment cleaners, helpers, laborers		
	813	Parking lot attendants
	865	Helpers, mechanics and repairers
	866	Helpers, construction trades
	867	Helpers, surveyors
	868	Helpers, extractive occupations
	869	Construction laborers
	874	Production helpers
	875	Garbage collectors
	876	Stevedores
	877	Stock handlers and baggers
	878	Machine feeders and offbearers
	883	Freight, stock, and material handlers, NEC
	885	Garage and service station related occupations
	887	Vehicle washers and equipment cleaners
	888	Hand packers and packagers
	889	Laborers, except construction

References

Abowd, John M., and Zellner, Arnold. 1985. "Estimating Gross Labor-Force Flows." *Journal of Business and Economic Statistics* 3: 254-93.

Abraham, Katharine G. 1983. "Structural/Frictional vs. Deficient Demand Unemployment: Some New Evidence." *American Economic Review* 73, no. 4 (September): 708–24.

———. 1987. "Help-Wanted Advertising, Job Vacancies, and Unemployment." *Brookings Papers on Economic Activity*, no. 1: 207–48.

Akerlof, George; Rose, Andrew; and Yellen, Janet. 1988. "Job Switching and Job Satisfaction in the U.S. Labor Market." *Brookings Papers on Economic Activity*, no. 2 :495–592.

Arrow, Kenneth J., and Capron, William M. 1959. "Dynamic Shortages and Price Rises: The Engineer-Scientist Case." *Quarterly Journal of Economics* 73, no. 2 (May): 292–308.

Belous, Richard S. 1989. *The Contingent Economy: The Growth of the Temporary, Part-Time and Subcontracted Workforce*. Washington, D.C.: National Planning Association.

Bishop, John H. 1992a. "Is a Skills Shortage Coming?" *Workforce* 1, no. 1 (Spring): 15–30.

———. 1992b. *Workforce Preparedness*. Working Paper No. 92-03. Ithaca, N.Y.: National Center on the Educational Quality of the Workforce; Cornell Institute for Youth and Work; Center for Advanced Human Resource Studies, New York State School of Industrial and Labor Relations, Cornell University.

Bishop, John H., and Carter, Shani. 1990. *The Deskilling vs. Upskilling Debate: The Role of BLS Projections*. Working Paper No. 90-14. Ithaca, N.Y.: Center for Advanced Human Resource Studies and Cornell Institute for Labor Market Policies, New York State School of Industrial and Labor Relations, Cornell University.

Blanchard, Olivier Jean, and Diamond, Peter. 1989. "The Beveridge Curve." *Brookings Papers on Economic Activity*, no. 1: 1–76.

———. 1990. "The Cyclical Behavior of the Gross Flows of U.S. Workers." *Brookings Papers on Economic Activity*, no. 2: 85–155.

Blank, David J., and Stigler, George J. 1957. *The Demand and Supply of Scientific Personnel*. New York: National Bureau of Economic Research.

Borjas, George J. 1990. *Friends or Strangers: The Impact of Immigrants on the U.S. Economy*. New York: Basic Books.

Burke, Thomas P., and Jain, Rita S. 1991. "Trends in Employer-Provided Health Care Benefits." *Monthly Labor Review* 114, no. 2 (February): 24–30.

Butcher, Kristin F., and Card, David. 1991. "Immigration and Wages: Evidence from the 1980s." *American Economic Association Papers and Proceedings* 81, no. 2 (May): 292–96.

Cohen, Malcolm S. 1985. "Deriving Labor Turnover Rates from Administrative Records." In *Record Linkage Techniques—1985*. Washington, D.C.: U.S. Department of Treasury, Internal Revenue Service.

———. 1990. "Study on the Feasibility of Using Labor Market Information for Alien Labor Certification Determination." Final report to U.S. Department of Labor, Employment and Training Administration. Ann Arbor: Institute of Labor and Industrial Relations, University of Michigan.

Cohen, Malcolm S., and Schwartz, Arthur R. 1979. *New Hire Rates by Demographic Group.* Ann Arbor: Institute of Labor and Industrial Relations, University of Michigan.

———. 1980. "New Measures of Labor Turnover." *Monthly Labor Review* 103, no. 11 (November): 9–13.

———. 1983. "A New Hires Model for the Private, Non-farm Economy." In *The Economic Outlook for 1984*, proceedings of the Thirty-first Annual Conference on the Economic Outlook, sponsored by the Research Seminar in Quantitative Economics, University of Michigan, Ann Arbor, November 17–18.

Cohen, Malcolm S., and Solow, Robert M. 1967. "The Behavior of Help-Wanted Advertising." *Review of Economics and Statistics* 49, no. 1 (February): 108–10.

———. 1970. "The Behavior of Help-Wanted Advertising: A Reply." *Review of Economics and Statistics* 52, no. 4 (November): 442–3.

Cooke, William N. 1990. *Labor-Management Cooperation: New Partnerships, or Going in Circles*. Kalamazoo, Mich.: W. E. Upjohn Institute for Employment Research.

Cooke, William N., and Meyer, David G. 1991. "Union-Management Cooperation: Choice, Implementation, and Effects." In *Proceedings of the Forty-third Annual Meeting of the Industrial Relations Research Association*, edited by John F. Burton, Jr. Industrial Relations Research Association Series. Madison: Industrial Relations Research Association, University of Wisconsin.

DRI/McGraw-Hill. 1992. "The Impact of the North American Free Trade Agreement on U.S. Regional and Sectoral Labor Markets." In *The Employment Effects of the North American Free Trade Agreement: Recommendations and Background Studies*. Special report. Washington, D.C.: National Commission for Employment Policy.

Ehrenberg, Ronald G., and Smith, Robert S. 1982. *Modern Labor Economics: Theory and Public Policy*. Glenview, Ill.: Scott, Foresman and Co.

Freeman, Richard B. 1976. "A Cobweb Model of the Supply and Starting Salary of New Engineers." *Industrial & Labor Relations Review* 29, no. 2 (January): 236–48.

Fullerton, Howard N. 1992. "Labor Force Projections: The Baby Boom Moves On." In *Outlook 1990–2005*. Bulletin 2402. Washington, D.C.: U.S. Department of Labor, Bureau of Labor Statistics.

Greenwood, Michael J., and McDowell, John M. 1986. "The Facor Market Consequences of U.S. Immigration." *Journal of Economic Literature* 24 (December): 1738–72.

Hall, Robert. 1972. "Turnover in the Labor Force." *Brookings Papers on Economic Activity*, no. 3: 709–56.

Herz, Diane E. 1991. "Worker displacement still common in the late 1980's." *Monthly Labor Review* 114, no. 5 (May): 3–9.

Holzer, Harry. 1989. *Unemployment Vacancies and Local Labor Market*. Kalamazoo, Mich.: W. E. Upjohn Institute for Employment Research.

Iowa State Occupational Information Coordinating Committee, National Crosswalk Service Center. 1993. General description of Version 4 of the NOICC master crosswalk data base. Des Moines: Iowa State Occupational Information Coordinating Committee, National Crosswalk Service Center.

Levine, Phillip B., and Mitchell, Olivia S. 1991. *Expected Changes in the Workforce and Implications for Labor Markets*. Working Paper No. 3743. Cambridge, Mass.: National Bureau of Economic Research.

Malitz, Gerald. 1981. *A Classification of Instructional Programs*. Report prepared for the National Center for Education Statistics, U.S. Department of Education. Washington, D.C.: U.S. Government Printing Office.

Medoff, James L. 1992. *The New Unemployment*. Report prepared for the Subcommittee on Economic Growth, Trade and Taxes, Joint Economic Committee.

National Center on Education and the Economy. 1990. *America's Choice: high skills or low wages!* Rochester, N.Y.: National Center on Education and the Economy.

President. 1990. *Economic Report of the President*. Transmitted to the Congress February 1990. Washington, D.C.: U.S. Government Printing Office.

Saunders, Norman C. 1993. "Employment Effects of the Rise and Fall in Defense Spending." *Monthly Labor Review* 116, no. 4 (April): 3–10.

Scheetz, L. Patrick, and Klefstad, Scott. 1992. *Estimated Supply and Demand for Michigan's College and University Graduates of 1992–93*. Lansing: Collegiate Employment Research Institute, Career Development and Placement Services, Michigan State University.

Schwartz, Arthur R.; Cohen, Malcolm S.; and Grimes, Donald R. 1986. "Structural/Frictional vs. Deficient Demand Unemployment: Comment." *American Economic Review* 76, no.1 (March): 268–72.

Shapiro, Harold T. 1992. "The U.S. Health Care System: Some Current Challenges and Future Prospects." In *The Economic Outlook for 1993*, proceedings of the Fortieth Annual Conference on the Economic Outlook, sponsored by the Research Seminar in Quantitative Economics, University of Michigan, Ann Arbor, November 19–20.

Silvestri, George, and Lukasiewicz, John. 1992. "Occupational Employment Projections." In *Outlook 1990–2005*. Bulletin 2402. Washington, D.C.: U.S. Government Printing Office.

Solow, Robert M. 1964. "The Nature and Sources of Unemployment in the United States." In *Wicksell Lectures*. Stockholm: Almqvist and Wicksell.

———. 1990. *The Labor Market as a Social Institution*. Cambridge, Mass.: Basil Blackwell.

Sorensen, Elane; Bean, Frank D.; Ku, Leighton; and Zimmermann, Wendy. 1992.

Immigrant Categories and the U.S. Job Market: Do They Make a Difference? Urban Institute Report 92-1. Washington, D.C.: Urban Institute Press.

Stern, Robert M.; Deardorff, Alan V.; and Brown, Drusilla K. 1992. "A U.S.-Mexico-Canada Free Trade Agreement: Sectoral Employment Effects and Regional/Occupational Employment Realignments in the United States." In *The Employment Effects of the North American Free Trade Agreement: Recommendations and Background Studies*. Special report. Washington, D.C.: National Commission for Employment Policy.

Taylor, Frederick W. 1911. *The Principles of Scientific Management*. New York: Harper and Brothers.

Thurow, Lester. 1992. *Head to Head: The Coming Economic Battle Among Japan, Europe, and America*. New York: William Morrow.

Trutko, John W.; Barnow, Burt S.; Chasanov, Amy B.; and Pande, Abhay. 1991. *Labor Shortage Case Studies*. Washington, D.C.: Employment and Training Administration, U.S. Department of Labor.

U.S. Congress. Congressional Budget Office. 1991. *Universal Health Insurance Coverage Using Medicare Payment Rates*. Congressional Budget Office Report.

———. 1992. *The Economic Effects of Reduced Defense Spending*. Washington, D.C.: U.S. Government Printing Office.

U.S. Congress. Office of Technology Assessment. 1986. *Technology and Structural Unemployment: Reemploying Displaced Adults*, OTA-ITE-250. Washington, D.C.: U.S. Government Printing Office.

———. 1990. *Worker Training: Competing in the New International Economy*, OTA-ITE-457. Washington, D.C.: U.S. Government Printing Office.

———. 1992. *U.S.-Mexico Trade: Pulling Together or Pulling Apart?* ITE-545. Washington, D.C.: U.S. Government Printing Office.

U.S. Department of Commerce. 1992. *Survey of Current Business* 72, no. 4 (April): C–25.

U.S. Department of Commerce. Bureau of the Census. 1989. *The Relationship between the 1970 and 1980 Industry and Classification Systems*. Technical paper 59. Washington, D.C.: U.S. Government Printing Office.

U.S. Department of Commerce. Office of Federal Statistical Policy and Standards. 1980. *Standard Occupational Classification Manual*. Washington, D.C.: U.S. Government Printing Office.

U.S. Department of Education. National Center for Education Statistics. 1988. *Digest of Education Statistics 1988*. Washington, D.C.: U.S. Government Printing Office.

U.S. Department of Labor. Bureau of Labor Statistics. 1981. *Job Openings Pilot Program: Final Report*. Washington, D.C.: U.S. Government Printing Office.

———. 1982. *Technical Description of the Quarterly Data on Weekly Earnings from the Current Population Survey*. Bulletin 2113. Washington, D.C.: U.S. Government Printing Office.

———. 1986. *Occupational Projections and Training Data*. Bulletin 2251. Washington, D.C.: U.S. Government Printing Office.

———. 1991a. *Employee Turnover and Job Opening Survey: Results of a Pilot Study on the Feasibility of Collecting Measures of Imbalances of Supply and Demand for Labor in an Establishment Survey*. Washington, D.C.: U.S. Government Printing Office.

———. 1991b. *Total and Net Occupational Separations: A Report on Recent Research*. Washington, D.C.: U.S. Department of Labor, Bureau of Labor Statistics, Office of Employment Projections.

———. 1992a. *Occupational Outlook Handbook*. Bulletin 2400. Washington, D.C.: U.S. Government Printing Office.

———. 1992b. *Occupational Projections and Training Data*. Bulletin 2401. Washington, D.C.: U.S. Government Printing Office.

———. 1992c. *Outlook 1990–2005*. Bulletin 2402. Washington, D.C.: U.S. Government Printing Office.

———. 1992d. *Occupational Employment Statistics, Dictionary of Occupations, 1988-1993*. Washington, D.C.: U.S. Government Printing Office.

———. 1992e. *News*. USDL 92-530. Washington, D.C.: U.S. Department of Labor, Bureau of Labor Statistics.

———. 1992f. *BLS Handbook of Methods*. Bulletin 2414. Washington, D.C.: U.S. Government Printing Office.

———. 1992g. *Employment and Earnings*. Washington, D.C.: U.S. Government Printing Office.

———. 1993. "Current Labor Statistics: Comparative Indicators" (Table 30, "Consumer Price Indexes for All Urban Consumers and for Urban Wage Earners and Clerical Workers: U.S. city average, by expenditure category and comodity or service group"). *Monthly Labor Review* 116, no. 2 (February): 101–3.

———. 1994. *How the Government Measures Unemployment*. Report 864. Washington, D.C.: U.S. Government Printing Office.

U.S. Department of Labor. Employment and Training Administration. 1991. *Dictionary of Occupational Titles*. 4th ed., 2 vols. Washington, D.C.: U.S. Department of Labor, Employment and Training Administration, U.S. Employment Service.

———. 1993. *Federal Register*, March 19, Part V, 20 CFR Part 656: "Labor Certification Process of Permanent Employment of Aliens; Labor Market Information Pilot Program; Proposed Rule." Washington, D.C.: U.S. Government Printing Office.

U.S. House. 1992. Committee on the Judiciary. *Immigration and Nationality Act*. 9th ed. Washington, D.C.: U.S. Government Printing Office.

Utter, Carol. 1982. "Labor Turnover in Manufacturing: The Survey in Retrospect." *Monthly Labor Review* 105, no. 6 (June): 15–17.

Index